Addressing the Needs of
All Learners in the Era of
Changing Standards

Addressing the Needs of All Learners in the Era of Changing Standards

Helping Our Most Vulnerable Students Succeed through Teaching Flexibility, Innovation, and Creativity

Edited by Katherine S. McKnight

ROWMAN & LITTLEFIELD
Lanham • Boulder • New York • London

Published by Rowman & Littlefield
A wholly owned subsidary of The Rowman & Littlefield Publishing Group, Inc.
4501 Forbes Boulevard, Suite 200, Lanham, Maryland 20706
www.rowman.com

Unit A, Whitacre Mews, 26-34 Stannary Street, London SE11 4AB

British Library Cataloguing in Publication Information Available

Library of Congress Cataloging-in-Publication Data

Names: McKnight, Katherine S. (Katherine Siewert), editor.
Title: Addressing the needs of all learners in the era of changing standards : helping our most
    vulnerable students succeed through teaching flexibility, innovation, and creativity / edited by
    Katherine S. McKnight.
Description: Lanham, Maryland : Rowman & Littlefield, 2016. | Includes bibliographical references.
Identifiers: LCCN 2016005948 (print) | LCCN 2016019166 (ebook) | ISBN 9781475818567 (cloth :
    alk. paper) | ISBN 9781475818574 (pbk. : alk. paper) | ISBN 9781475818581 (Electronic)
Subjects: LCSH: Common Core State Standards (Education) | Education—Standards—United
    States—States. | Educational equalization—United States.
Classification: LCC LB3060.83.A34 2016 (print) | LCC LB3060.83 (ebook) | DDC 379.1/58—dc23
LC record available at https://lccn.loc.gov/2016005948

♾ ™ The paper used in this publication meets the minimum requirements of American National Standard for Information Sciences Permanence of Paper for Printed Library Materials, ANSI/NISO Z39.48-1992.

Printed in the United States of America

For Ellie, Colin, and David.

For our teachers who believe that *all* children can learn.

Contents

Acknowledgments

This book was a special undertaking, since the contributors are professionally recognized in their respective fields. As I worked with my colleagues on this book, their professional dedication to the success of all children inspires me. I know that their words will inspire you as well. Without their wisdom, passion, knowledge, and generosity, this project would not have addressed the challenges of the student achievement gap in the era of new standards as comprehensively. Thank you to the contributors, whom I adore personally and professionally:

Diane Arrington
LeAnn Nickelsen
Richard Cash
Melissa Dickson
Seema Imam
Elizabeth Knost
Nicole Lambson
Eileen Murphy
Elizabeth Perry
Brenna Sherwood
Michael Troop

I also want to express my appreciation for my assistant, Elaine Carlson. I cherish Elaine's ability to edit, organize, and make me laugh. Kris Lantzy also makes me laugh and I appreciate her skills in checking sources and references. Many thanks to my awesome editor, Suzanne Canavan. My children, Ellie and Colin, always inspire me and remind me of what is really important in the development of all children. I also want to acknowledge David Gade. For me, he embodies the proverb, "when one door is closed, another has opened." His unconditional love and support for my work makes me stronger and even more committed to closing the achievement gap.

Most of all I want to recognize my mother, Patricia Suever Siewert (1934–2008), a Chicago Public School teacher of over forty years. Mom was my first teacher, my mentor, and best friend. She and my father fostered a strong drive for social justice in their children and their legacy is with me in my professional life. It was my mother who would always remind me, especially when I was discouraged by poor decision making, which was often politically driven in public schools, that teaching is an act of love and social justice. As you read through the chapters and think about all of our children and the education that they currently receive, please remember my mom's words, "teaching is an act of love and social justice."

ONE

Introduction

How Does the Common Core Address the Needs of All Students?

Katherine S. McKnight

As I write this chapter, the United States has been in the midst of transitioning to the new college and career standards for several years. The Common Core State Standards (CCSS) were released in 2010, and for five years, individual states have been grappling with the meaning and impact of the new standards. Like prior educational initiatives, politics soon became entangled in this paradigm shift. In the two to three years after CCSS was introduced, more than forty-five states and territories adopted this new framework. In the year prior to this publication, more states that had previously adopted CCSS created their own standards. Interestingly, as I studied CCSS, I discovered that there really wasn't much of a difference between standards in states such as Texas, Indiana, and Oklahoma and the original CCSS framework. We can continue to argue the difference, but there is a common focus for all of these standards. All of these standards articulate skills that are focused on college and career readiness for *all* students.

The idea of college and career readiness is not new. It has been part of our educational dialogue for quite some time. The College Board and Committee of Ten (from the early twentieth century) articulate the skills and content knowledge that students need in order to be career and college ready (Holcomb, 2006). Although there are many disagreements regarding the manner in which the development of skills and content knowledge should be conducted, there is overlapping consensus that stu-

1

dents must possess higher-order thinking skills as preparation for career readiness and college. Higher-order thinking skills accompanied by strong self-regulation skills and independence are foundational for student college and career readiness.

When the CCSS were developed, the architects examined individual states' standards and created a national, unifying set of educational goals. This framework placed emphasis on the development of the skills that students need to possess in order to demonstrate what they know and understand about content knowledge and higher-level problem solving. There is misunderstanding about the CCSS and the college and career readiness movement that I wish to dispel.

Educators, not politicians or bureaucrats, developed the CCSS. Educators are our most precious resource, and unlike other written standards, their expertise is reflected in the CCSS. It is unfortunate that this reality has been mythologized. Many colleagues argue that they did not have a voice in the development of the new standards, which are confused when they are largely muted by state and district bureaucrats during the implementation process. New initiatives such as performance-based teacher evaluations are often paired with the implementation of new standards. There is not one place in the actual text of the CCSS and many of the individual state counterparts that outlines policy and implementation considerations. In fact, unlike previous national initiatives, CCSS identifies that it is teachers and curriculum specialists who know best how to develop the skills that are articulated in this new framework (NGA and CCSSO, 2010). Unfortunately, like so many educational initiatives, there is a gross misunderstanding of what CCSS is designed to do that is perpetuated by special interest groups and political entities.

THE NEED FOR NEW STANDARDS AND NEW EXPECTATIONS FOR *ALL* STUDENTS

In response to research reports in the past decade that there has a growing decline in the complexity and rigor of assigned texts in school, the authors of CCSS addressed this reality in the new framework. Other individual states have also followed suit.

Recent reports indicate that students have low-level reading proficiency that has rendered them devoid of the skills that are needed for college and career readiness. Appendix A of the CCSS identifies a 2006 ACT report, *Reading Between the Lines*, to evidence these concerns. It is important to remember that this report focuses on students who are largely college bound. What about our students who do not plan on attending college? CCSS recognizes these issues and the developers brought together a task force to collect and examine the texts used for freshmen college and university level courses as well as texts used for individuals entering the workforce. As the CCSS developers examined the texts, it was evident that the high school texts were not at the same level of difficulty and rigor. It became evident that a significant gap existed between the level of text complexity and work required in high school and what was needed for success in college and careers.

In the past, many educational initiatives focused primarily on college preparation. CCSS includes students who transition directly from high school to careers. The CCSS developers focused on the mathematical and literacy skills that students need to be prepared for in the twenty-first-century marketplace whether the students embarked on the college or career path directly from high school. This is important to note since the CCSS developers examined the needs of *all* students, not just those who were college bound.

Since the CCSS framework is designed to have consistent anchor standards from kindergarten through twelfth grade, with grade level articulations for each grade level, it makes it easier for educators to differentiate instruction. For example, a student with special needs who is in seventh grade but may be performing on a fifth-grade level can work on the same skill as their peers since it is the same anchor standard, but at an appropriate skill and grade level. Conversely, an academically accelerated student could work at a higher level on the same skill. This is in contrast to previously written standards that were mostly focused on content knowledge, rather than skills. This is not to say that content is not important or significant in the new standards. Instead, content is the vehicle used to develop skills as they are articulated in the new standards.

Another way in which the new standards address the needs of all students is that during the first round of standards in the late 1990s, individual states developed and created their own standards and assessments. The National Assessment for Educational Progress (NAEP), administered by the U.S. Department of Education, has been our primary resource for comparing the performance of students on a state-by-state basis (NCES, n.d.). The data from NAEP have consistently revealed significant differences among states and of different socioeconomic backgrounds. The new standards afford us for the first time to have some consistency among standards and assessments to accurately determine student performance.

More Rigorous Expectations

As I work with fellow educators in the United States, many note that the expectations with the new standards are high, with more rigorous texts, evidence-based writing, and mathematical practices requiring students to apply mathematical concepts to contextualized problems. These raised expectations for all students include:

- The ability for students to understand complex texts. They need to be able to identify the main idea key details, text structures, and the integration of knowledge and ideas. Students are also expected to make comparisons between texts and draw conclusions.
- Students are also expected to read at a more accelerated level of difficulty. Many of the new standards require students to read about two hundred Lexile points higher than the current expectations.
- There is also greater emphasis on reading informational text. Since we gain the majority of content knowledge through text, it is important that students are able to effectively read informational text to learn about social studies, science, mathematics, technical subjects, and English.
- Students are expected to be malleable in their reading, meaning that they can develop skills while reading and through analysis that allow them to critically examine text. They are also expected to be able to demonstrate what they know and understand about content through effective literacy skills: reading, writing, speaking and listening, and language.
- The ways in which we read text, write text, use text, and how text affects us have changed in the twenty-first century. In this information age, students need to be able to sort through and analyze large volumes of information. This is very different from how most of us were educated. Our teachers and professors were largely the dispensers of content when I attended college. Now, there is more recorded information in human history and students need to be able to make sense of it. Students are no longer dependent on their teachers, professors, and textbooks for information. Widely available and abundant information is no longer a time-intensive process.
- There is also greater emphasis in the new standards on argumentation in writing. This is not to say that other types of writing like personal narratives and expository writing are not important. The new standards recognize that students must be skilled in their ability to articulate an argument. Written arguments also must be supported with relevant evidence. Can students make an assertion and support it with evidence?
- Speaking and listening standards also place emphasis on a student's ability to articulate an argument or analysis in a small or large group setting. The new standards emphasize the importance of these communication tools.
- Another key feature of the literacy standards is the importance of word learning. As students progress through school, there is more general academic and domain-specific vocabulary. Learning strategies for the development of academic and content vocabulary al-

lows students to better understand and comprehend specific subjects like science, social studies, and technical subjects.

- In mathematics, students are expected to have speed and accuracy with simple calculations. Additionally, it is expected that educators teach more than "how to get the answer" and instead develop and nurture a student's ability to access concepts from a number of perspectives. Students demonstrate understanding by applying core mathematics concepts to new situations as well as writing and speaking about them. If students can talk about math, they will understand it.
- The new standards expect students to apply math concepts in real-world situations. Students are expected to choose the appropriate concept and apply it in various contexts.

A clear message has been sent in the new standards that students must be engaged in deeper learning. This deeper level of understanding and comprehension is communicated through a more sophisticated and independent level of applied literacy skills. Combining deep understanding of content and literacy development is a hallmark feature in the new standards. This expectation encourages teachers to vary learning experiences for their students through differentiation of text, materials, activities, and assessment. As educators, we already know that providing students with these kinds of learning experiences facilitates their growth and development, regardless of their socioeconomic status, identified special need, or academic ability. In short, the new standards remind us of what it means to close the achievement gap and prepare *all* of our students to be college and career ready.

How This Book Addresses the Needs of All Students in Closing the Achievement Gap

Although there are success stories in different districts and schools across the United States, the challenges in closing the achievement gap among students continue to vex us. This book addresses these challenges and possible solutions for closing the achievement gap in this era of new standards and more rigorous expectations.

LeAnn Nickelsen, a leading expert on brain-based learning, shares her work about how the brains of those who are poverty stricken differ from those who live in higher socioeconomic status environments. Nicklelsen focuses on language and cognitive differences that can affect students who live in poverty and their potential to meet the expectations of the new standards. She shares key research and offers strategies to help students achieve and develop the skills and expectations that are articulated in the new standards.

Building on the work of Stanford professor Carol Dweck (2006), Richard Cash addresses a critical component in achievement: the effectiveness of the learner's application of and focus toward self-regulation and self-efficacy. Both are necessary for turning struggling learners into active and independent learners. Fostering greater independence in learners is a key focus for the new standards. His chapter provides a review of promotion and prevention orientation of self-regulation and how these are related to college and career readiness. Cash also shares his expertise in providing a self-regulatory model that fosters student self-efficacy that educators can implement in schools and classrooms.

Experienced literacy coach and classroom teacher Melissa Dickson explores the ways in which differentiated instruction can increase the likelihood of student success. After surveying the characteristics of a standards-based classroom and the elements of authentic differentiation, Dickson itemizes ways in which pre-assessment data can be effectively used to help teachers determine what to teach, who to teach, and how to teach. Differentiating content, the educational process, and the final product creates an environment in which each student can achieve success and each educator can employ the ideal blend of the art and the science of teaching.

As there is greater emphasis in the new standards on evidence-based argumentation in writing, Eileen Murphy addresses writing and argumentation in her chapter. This chapter addresses the benefits and challenges of developing a stable systemwide vocabulary for discussing critical literacy across disciplines. In creating a common language and working toward the development of an explicit progression of argumentation skills, students become more independent and successful. Murphy has had extensive experience closing the achievement gap through her critical analysis model in reading and writing in many schools and districts throughout the United States.

Developing a mathematics curriculum that involves teaching key concepts that promote a student's ability to analyze and apply his or her skills to different contexts is addressed in Michael Troop's chapter. Using his expertise in both mathematics and science, Troop examines the new mathematics standards and implications for teaching and learning in the twenty-first-century classroom.

The need to carefully select and integrate appropriate educational technologies that enhance classroom teaching and learning is crucial to the success of meeting the new standards. Teachers have the options of how they decide what strategies they use for their teaching, but to be effective, they must engage the students according to the standard (or academic skill) and not to the technologies available. It is tempting to select technology that appears to be engaging for students, yet the use of technology in isolation or without adequate planning causes one to lose sight of the real purpose of the classroom activity. Seema Imam addresses the effective application of educational technologies within the new standards and how these can potentially close the achievement gap.

Without both preassessment and formative assessment, teachers would not know when and how to differentiate instruction for learners. However, teachers frequently feel overwhelmed with the need to design, facilitate, and then analyze formative assessment data as well as find the time to do so. In the formative assessment chapter, I address how teachers can gather formative data to make instructional decisions but also actively engage students in nonthreatening assessments. The new assessments and initiatives have created a threatening environment for teachers and students. Many critics of CCSS claim that the new framework has subjected students to more high-stakes testing. This is simply untrue. Districts and states make these decisions. The new standards, including CCSS, do not necessitate more testing. My chapter focuses on the need to have reliable assessment and data sources that are well reasoned and not threatening.

We have the opportunity to hear from ninth-grade ELA teachers Elizabeth Knost and Elizabeth Perry. They offer an insight into how real teachers are incorporating the new standards in some of our most challenging classrooms. Their frank acknowledgement of obstacles that will seem familiar to many teachers, plus case studies of four students, provide a valuable backdrop to what can sometimes seem a theoretical discussion of college and career readiness. By focusing on appropriately complex texts, using an integrated literacy model, and incorporating learning centers and a gradual release of responsibility, these talented educators help close the achievement gap for students who have entered high school reading well below grade level–and they redefine the possibilities for teachers who are called upon to achieve the impossible.

I also address the importance of reading as the foundation for all learning. The foundational core skills needed to prepare students for careers and college readiness are fundamental in the new standards. This strong focus on expectations for the development of reading skills is long overdue and a welcomed change from the previous generation of standards. Students must develop reading skills with greater independence and rigor in order to access, learn, and comprehend content at all grade levels. My chapter will explore how the development of reading skills in all content areas develops college and career readiness. In addition there is special emphasis on reading and associated literacy skills in writing, speaking, listening, and language for at-risk students and how educators can close the achievement gap.

The focus of this text is on closing the achievement gap for *all* students in this era of new standards. There are two specific chapters dedicated to students with special needs, and English-language learners are included. Brenna Sherwood and Nicole Lambson share the model that they developed in Farmington, New Mexico, for differentiating instruction in meeting the individual education plans (IEP) for students with special needs. Their work provides a model for us to consider in creating rigor and achievement for our students with special needs. Their colleague, Diane Arrington, examines how the new standards impact English-language learners. Arrington addresses how the standards allow for greater differentiation and targeted instruction for language development.

Creating a Dialogue for Student Achievement and Success

The CCSS and parallel individual state standards were written to address the harsh realities of poor performance of American students across all grade levels, kindergarten through twelfth grade. According to NAEP data, more than 60 percent of our students in grades four, eight, and twelve are not proficient readers, and the United States is one of the lowest performing nations in mathematics. The statistics are even more staggering for our children who live in poverty, are differently abled, and English-language learners. This book envisions the new standards as a vehicle and opportunity to provide more rigorous instruction that is comprised of articulated skills and places the trust in teachers and the curriculum specialist to determine which methods are most effective in developing skills in their students.

This book was written for fellow educators, preservice teachers, and administrators who are seeking understanding and potential solutions and models to address the achievement gap. A common theme that emerged from the contributors and their chapters is that creativity, flexibility, and innovation must be the primary focus in closing the achievement gap.

At this point as you embark on this text I want to remind you of the political climate at the time this book was written. The new standards have been attacked and are frequently misrepresented. Comments like "the new standards dictate a list of books to be read" or "the new standards are creating teacher evaluation systems," or "the students are subject to increased standardized testing" are prevalent, but none of these are ever articulated in the original CCSS document or in their individual state counterparts. Instead, these are policy decisions that are made at the district and school levels. I believe that the philosophy and intent of the new standards is not harmful to students. Instead, the emphasis on academic rigor is overdue. I have become increasingly worried when the intentions of CCSS and individual state standards become mired in political agendas and misunderstanding of the research and intent of the new standards.

It is not the first time in the history of education in the United States that well-intentioned educational initiatives become misrepresented and politicized. I implore my colleagues to keep an open mind. Let's remember why educators became educators. It's always about the students and how we can prepare them to be college and career ready, but more importantly, it is about preparing our students to be active and productive citizens in our democratic society. Let's not lose sight of that in this politically charged environment regarding the new standards.

REFERENCES AND RESOURCES

American College Testing (ACT). (2006). *Reading between the lines: What the ACT reveals about college readiness in reading.* Iowa City: Author.

Dweck, C. (2006). *Mindset: The new psychology of success.* New York: Random House.

Holcomb, S. (2006, February 21). Answering the call: The history of NEA, part 2. Rss. National Education Association.

National Assessment Governing Board. (2008). *Reading framework for the 2009 National Assessment of Educational Progress.* Washington, DC: U.S. Government Printing Office.

National Center for Education Statistics (NCES). "NAEP Nations Report Card." Retrieved from nces.ed.gov/nationsreportcard/reading/achieve.aspx.

National Governors Association Center for Best Practices (NGA) and Council of Chief State School Officers (CCSSO). (2010). *Common Core State Standards.* Washington, DC: Authors.

TWO

Empower Poverty-Stricken Students for Common Core State Standards Mastery

LeAnn Nickelsen

The Common Core State Standards (CCSS) were designed to meet student needs based on the nationwide data that have been reported. To sum up the data, students are not as prepared for the college and career ready standards that they will encounter in higher education. The National Center for Education Statistics (based on our nation's report card: National Assessment of Educational Progress) reported that only 38 percent of twelfth graders have the reading skills for entry-level college courses. Scores from 2014 were in the same range as the last time the test had been taken in 2009 (the test is administered every four years). In other words, scores have flat-lined—no growth! On top of that research, students with disabilities, low background knowledge, and those who live in poverty have an even larger gap in being prepared for college and career routes. This chapter will address how we can help students who live in poverty (and students who don't live in low socioeconomic conditions as well) achieve these high standards. The research, ideas, and strategies in this chapter are powerful methods that are extremely effective for high student achievement.

Recent research from Southern Education Foundation (SEF, 2015) reported that more than half of U.S. public school students are from low-income families. The highest concentration of low-income students resides in the southern and western states, according to SEF's research, but they are prevalent in all states.

We know through numerous studies that poverty has adverse effects such as impaired cognitive development, high levels of stress and cortisol, emotional and social problems, increased health concerns, and myriad other problems that are synergistic. Chronic exposure to poverty conditions causes negative physical changes in the brain that affect learning.

RESEARCH ABOUT POVERTY-STRICKEN BRAINS

The following list provides information about students from different socioeconomic statuses taken from the American Psychological Association website (www.apa.org/pi/ses/resources/publications/factsheet-education.aspx):

- Children from low-SES households develop academic achievement more slowly compared to children from higher-SES groups (Morgan, Farkas, Hillemeier, and Maczuga, 2009).
- Children from low-SES environments acquire language skills more slowly, exhibit delayed letter recognition and phonological awareness, and are at risk for reading difficulties (Aikens and Barbarin, 2008).
- Children with higher-SES backgrounds were more likely to be proficient on tasks of addition, subtraction, ordinal sequencing, and math word problems than children with lower-SES backgrounds (Coley, 2002).
- Students from low-SES schools entered high school 3.3 grade levels behind students from higher-SES schools. In addition, students from the low-SES groups learned less over four years than children from higher-SES groups, graduating 4.3 grade levels behind those of higher-SES groups (Palardy, 2008).
- In 2007, the high school dropout rate among persons sixteen to twenty-four years old was highest in low-income families (16.7 percent) as compared to high-income families (3.2 percent) (National Center for Education Statistics, 2008).
- Families from low-SES communities are less likely to have the financial resources or time availability to provide children with academic support.
- Children's initial reading competence is correlated with the home literacy environment, number of books owned, and parent distress (Aikens and Barbarin, 2008). However, parents from low-SES communities may be unable to afford resources such as books, computers, or tutors to create this positive literacy environment (Orr, 2003).
- In a nationwide study of American kindergarten children, 36 percent of parents in the lowest-income quintile read to their children on a daily basis, compared with 62 percent of parents from the highest-income quintile (Coley, 2002).

- When enrolled in a program that encouraged adult support, students from low-SES groups reported higher levels of effort toward academics (Kaylor and Flores, 2008).

One of the most significant pieces of research that shows the detailed differences in children of poverty brains versus children of a higher socioeconomic status is by Noble, Norman, and Farah in 2005. This study scanned brains and compared kindergartener low-SES students with kindergartener higher-SES students and found that there were several differences in their cognitive functioning—in their cognitive control, reward processing systems, spatial and visual cognition—but the largest effect sizes were in language (almost 1.0 effect size), memory, and working memory. Several other pieces of research have been done comparing their neurocognitive systems, and all of the results showed that there are significant differences in their brains across the age and grade levels. Because language skills and memory tasks had the largest differences or deviations, this chapter will focus on strategies for building language skills, executive function skills (working memory; see Richard Cash's chapter on self-regulation), and long-term memory skills.

There Is Hope!

The environment that we are in consistently affects our brain. Just as it is true that poverty-stricken environments of stress, hunger, and lack of resources and needs affect the brain in negative manners, our schools can provide highly enriched, complex learning environments that change brains for the better. Because we have the research on this, we now know which factors affect students positively.

Dr. Marian Diamond, a top brain researcher from University of California, Berkeley, found that enriched environments can increase the dimensions of the cellular constituents of the cortex part of the brain at *any* age from prenatal to extremely old age (around ninety years). Four days of being in an enriched environment can create statistically significant growth, just as four days of living in an impoverished environment can cause statistically significant decrease in cortical development. This is great news! When she and her researchers placed rats in a highly enriched environment (rotated toys for novelty effect, introduced other rats for socialization, increased space, provided exercise toys) versus a single rat in a large cage with no toys, in as little as eight days of time, the enriched pups' cortex went from 7 to 16 percent thicker than in the other rats that were in impoverished environments (no friends, isolation, no toys). Not only did they have thicker cortexes, but the neurons in the brain had more dendritic growth and connections. Diamond has defined enriched environments as (Diamond and Hopson, 1998):

- A steady source of positive emotional support
- Nutritious diet with enough protein, vitamins, minerals, calories, and antioxidants
- Multisensory strategies and toys
- Atmosphere free from high stress and pressure, but a degree of pleasurable intensity
- Novel challenges available that are just right for the stage of development that the child is at
- Social interactions for a significant percentage of activities
- Broad development of mental, physical, aesthetic, social, and emotional skills and interests
- Many choices present for the children
- Opportunities for assessing growth and efforts and time to modify them
- Enjoyable atmosphere that promotes exploration and fun of learning
- Enriched environments that allow a child to be an active participant rather than a passive observer

We can do this, educators! We have the tools, books, strategies, and learning opportunities to promote and create this type of enriched environment in all of our schools—we must make the choice to take the time and effort to think through how this will look in our classrooms every day. Poverty-stricken children must have this enriched environment.

Did you know that our environments can actually produce new brain cells? There were years where neuroscience stated that we were born with 100 billion neurons, and that was it! It was all downhill after that—how discouraging (especially at my age). In the 1990s, we learned through research that new brain cells are formed when certain factors are in place. This formation of new brain cells in certain parts of the brain is called neurogenesis. We know that neurogenesis is reduced in certain parts of the brain when it experiences distress, boredom, depression, poor nutrition, isolation, inactivity, and low social status. On the other hand, neurogenesis can be enhanced by positive social situations, low stress, healthy nutrition, new learning opportunities, complex and challenging environments, and exercise, the latter being the most powerful!

Exercise is one of the best activities for a better brain. Exercise stimulates brain-derived neurotrophic factor (BDNF), a "Miracle-Gro" for the brain. John Ratey, author of *Spark: The Revolutionary New Science of Exercise and the Brain* (2008), explained that when researchers sprinkle BDNF onto neurons in a petri dish, the cells spontaneously sprout new dendrites, which is the same structural growth required for learning. Make sure your students never miss recess or exercise opportunities. Neurogenesis gives everyone hope—that our choices and our environment can improve our brains.

Brains Change

Our brains change depending on many factors. We know that every time learning takes place, the structure of the brain cell, called the neuron, changes physically. Dendrites extend out from the neuron and synapses are formed among neuronal dendrites and axons from another neuron, creating neural networks. We also know that certain environments that we are in affect our brain physically, mentally, and academically. Neuroplasticity is when region-specific changes in the brain (synapses and pathways) occur because of the changes in that person's experiences that are made up of the environment, emotions, thinking, behavior, injury, and disease. In other words, the brain can reorganize itself by creating new connections because of the new environment it is in. This is amazing and gives everyone hope! For example, Gottfried Schlaug, Harvard neurologist, conducted a study in 2003 that showed that after fifteen months of musical training in early childhood, structural brain changes associated with motor and auditory improvements begin to appear. Other studies found an increase in volume of white matter among the neurons. On the other hand, children playing and engaging in violent video games caused more aggression in those children. Experiences change our brains—for the good and for the bad!

Research from Gottfredson in 2004 suggests that low socioeconomic status students begin school with lower intelligence quotients (IQs). Just how much is IQ inherited or affected by nature versus nurture? We know IQ is not fixed but is affected by environments, nutritious factors of food eaten, and early childhood learning opportunities and interventions. Research conducted by Capron and Duyme (1989) found that by changing a low-SES, adopted child's environment to a high-SES environment, IQ can be raised significantly (19.5 points). Again, very encouraging research to show us that brains can change for the better with time and other powerful factors.

The Power of the Teacher

According to John Hattie's research (2009), the teacher has more power on student achievement than a student's socioeconomic status, student language, and even class size. Socioeconomic status (parental income, education and occupation are three main indicators of SES) still has an effect on student achievement, an effect size of 0.57, but doesn't come close to the power of an effective teacher who engages in the formative assessment process (0.90), encourages student self-assessment (1.44), models and teaches students reciprocal teaching reading/discussion tool (0.74), teacher credibility (in eyes of student) (0.90), teacher clarity (0.75), feedback (0.73), teacher-student relationship (0.72), and teacher's strategies chosen (0.60). Everything listed here (and many more items that I didn't even mention) has a greater effect on student achievement than a student's background or his or her home environment.

So, have I convinced you yet? Even though there are many factors that work against poverty-stricken children's education and learning, we can make a *huge* difference in their ability to master high standards, such as the new CCSS. If so, read on for some of the most powerful tools and strategies that we can use in our schools.

THE MOST POWERFUL FACTORS, TOOLS, AND STRATEGIES: PART I

So how do high-performing, high-poverty schools reach high standards? Numerous books have collections of these schools' stories, such as Karin Chenoweth's book, *How It's Being Done: Urgent Lessons from Unexpected Schools* (2009), and Eric Jensen's book, *Teaching with Poverty in Mind* (2009). There are researched factors that many of the schools had in common and all of the stories start with a leader who knows and believes that these students can learn at high levels and persevere through their tough situations. The first section of this second part of the chapter will deal with our mindsets, attitudes, thoughts, and expectations for our students. They greatly affect how much these children can accomplish in our classrooms. The second part of this section will present specific tools and strategies teachers can use in their classrooms with the CCSS English language arts (ELA) standards in mind — remember, every subject area has incorporated the ELA reading and writing standards (note to middle school and high school teachers).

The Growth Mindset Leader at High-Poverty Schools

I consider the best leaders to be those who want to inspire positive change in their school buildings so that the powerful tools they are encouraging become "contagious" around the whole building! So, leaders can be administrators, coaches, teachers, and other educators in different roles. Our beliefs totally affect our actions.

The number one place to start is by building growth mindsets among all the stakeholders: district-level administrators, principals, teachers, parents, and students. Leaders with a growth mindset can lead teachers to have that same mindset of hope, effort, tenacity, and goal orientation. Characteristics of a leader with a growth mindset include:

- *Their praise toward others*: Carol Dweck's research (2006) found that when we praise intelligence, mental power, and abilities, those who receive the praise didn't want or appreciate too much challenge — they wanted to be comfortable, not make mistakes, and receive more praise for their "status quo" intelligence that received the praise in the first place. So, a growth mindset leader will be praising others' attitudes, efforts, and strategies used to accomplish tasks. They also embrace challenges and persist through them.

- *Wanting to try new things*: Growth mindset leaders will not be afraid to try new strategies and tools. They are not afraid of making mistakes since they view them as a way to growth and learn rather than feel threatened about others thinking they are failures for a mistake. It was 10,000 mistakes that finally helped Thomas Edison invent the lightbulb—now that is an amazing growth mindset example!
- *Effort is a necessary belief*: Growth mindset leaders believe that effort is the path to mastery, and through much time and practice one can achieve anything he or she wants.
- *Inspired by others' success*: These leaders want others to succeed and are grateful for others' accomplishments and hard work that they achieved rather than looking at successful people as threats.
- *Potential is developed belief*: These leaders believe that goals should be set to reach their full potential—by the way, their full potential is not even defined—they just keep on growing, learning, building, creating, and doing toward a goal they know they can accomplish over time and with effort!
- *Powerful impact on others*: These leaders invite cooperation, feedback, and suggestions that make them "partners" in learning rather than being the "know-it-all." They listen, research, inspire others to try new things, and praise those stakeholders appropriately.

For more specific ideas for encouraging growth mindsets in the children at a school, please see my article on the website www.brain-basedlearning.net. This extremely important concept called growth mindsets is the beginning or the foundation of truly changing environments in a high poverty school.

Tenacity Tools

Children living in high poverty oftentimes have seen their parents struggle with no apparent way out of their problems (refrigerator breaks and can't purchase a new one, utility bill can't be paid, car just broke down, etc.). Stressor after stressor occurs. In fact, research shows that low socioeconomic children are more subject to both acute stress (stress resulting from onetime events) and chronic stress (high stress that is sustained over time) than their more affluent peers. Children living in poverty experience significantly more chronic stressors daily (Almeida et al., 2005). Chronic stress greatly affects childrens' physical, psychological, emotional, and cognitive functioning—all of which affect daily learning.

These students will need tenacity-building tools (those that give them hope) on a daily basis. The tenacity-building tools include:

1. Positive relationships: These relationships are built on trust, concern, compassion, growth, and fun. These kids need someone they can discuss problems or concerns with—someone who will encourage them to be the best they can be. Research shows that if a child even has just one person in his or her life that believes in him or her, the child can make it through some of the toughest obstacles in life. Mentorship programs and a teacher who cares can make a huge difference in these children's lives.

2. Meaning-making in lessons: Educators need to ensure relevancy and opportunities for meaning-making in every lesson. If there is buy-in, there is a greater chance for memory of the concepts. Think about it: we like to read books and listen to podcasts that are relevant to our lives and interests. Educators can make lessons more relevant by explaining to the students why they need to learn that particular standard and how it can be used in the future and present time. When possible, educators should plan activities or problem-based learning projects that children work through that truly solve problems that are around them.

3. Celebrate their strengths, teach with their interests in mind, and encourage their passions: In other words, get to know your students well and deeply in order to meet their inner needs and show them they have strengths and purpose.

4. Encourage books and peripherals in your classroom about hope and about persistence: These students need to see others who struggled and yet made it—perhaps made it big! These role models and examples can give them hope. If someone has hope, they can conquer much. Once hope is gone, motivation to keep going is gone.

5. Provide the just right amount of challenge with hope and scaffolding: When teaching your high standards, educators will need to know students' background knowledge before teaching so they provide the right amount of challenge with the right amount of support to reach these high standards. In other words, do not give these children too high of a challenge with no support; that is a recipe for hopelessness and giving up. Daniel Pink in his book, *Drive* (2009), states that people are motivated when there is purpose, autonomy (not forcing, but giving choices), and mastery. Mastery is one of the best tools to *want more* and *master more*!

6. Feedback along the learning journey: We know that the best feedback relates to students' efforts, attitudes, and strategies that they use, but we must also give them feedback about where they are with the standards and daily learning targets. They must know

how close they are to closing gaps and which strategies to use to close the gaps in achieving the learning targets. We help them self-evaluate and move the work closer to those daily learning goals. I call it baby-step feedback.

There are so many more tenacity tools that these students need, but these are some of the most powerful tools.

Teacher High Expectations

A study from the Center for American Progress (Boser, Wilhelm, and Hanna, 2014) concluded that teachers' expectations for their students are strongly correlated with students' graduation rates. The unfortunate part of this study was that they found that teachers who worked with poverty-stricken students, specifically secondary teachers, viewed high-poverty students as 53 percent less likely to graduate from college than their classmates from wealthier backgrounds. Another long-term study from the National Center for Educational Statistics (2008) found that high school teachers who had high expectations for their students had three times the rate of students who graduated from college than from those with low expectations.

Many teachers wonder how they can help students with low background knowledge and thinking skills come close to the very rigorous standards. The above study focused on a theory that has been around for a while called the "Pygmalion effect," the theory holding that higher expectations of a person lead to higher performance. It also can be true that those who have lower expectations of others are more likely to perform poorly. This amazing work by Rosenthal and Jacobsen (1968) showed that teacher expectations influence student performance. "When we expect certain behaviors of others, we are likely to act in ways that make the expected behaviors more likely to occur" (Rosenthal and Babad, 1985). To help students get to these high standards, the teachers will need to preassess to determine where the students are with the standards before explicitly teaching them, create a scaffolding plan for teaching, and differentiate the instruction to help students achieve these high standards on different days and with different tools.

Challenge Students: The Academic Rigor at High Poverty Schools

There is a common myth in the education world: If information feels easy to absorb, then our students have learned it well! Research suggests that when students put forth great effort to understand information and learn it, they actually can recall it much better. In other words, we should design lessons, activities, and assessments that challenge students to think deeply about the information. This action tells the brain "Hey this is important, so please remember it!"

Psychologists performed this research by having one group of students read difficult material in unfamiliar fonts and another group read the same article with conventional, familiar fonts. They found that the students who read the difficult material in unfamiliar fonts actually learned the content from the article more deeply than the latter group. This phenomenon is called cognitive disfluency. They also created passages with punctuation mistakes, deliberately leaving out letters, shrinking the font size, and making the page blurry to challenge the reader. Same results.

Teachers and students may think that learning material with ease and speed is the better route, but the researchers showed that "making material harder to learn can improve long-term learning and retention. More cognitive engagement leads to deeper processing, which facilitates encoding and subsequently better retrieval" (Diemand-Yauman, Oppenheimer, and Vaughan, 2010).

Many other experiments suggest that the more effort one puts toward learning, the more the information may sink in more deeply. "Disfluency" during the learning process can produce greater retention. The careful, deep thinking of learning something that is "disfluent" can be very beneficial to memory encoding of that content.

I personally like the analogy that James M. Lang, professor of English at Assumption College and author of *On Course: A Week-by-Week Guide to Your First Semester of College Teaching* (2008), created about cognitive disfluency:

> To put this as (over)simply as possible, learning material in fluent conditions—easy-to-read fonts, clear causal connections—is like driving to the grocery store on cognitive automatic pilot. You get from Point A to Point B, but you are not really paying close attention, and, hence, are unlikely to remember your trip in any detail later. (Lang, 2012)

There are several ways to respond to this research in our classrooms. Educators could preassess their students to know if a concept will be challenging or too easy for the students and plan accordingly. Assignments could be "interleaved," which mixes concepts apart from one another so students cannot easily complete the assignment based on a familiar pattern, rule (grammar rule, etc.), or theorem. They have to think about how to solve the problem versus just determine, "Oh this group of math problems all follow the same pattern or equation." Therefore, the students' brains will have to think deeper about the problems since they are not grouped by similar type. Making mistakes takes kids out of autopilot mode and into "I'm trying to figure out what just happened." The CCSS give students more opportunities to enter into this cognitive disfluency mode.

THE MOST POWERFUL FACTORS, TOOLS, AND STRATEGIES:
PART 2

The following CCSS expectations are definitely going to challenge students if teachers use them effectively: close reading of complex text with text-dependent questions that teachers take students through while reading; argumentative and informational writing by using academic vocabulary that students think, speak, and write with. Within each section explaining these strategies and tools, critical thinking and executive function skills will be emphasized.

Complex Text and Text-Dependent Questions

The CCSS created Anchor Reading Standard 10 in order to truly challenge brains: "Read and comprehend complex literary and informational texts independently and proficiently" (www.corestandards.org). Educators must plan more lessons using complex text. The clearest differentiator in reading between students who are college ready and students who are not is the ability to comprehend complex texts. This is one reason why the CCSS is asking teachers to give their students more opportunities to grapple with complex text (ACT, 2004). I wonder if the creators of CCSS knew about cognitive disfluency?

During a close read of complex texts, teachers want to make sure that students are thinking deeply about the text and the purpose of the text. The goal is for the students to deeply comprehend this text, build stamina with challenging meaning and possibly terms, and use the most powerful reading strategies and skills from their toolkit that is constantly being developed. These lessons need much teacher support and predesigned text-dependent questions that force the students back into the text in order to find the answer. These questions are not "right there," easy to find, one-word answers. The questions start out simple and gradually increase in depth, using inference by studying syntax and sentence structure, determining how words and phrases change meaning throughout the text, determining the author's purpose, and even how the students respond to this text. Douglas Fisher and Nancy Frey created a powerful visual to explain the progressions of questions: Moving Beyond the Literal (education.illinoisstate.edu/downloads/casei/4-02A-Engaging%20fisher.pdf). You can ask questions about words, sentences, paragraphs, segments, entire texts, and even across texts. Questions can be about any of those pieces asked at the general understanding and key detail level, then studying the vocabulary and text structure of the text, with a focus on the author's purpose. Finally, questions can be designed to ask the reader opinions, arguments, and questions about intertextual connections. Figure 2.1 presents a list of text-dependent questions for ideas of how to form these questions.

Type of TDQ	Informational Text	Literary Text
General Understanding of Text	• What is the gist of this text based on title, headings, pictures, captions, etc.? • What is the main idea? • •	• What might this story be about based on cover pages, pictures, title, etc. •
Key Details	• What was an interesting fact that you read about? • What details do you think should be part of this text and are not? • What did you learn from paragraph _____? • What supporting details did the author include to help you learn _____?	• Who, did what, where, when, why and how? • Who is telling this story and why? • Who is the story being written to?
Vocabulary & Text Structure	• What does the author mean when he/she said: ____? • How does this sentence, passage or section connect with the rest of the whole text? • What words are confusing or stand out? • How do the transition words that the author uses help your brain transition from paragraphs or ideas? • How do the text features help you understand the text better? Would you change any of them? • How does the author organize this writing? Which text structures did he/she use? Good choice?	• Which words were rich in meaning or created a particular emotion within you? • How did the characters change based on what they experienced (plot events)? • How did the setting impact the plot? How did that impact the characters? • Which words are confusing? • If _____ word was changed to _____ how might the meaning change? • What figurative language or symbols made the visualization process better? • How does the sequence of the story develop the plot, characters, climax, etc? • What major events affected the behaviors of the characters? • What words resonate with you? Which phrases do you love?

Author's Purpose	• What is the author telling us about this topic (point of view)? Does he/she have any biases? Purpose? • Is the author trying to persuade the reader to believe/do something? • What resources is he/she using to support topic? • What does the author want me to believe or understand? What is his/her connotation?	• What does the author want me to believe and/or understand? • What are some themes within this story? • What tone or mood is the author portraying? • What assumptions is the author making during _____. • What does the author want me to believe or understand? What is his/her connotation?
Inferences Or conclusions	• What facts do you believe are missing from this text? • What caused _____? • How can you determine if this author is credible to write about this topic? • Research the author's life – what factors in his/her life have contributed to this piece of writing?	• What two events could have prevented the problem? • Why did the character do _____ or say _____? • Does the story describe a particular culture? Belief system? • Research the author's life – what factors in his/her life have contributed to this piece of writing?
Self-Expression with opinions, arguments and comparisons to other texts	• What is your opinion about this topic? How would you create an argument for or against it? • Compare this topic to what we read yesterday about _____.	• How does this story connect with other stories you read? • How is this author's style like his/her other book called _____? • How would you rate this book? Which audience would appreciate this book the most? • How does the internet site _____ help us understand this book better?

Every **TDQ** should force the student **BACK** to the text to retrieve the answer. Always include follow-up phrases such as:

- Where did you find that?
- Why did you say that?
- Support your answer. Show me where you found that.
- What is the evidence to prove what you just said?
- Explain your thinking?
- How do you know that?

Figure 2.1.   Text-Dependent Questions.

Argumentative and Informational Writing

Formulating opinions and supporting them can definitely challenge the brain since the brain has to evaluate many pieces of evidence to determine whether or not they are strong enough to make a solid claim and then argue for or against them. Writing Anchor Standard 1 states: "Write arguments to support claims in an analysis of substantive topics or texts using valid reasoning and relevant and sufficient evidence" (www.corestandards.org).

To really help students of poverty reach this high standard, you will need to break it down into smaller units, or daily learning targets. Here are some steps to help you be more successful: Help the students choose a high interest topic that is part of your curriculum. You want the students to be familiar with this topic so you might have some ideas ready for them. The website www.procon.org has many topics in several categories that will help your students get a quick perspective on many pressing issues. During this stage of finding a topic, I encourage small group discussions so their brains get primed and possibly provide feedback.

The next step is to make sure you teach the vocabulary terms that go along with argumentative writing like: claim versus opinion, counterclaim, evidence, reason, warrants. The following website will explain each component and even give you mini-lessons about how to explicitly teach your students about argumentative writing: www.ThinkCerca.com. The other learning targets that must be taught in order to get their best opinion writings are:

- Identifying support for the main ideas
- Detecting bias
- Distinguishing arguments and counterarguments
- Evaluating the strength of the argument
- Drawing conclusions
- Describing vocabulary words

This scaffolding will help students be more successful with their writing if they understand these very important skills before pulling the pieces together. This is called providing the scaffolding so each step will give them success—it is needed when they are surrounded with environments that are violent, sometimes hopeless, and often very stressful. Provide your utmost support!

Once the students understand the pieces that make up a great argumentative writing piece, it's time for them to brainstorm their claim, evidence, and warrants for their argument. The warrant is a statement that connects the evidence to the claim. Students can create a web showing how these pieces come together. They can visually brainstorm their claims or position on the matter, give their evidence and reasons for that claim, and then finally write the warrant to bring them together. You will need to model this process. After you teach them what a counterclaim is and you have modeled one for them with one of your arguments, help them brainstorm that piece to conclude their writing. Make sure to give them feedback on their brainstorm so they have the tenacity and excitement to start the writing. Children with low background knowledge have a harder time starting the writing process.

Some students may be reluctant to want to get started with this challenging task. Researchers and teachers have found that the following three pieces motivate students to get started more quickly. First, they should know much about their topic—get them reading lots about their topic. Second, they should discuss their topic with others to ensure they are going in the right direction. Finally, they should brainstorm their ideas in a web-like format so they have a writing plan in front of them. Don't forget to give them the criteria for success that is based on the rubrics. I really like the rubrics created by www.schoolimprovement.com for all the grade levels, but I do not give them this rubric. Instead, I make it kid-friendly by writing "I can" statements in the criteria boxes. They then self-assess and get a peer to assess as well.

After you have gone over every criterion (and ensured that they understand and have been taught explicitly each of the criteria), it's time to help them organize their pieces. You could give them organizational ideas such as introduction, claim one with reasoning, claim two with reasoning, counter-claim, rebuttal, conclusion. This is just an idea, but we do know that an executive function skill that these students sometimes struggle with is sequencing and prioritizing. So make sure you know which students need this type of support, and pull a small group of students to explicitly teach sequencing and prioritizing of their ideas for their writing.

To make this type of writing even more challenging, ask students to debate the opposite view after writing on his or her opinion. We know that the CCSS is asking students to write argumentative/opinion pieces about *their* opinions and claims, but what if we asked students to study the opposite view of the unfamiliar perspective of what they actually hold and *try* to persuade others through speaking and writing? Based on the cognitive fluency research, educators know to take the time to plan strategies and activities that challenge the brain into thinking more deeply so that memory can be enhanced.

Argumentative writing opportunities are highly memorable too, as they engage emotions in the writing and because they have a choice on which stance to take and support. Encourage them to present their arguments and debate verbally too. I love to have Socratic seminars and even official debates after argumentative writings are complete and shared. After all, the CCSS have speaking and listening standards that are pretty high too.

Informational writing or nonfiction writing is powerful for challenging the brain as well. It's not easy to analyze information from several sources and then pull them together to synthesize what was learned in a logical, evidence-based manner. High-achievement, high-poverty schools made nonfiction writing across the curriculums a top priority according to Douglas Reeve's research called, 90-90-90 Schools (those with 90 percent or more free and reduced lunch, 90 percent ethnic minorities, and yet 90 percent or above achievement).

Informational Writing: Writing to Learn Across the Curriculums

The CCSS has the common Writing Anchor Standard 2: "Students will write informative/explanatory texts to examine and convey complex ideas and information clearly and accurately through the effective selection, organization and analysis of content." Informational writing enhances students' comprehension of text and strengthens students' reading comprehension. Writing about what they read improves comprehension as well. Applebee and Langer said in their book, *Writing Instruction That Works: Proven Methods for Middle and High School Classrooms* (2013, 217): "Rather than use writing to measure what has been learned, we need to move it forward, in conversations appropriate to the disciplines, to using writing in order to learn. . . . When students are afforded the opportunity to use writing to develop understandings, sort out ideas, and engage in discussions within the community of the classroom, students are likely to develop a deeper understanding of the underlying principles."

With all assignments, we need to be clear about the expectations. We can explain this criterion for success to the students by showing an exemplar, explaining the details of a rubric, conferencing, and creating a student self-assessment with the criteria listed. A fifth-grade example of some of the Informational Writing Expectations from CCSS is shown Figure 2.2. Notice there is a place for the student and peer to assess where the piece of writing is in relation to the standards of expectations. Give students plenty of time to change their writing to better meet the standards before giving them the final score. Much feedback should have been given to them about their writing before the final grade.

Writing should happen daily in all classrooms to show what was learned (formative) and what still needs to be learned. Here are some examples of how to incorporate writing in numerous subject areas.

Social Studies Ideas

- Read, Discuss, Write: Create an outcome for your lesson based on your standards at hand. Have students acquire information about this topic by asking them to read articles (www.newsela.com or www.ReadWorks.org) or texts. Then, give students question stems to discuss with one another in small groups about what they read. Writing becomes easier when we have ideas discussed and confirmed by others. Finally, give the writing task to the students. The task should reflect the outcome, reading, and discussion.
- End of Unit Writing: Have students answer the Essential Questions of the Unit in essay format with topic sentences and supporting

Criteria for Informational Writing

0 = Not there
1= Parts of the criteria were included
2= Good effort; more elaboration needed
3 = All criteria in writing

Criteria	Student	Peer	Teacher
1. I introduced a topic clearly with topic sentences (claim). My lead grabbed reader's attention.			
2. The middle section of my writing was organized/grouped logically.			
3. I used headings, illustrations, graphics, and multimedia appropriately.			
4. My topic was developed with evidence such as: facts, definitions, concrete details, quotations or other information and examples related to the topic.	5th grade Standards W.5.2A-E		
5. The answer has at least three text-based or note-based references to support it (sourced accurately, truly support answer).			
6. Ideas are linked appropriately with words, phrases and clauses.			
7. At least _____ vocabulary words are used to explain the answer (underline) (Tier 2 or 3).			
8. I wrote a strong concluding statement related to the information in my writing. It makes the reader think.			
9. Conventions (spelling, grammar, usage, punctuation, capitalization, etc.)			

Figure 2.2.   Fifth-Grade Writing Self-Assessment.

details. Make sure it is open notes/texts and done in the classroom. They will need to construct their answers (make sure to talk about plagiarism).

- Research Projects: In each unit, students should do several small and large research projects based on interest. Teachers can provide the list of topics that support the curriculum. Ask students to create an opinion about the event, write an argumentative paper about it with supporting details, and then present it.

Science Ideas

- While reading text or articles in science that help students get to the daily outcome, they should always summarize their learning, argue for or against the learning, and/or respond to a question in writing.
- Writing lab reports is a powerful way to process what was learned during the labs. Have a rubric/checklist for expectations and show the students an exemplar. Invite them to think analytically and critically.
- RAFT writing is powerful in the science classroom. R = Role of writer; A = Audience; F = Format; T = Topic. Example: R = Frog; A = Tadpole; F = Letter; T = Life Cycle. Let students choose some of the

pieces of RAFT, give them the expectations and rubric for writing, and have students give each other feedback on their ideas. This is a great creative writing activity!

- Interactive Notebook (many daily writing activities to reinforce content): Students take notes on the right-hand side and respond to those notes or articles read on the left-hand side. Their thinking in writing on the left-hand side can be done daily in response to the learning.
- Compare and Contrast Writings (compare an animal cell to a plant cell): Use the graphic organizer of a Venn diagram first, then summarize in paragraph format.

Math Ideas

Marilyn Burns, math expert, said, "I can no longer imagine teaching math without making writing an integral aspect of students' learning. Writing in math class requires students to organize, clarify, and reflect on their ideas."

- During a multiple choice quiz or test, ask students to write explanations for why any one of the choices is wrong. After a test, ask students to explain in writing why they missed a problem and how they can fix it to make it correct.
- Show students a vocabulary word web for the unit you are about to encounter and then ask students to explain what words mean and how they connect to bigger concepts.
- Ask students to write about the similarities and differences among two concepts (multiplication and division; percentages, fractions, and decimals).
- Students can write as if they were the math concept. Ask them to become a decimal or fraction and explain their importance in this world, town, and their home.
- Use the Math Writing Prompts for daily journal entries or Exit Tickets at the end of the class. It's important to ask the student to explain mathematical concepts by using the vocabulary terms that were taught. Hold students accountable for speaking and writing these words that you took the time to teach!
- Have students write their own word problems.

One of the number-one ways to make classrooms more rigorous is by asking students to write with clear, challenging expectations by using the skills that have been explicitly taught, modeled, and given feedback across the disciplines in every single classroom. These latter examples show the powerful connection of reading, questioning, discussing with academic vocabulary, and pulling those pieces together for a beautiful piece of writing that shows the deep thinking, deep learning, and what else still needs to be learned. Writing is one of the best formative assessments as well, since a teacher can see a student's thinking in print.

REFERENCES AND RESOURCES

ACT, Inc. (2004). *Crisis at the Core: Preparing All Students for College and Work.* Iowa City: Author.

Almeida, D. M., Neupert, S. D., Banks, S. R., and Serido, J. (2005). "Do daily stress processes account for socioeconomic health disparities?" *Journals of Gerontology Series B–Psychological Science and Social Sciences, 60*(2), S34–S39.

Aikens, N. L., and Barbarin, O. (2008). "Socioeconomic differences in reading trajectories: The contribution of family, neighborhood, and school contexts." *Journal of Educational Psychology* 100, 235–251.

Applebee, A. N., and Langer, J. A. (2013). *Writing Instruction that Works: Proven Methods for Middle and High School Classrooms.* New York: Teachers College, Columbia University Press.

Boser, U., Wilhelm, M., and Hanna, R. (2014, October 6). "The power of the Pygmalion effect: Teachers expectations strongly predict college completion." Center for American Progress. Retrieved from www.americanprogress.org/issues/education/report/2014/10/06/96806/the-power-of-the-pygmalion-effect/.

Capron, C. and Duyme, M. (1989). "Assessment of the effects of socio-economic status on IQ in a full cross-fostering study." *Nature, 340*: 552–554.

Chabris, C., and Simons, D. (2010). *The Invisible Gorilla: How Our Intuitions Deceive Us.* New York: MJF Books.

Chenoweth, Karin. (2009). *How It's Being Done: Urgent Lessons from Unexpected Schools.* Cambridge, MA: Harvard Education Press.

Coley, R. (2002). *An Uneven Start: Indicators of Inequality in School Readiness.* Princeton, NJ: Educational Testing Service.

Diamond, M., and Hopson, J. (1998). *Magic Trees of the Mind: How to Nuture your Child's Intelligence, Creativity, and Healthy Emotions from Birth Through Adolescence.* New York: Plume.

Diemand-Yauman, C., Oppenheimer, D. M., and Vaughan, E. B. (2011). "Fortune favors the bold (and the italicized): Effects of disfluency on educational outcomes." *Cognition, 118*(1): 111–115.

Dweck, Carol. (2006). *Mindset: The New Psychology of Success.* New York: Random House.

Gottfredson, L. S. (2004). "Intelligence: Is it the epidemiologists' elusive fundamental cause of social class inequalities in health?" *Journal of Personality and Social Psychology, 86*: 174–199.

Hattie, J. (2009). *Visible Learning: A Synthesis of over 800 Meta-Analyses Relating to Achievement.* New York, NY: Routledge.

Jensen, E., and Nickelsen, L. (2014). *Bringing the Common Core to Life in K–8 Classrooms.* Bloomington, IN: Solution Tree.

Jensen, E., and Nickelsen, L. (2008). *Deeper Learning: 7 Powerful Strategies for In-Depth and Longer-Lasting Learning.* Thousand Oaks, CA: Corwin Press.

Jensen, E. (2009). *Teaching with Poverty in Mind: What Being Poor Does to Kids' Brains and What Schools Can Do About It.* Alexandria, VA: Association for Supervision and Curriculum Development.

Jihyun, L. (2014). "Universal factors of student achievement in high-performing Eastern and Western countries." *Journal of Educational Psychology, 106*(2): 364–374.

Kaylor, M., and Flores, M. M. (2008). "Increasing academic motivation in culturally and linguistically diverse students from low socioeconomic backgrounds." *Journal of Advanced Academics, 19*, 66-89.

Lang, J. M. (2012, June 3). "The benefits of making it harder to learn." *Chronicle of Higher Education*. chronicle.com/article/The-Benefits-of-Making-It/132056/.

Morgan, P. L., Farkas, G., Hillemeier, M. M., and Maczuga, S. (2009). "Risk factors for learning-related behavior problems at 24 months of age: Population-based estimates." *Journal of Abnormal Child Psychology*, 37: 401–413.

National Center for Education Statistics. (2002). "Education longitudinal study of 2002: Third follow-up restricted-use data file," United States Department of Education. Available by request from the Institute of Education Sciences.

National Center for Education Statistics. (2008). *Percentage of high school dropouts among persons 16 through 24 years old (status dropout rate), by income level, and percentage distribution of status dropouts, by labor force status and educational attainment: 1970 through 2007*. Retrieved from nces.ed.gov/programs/digest/d08/tables/dt08_110.asp.

NGA Center for Best Practices. (2005). *Reading to Achieve: A Governor's Guide to Adolescent Literacy*. Washington, DC: Author.

Noble, K. G., Norman, M. F., and Farah, M. J. (2005). "Neurocognitive correlates of socioeconomic status in kindergarten children." *Developmental Science, 8*: 74–87.

Orr, A. J. (2003). "Black-White differences in achievement: The importance of wealth." *Sociology of Education, 76*: 281–304.

Palardy, G. J. (2008). "Differential school effects among low, middle, and high social class composition schools: A multiple group, multilevel latent growth curve analysis." *School Effectiveness and School Improvement, 19*: 21–49.

Pink, D. (2009). *Drive: The Surprising Truth About What Motivates Us*. New York, NY: Riverhead Books.

Ratey, J. (2008). *Spark: The Revolutionary New Science of Exercise and the Brain*. New York: Little, Brown.

Rosenthal, R., and Babad, E. Y. (1985). "Pygmalion in the gymnasium." *Educational Leadership, 43*(1): 36–39.

Rosenthal, R., and Jacobson, L. (1968). "Pygmalion in the classroom." *The Urban Review, 3*(1): 16–20.

Schlaug, G., and Gaser, C. (2003). "Brain structures differ between musicians and nonmusicians." *The Journal of Neuroscience, 23*(27): 9240–9245.

Southern Education Foundation. (2015, January). *A New Majority: Low Income Students Now a Majority in the Nation's Public Schools*. Atlanta, GA: Author.

THREE

Self-Regulation for Learning

Richard Cash

Learning is a complex process of interrelated dimensions. To be literate, students must not only possess the tools and skills, they must also be confident, resilient to adversity, understand the effect of behavior, be self-reflective, value the activity, and have motivation and interest, to name a few. These interactive dimensions all collaborate to produce what is known as self-regulation. In this chapter, the concept of self-regulation will be described, along with its interactive dimensions and the process students go through to engage in learning. Throughout the chapter, to emphasis self-regulation as a process *for* learning, strategies and ideas will be highlighted.

The concept of self-regulation has been a focus of research for well over forty years. Educational psychologists seeking to understand the complexity of learning have found an array of ways teachers can improve achievement through this multidimensional approach called self-regulation. Many educators already know that learning isn't a simple act that can be controlled by increasing standards, finding the "right curriculum," or putting in place policies that punish students or teachers for the lack of achievement. Educators, curriculum developers, and policymakers need to understand the holistic impact self-regulation has on student learning and achievement.

THE BRIEF HISTORY OF THE CONCEPT OF SELF-REGULATION

Educational psychologist and university professor, Barry Zimmerman (2000), states that self-regulated learning (SRL) is the "self-generated

31

thoughts, feelings, and actions that are planned and cyclically adapted to the attainment of personal goals" (14). Research on SRL originated as an outgrowth of psychological studies in adult and child development, oftentimes stemming from addiction or the therapeutic context. Researchers often taught patients to alter dysfunctional behavior such as aggression or depression. Based on these studies, researchers soon found that changing behaviors required comprehensive approaches for reaching goals. Not all patients were equally impacted through the same methods. This led researchers to explain not only behavioral differences, but also achievement differences between students. They believed understanding the nature of SRL could be a way to improve academic performance of all students.

Early research on the impact of SRL focused on cognitive strategies and behavioral modification. Teaching students how to monitor their thinking (metacognition), rehearsing, goal setting, and time management would set the stage for a productive learning environment. Most recently, studies indicate that the affective dimension of motivation, interest drive, focus of emotional response, self-efficacy, and self-confidence of the individual plays as important a role in learning as does cognition and behavior. The significance of SRL is the sustainability and interaction between the three critical dimensions I define as affect, behavior, and cognition (ABC) (figure 3.1). For a learning goal to be achieved, learners must have an understanding of the impact and learn to balance their ABCs.

Throughout my years of teaching, curriculum development, program direction, and professional development, I have found that students who struggle in school or underperform are often lacking the awareness, attention toward, or understanding of SRL. I believe that prior to being successful in school students must possess the tools to build, manage, and adapt their own self-regulation. Therefore, in this chapter, the focus of self-regulation will be toward becoming a learner: developing self-regulation *for* learning. Additionally, because SRL is a multifaceted and highly complex concept, this chapter will highlight a limited number of aspects of the studies. This chapter will distill primary facets for educators to begin the discussion and develop effective strategy development toward self-regulation for learning. Under each of the primary categories of SRL, a couple of ideas are shared. (For more complete information as to strategy development, see Cash, 2016.)

A IS FOR AFFECT

Affect is either physical or mental states of emotions and feelings, generally understood as ranging from pleasure to pain, sorrow to joy, and

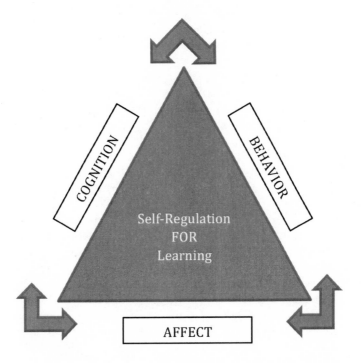

Figure 3.1. The Balance within Self-Regulation for Learning (Cash, 2016).

desire to need. Theories abound as to the differences between feelings and emotions (de Sousa, 2014).

Neuroscientist Antonio Damasio (1995) states that an emotion is an involuntary bodily response. Emotion, in this case, is the chemical reaction within the limbic system of the midbrain. These chemical reactions are innate or instinctual to our being and in most cases are uncontrollable.

The term *feelings* is referenced as physical reactions to the emotion/ chemical stimuli produced by the midbrain. When the prefrontal cortex becomes aware of the chemical stimuli produced by the midbrain, it will signal the body to react, creating a feeling. These physical reactions often appear as facial expressions, body movements, or modulation voice tones. Subjectively, these feelings can be the focusing of attention, desires, or motivations. Therefore, feelings are the external "read-out" to emotion. How a learner feels about a situation has a direct effect on how the learner will approach, attend to, value, or accomplish a task or experience.

Affect as Motivation

Motivation is our driving force. Whether extrinsically produced from outside of us or intrinsically initiated from inside of us, motivation has an effect on the learning process. Our self-control or self-discipline is directly related to our motives toward goals and ideals (English and English, 1958). Our sources of motivation have a strong effect on goal orientation, self-efficacy beliefs, confidence, social interactions, values, and interests. Sources of motivation come from our self-beliefs regarding our abilities, competence, and impact on outcomes.

Those students who were more motivated by external factors, such as pleasing others or avoiding punishment, had a lower rate of achievement than did those who were motivated by a personal desire to accomplish or be challenged (Lepper, Corpus, and Iyengar, 2005). Additionally, students who were motivated to set quality learning goals, implement effective strategies, monitor their goal progress, seek assistance, and evaluate their outcomes were significantly better at self-regulation in future learning experiences (Zimmerman and Schunk, 2008).

Motivation has four influential impacts on learning. First, as cited above, students who are motivated to learn focus their attention toward the process and the outcome. The trait of self-monitoring is important to understanding how well goals are set, actions are being implemented, and goals are being achieved.

Second, choice in learning options has a substantial effect on learner motivation. When students have the opportunity to select how they would like to learn material and present learning, they progress more fluidly toward achievement goals. Choices increase a sense of control over the learning environment and valuation toward the task at hand. Choices need not be extensive; simply providing students two or three options allows them the opportunity to develop direction and regulation for learning.

Carol Dweck (2006), a leading researcher in the field of motivation and professor of psychology at Stanford University, suggests that those who are more successful in life possess a growth mindset over a fixed mindset. The third factor in motivation is the growth mindset. Students who view learning as a challenge where effort is required are motivated to achieve. Putting effort forward and utilizing individual talent is what Dweck defines as a growth mindset. Students who believe their abilities are static and cannot be increased are considered to possess a fixed mindset.

Fourth, learners who are persistent and learn to overcome obstacles have greater levels of motivation. Students who persevere learn through repeated consistent practice. This type of practice, known as deliberate practice, is a framework of skill improvement to reach expertise. The process of deliberate practice requires the learner to break down the larger skill into discrete, conscious actions (or strategies) to define where they are proficient and where they lack proficiency (Cash, 2016).

These factors of motivation increase satisfaction and have a positive effect on learning (Zimmerman and Kitsantas, 1999). Students who lack motivation are less likely to set short- and long-term goals, may not find meaningfulness in learning tasks, feel less accomplished, and do not achieve success as often as those who have higher degrees of motivation.

What can teachers do to help students develop long-term forms of motivation?

1. Teach students how to monitor their learning. Focus on successes and how mistakes can be viewed as an opportunity.
2. Provide students with relevant and meaningful choices. Use interests, fun, and active learning options to engage students. Limit the number of choices so as to not overwhelm the students with making decisions.
3. Help students build their growth mindset. Focus students on what they are good at—recognizing their strengths and persistence toward achievement.
4. Demonstrate for students the qualities of persistence and effort application. Show students how overcoming obstacles can lead them to being more successful.

Affect as Self-Efficacy

For centuries, philosophers have understood the connection between how we feel about our capabilities and the application of our effort and outcomes. Psychologist Albert Bandura (1977) theorized that in addition to our beliefs about our capabilities, the outcomes of our efforts greatly influenced our self-regulation (figure 3.2).

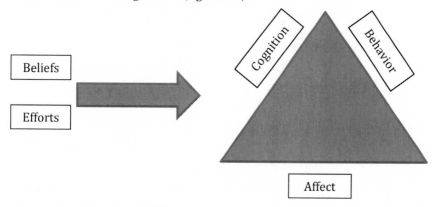

Figure 3.2. Affect as Self-Efficacy.

Social cognitive theorists have long known that improving beliefs about capabilities can be taught and learned. Teachers can help students build their academic self-confidence, which improves attention to detail (efforts), increases positive emotional states, assists in developing appropriate behavioral responses, and alters lines of cognition/thinking. For a student to develop a healthy level of self-efficacy, the awareness of capabilities, they need a nurturing learning environment, positive peer relationships within the classroom, and a supportive network of caring individuals.

Students who possess a strong sense of efficacy are resilient toward difficult tasks and approach challenges as developmental toward mastery rather than as a threat to be avoided. This approach versus avoidance volition has an effect on all learning and levels of success. Students who are approach oriented have greater intrinsic drive, set high standards, and persevere toward achievement. Avoidance-oriented students lack confidence, allow task accomplishments to define them through success or failure, and give up easily.

Self-efficacy is the belief that one has the capabilities to complete tasks. This "I can" mindedness is different from the concept of self-beliefs. What a student believes about him- or herself may bear little relationship to what a student can achieve. This is most apparent among gifted students who possess exceptional academic skills and achieve high marks, while being labeled by their peers as less desirable, such as geeks or nerds. Alternatively, low-performing students may have no loss of self-esteem when their confidence is nurtured on the football field or through being popular in social circles. Students who have strong academic self-efficacy have greater academic performance regardless of possessed knowledge and skills. Additionally, positive self-efficacy can increase the effect of possessed knowledge, skills, or other motivational factors on most academic performances (Pajares, 2002).

There are three sources in attaining a strong level of academic self-efficacy. As a student progresses from childhood through adolescence and into adulthood, the interpretations of information from these three sources influence how they develop their sense of self-efficacy. The most powerful source is the student's past experiences with success or *mastery experiences*. Success breeds confidence, which breeds success. An important factor in assisting students in developing mastery experience is for them to find small successes, no matter the arena (such as on the football field, in the band room, or through academics), which can build their self-confidence, and in turn provide them with greater successes. Mastery experience has an enduring effect on learning, regardless of situation, location, or content. Students who experience academic success are most likely to make wise decisions about their learning for many years.

Much of learning happens in a social context. Along with interpreting their own abilities, students are likely to compare themselves to others.

Vicarious experiences are those in which students observe the successes and failures of peers perceived as similar in capabilities. How students see others' performances can influence how they perceive their own. This can have both a positive and negative effect. For students who may fear taking on a challenge, seeing someone like themselves be successful in that challenge can influence their willingness to attempt the task.

Adversely, students who see someone like themselves fail can alter their way of thinking about the task and then avoid attempting it. Also consider that when students are discretely different from one another, such as a low-performing student compared to a high-achieving student, few positive vicarious experiences will be had by either student, as the likeness in academic success may be too great.

The third impact factor is known as *social persuasion*. How a student interacts within social groups and how the individuals within the group react to the student can influence learning outcomes. Whether the interactions or reactions are verbal or nonverbal, students will adjust their attitude toward achievement. Cohen, Garcia, Apfel, and Master (2006) found that positive identification with social groups had a significant effect on achievement among African American adolescent students. Finding the "right" social group, having the group communicate messages of strong achievement, and support can affect how students view achievement.

The strength of a student's self-efficacy serves as a filter through which learning new information is processed. If a student has a low sense of self-efficacy, either cultivated by lack of mastery experience, limited vicarious relationships, or negative social persuasion, his or her emotional state (affect) is influenced in a negative way. Conversely, those who have high self-efficacy will apply effort to challenges and interpret mistakes as learning tools and gain value from even small successes.

B IS FOR BEHAVIOR

In the context of self-regulation for learning, behaviors are the actions students take inside and outside the classroom to be successful in learning. Typically, the behaviors that students employ during learning are considered the behaviors of self-regulation. Our learning behaviors are an array of actions we perform to initiate, sustain, change, or develop based on internal and external factors. Behaviors can also be considered conscious and unconscious.

Behavior as Literacy Development

As renowned educator Paulo Freire stated, genuine literacy involves "reading the word and the world" (1985). This broader definition goes well beyond reading and writing as literacy. Literacy in the twenty-first century lies in the ability to read, write, interpret, influence, and infuse these critical skills to work and be successful in the world. In this broadened context of literacy skills, the behavioral aspect of self-regulation for learning would include:

- Determination: the level of commitment to the task
- Interest: the personal attention used to engage in the task
- Work habits: the strategies and techniques to learn through the task
- Communication: the effective use of speaking, writing, listening, interpreting, and nonverbal use and understanding
- Collaboration: the use of tools to be successful in a team, such as trusting, sharing, respectful interaction, asking for help, taking responsibility
- Goal focus: setting, managing, and achieving realistic goals

The interactions between and among these general behavioral skills are essential to school and life success. Assisting students in achieving quality behavioral patterns in learning requires students to practice in learning settings that are goal oriented and stimulating through hands-on activities, inclusive of students' interests, supportive of developing autonomy, and collaboration.

Behavior as Study Habits

Another crucial behavioral aspect of self-regulation for learning is that of study habits. To ensure students are college and career ready, they must possess the abilities to study. Study can be considered preparation for what's to come. I have defined ten important study habits that every student should know and be able to use (Cash, 2016):

1. *Set a regular study time each day,* whether it be right after school, before the evening meal, or prior to bedtime.
2. *Create a space* where distractions are few, lighting is ample, and clutter is at a minimum.
3. *Manage the time* devoted to studying by parceling out the total study time to each of the various tasks that need to be completed.
4. *Organize* yourself and your materials prior to studying for efficient use of the time.
5. *Be aware of the way you like to learn best,* whether you are an auditory, visual, or kinesthetic type of learner.
6. *Take a short break* of two to three minutes during your study time, which can help keep you motivated, refreshed, and focused.
7. *Know how to avoid distraction* by recognizing when you are wasting time or procrastinating.

8. *Plan for asking for help* by identifying those who can help you or where you can seek advice or information when you get stuck or are struggling.
9. *Check yourself* when you have completed a task to ensure you have done it correctly and have fulfilled the requirements.
10. *Reflect on your study time* by asking yourself the ABCs:
    a. How do I feel now that the study time is over?
    b. Were my behaviors successful?
    c. What will I do better next time?

C IS FOR COGNITION

Cognition is commonly defined as the mental process from simple to very complex levels of awareness. Simple cognition is the recognition of sensory inputs, movement at will, and recall of factual information. Complex cognition is the abstractions of thought from critical reasoning, interpretation, and creativity. Experience increases our cognition from a repetition at the factual level to practice at the procedural level to discovery at the conceptual level. In the classroom, cognition is the varied thinking processes students use in the learning process.

Metacognition: Thinking about the Self

The most often recognized level of cognition in the classroom is the act of metacognition: thinking about our own thinking. Reflective thinking is a process we all use every day as we think about what just occurred or what has happened in the past. Metacognition also includes the mental actions of planning, monitoring, and evaluating progress toward achievement of a task (Livingston, 2003). Metacognition is also essential to our abilities to manage our executive functioning. Using metacognition as a tool in self-regulation for learning requires oversight of control, which includes:

- Personal knowledge: how a student learns best
- Task knowledge: what's expected
- Strategy knowledge: what to do and when.

Effective learners know their strengths and limitations, know how to approach and solve problems, and apply strategies to successfully complete tasks.

Infra-Cognition: Thinking as a Process

Infra-cognition is the grand thinking processes used in school. As we progress through the twenty-first century, thinking at advanced levels has become more important than ever before in human history. Therefore, students need instruction in critical reasoning, creative thinking, problem-solving techniques, and decision-making strategies.

The act of thinking moves along a spectrum of thinking from convergent to divergent (figure 3.3). At one end of the spectrum is convergent thinking, thinking that is logical, step by step, and based on factual information. At the other end of the spectrum is divergent thinking, thinking that generates numerous ideas, creating new and imaginative ideas (Cash, 2011). Where the two types of thinking overlap is where true problem-solving happens. When students are able to use both convergent and divergent thinking strategies together, the best solutions are created.

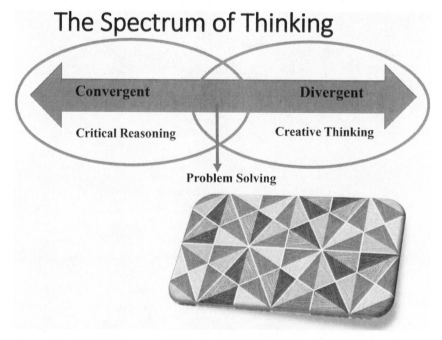

The Spectrum of Thinking

Convergent

Divergent

Critical Reasoning

Creative Thinking

Problem Solving

Figure 3.3.   The Spectrum of Thinking (Cash, 2016).

Metaphysical Thinking: Thinking beyond the Self

The most advanced level of cognition is metaphysical thinking, thinking beyond the self. Metaphysics is a philosophical line of abstract or theoretical thinking. Dorothy M. Emmet (1949), British philosopher, defined metaphysical thinking as being analogical thinking. There are two types of analogical thinking:

- Coordinated analogies: a form of reasoning in which similarities between two or more objects or ideas are compared, such as "The structure of an atom is like a solar system."

- Existential analogies: ideas from experiences to explain or make judgments about reality or our being. Often, poets will use existential phrases to explain the human condition for the search for meaning, such as in the poem:

> Grave me, near death, who see with blinding sight
> Blind eyes could blaze like meteors and be gay,
> Rage, rage against the dying of the light.
> *Do Not Go Gentle Into That Good Night* —Dylan Thomas

An important factor of self-regulation is the ability to move from the reflective process of metacognition to the structure thinking tools of infracognition to ultimately using knowledge to think beyond the self. To be productive in this new era, students must be able to reflect on experiences, consider the multiple ways to solve complex ambiguous problems, and then be able to communicate ideas beyond themselves (Cash, 2016).

THE BALANCE BETWEEN THE ABCS

Attainment of peak levels of academic and athletic performance requires more than talent and ability. For students to be successful, they must possess and act upon the balances between affect, behavior, and cognition. Discipline and determination along with a positive sense of self are instrumental in achieving proficiency and competence (Zimmerman and Kitsantas, 2005).

Students who are dependent and inflexible in their learning are less likely to seek out help, do not self-initiate, lack effective focus, and may require more sustained support. Conversely, students who are more efficient in self-regulation may struggle, but seek out effective role models, teachers, or additional resources to become successful. Self-regulated learners can adjust the coordinating system of the ABCs to find greater enjoyment, motivation, and autonomy in learning.

Using the idea of self-regulation as the balance across the three dimensions is a figurative way to help students in creating their own equilibrium. Without a strong affect (the motivational beliefs that one can achieve), behavior will not be focused and cognition will not be ignited. Without effective behaviors (study and learning skills) cognition is not refined and affect tumbles. Without the reflective, thoughtful cognitive aspects, affect (motivation) wanes and behavior instigates helplessness. Keeping students strong in all three dimensions or learning how to adjust one dimension to support the others is an essential tool for learning and success (Cash, 2016).

Stages of SRL Development

As in all learning, self-regulation is an ongoing process developed in stages. Barry J. Zimmerman (1989), a leading social cognitive researcher, describes the acquisition of self-regulation as a self-initiated multidimensional process of combining affect, behavior, and cognition in coordination with the environment to achieve valuable goals. This process is fluid in that there are continued adjustments a person makes throughout the developmental process when engaged in learning. Affectively, if a student feels stressed during performance, there may be a need to alleviate the stress through relaxation activities. If using a learning strategy such as Cornell Notes (a behavior) is not successful when it comes time to discuss information in class, the student must shift or employ a new strategy to be better prepared for the next day's discussion. If, after a class session, the student realizes he or she has little understanding of the concepts defined and worked on, then the student will need to plan for techniques (such as a mnemonic) to remember information for the next session. These are the conscious actions that self-regulated learners undertake to continually achieve at the highest level (Cash, 2016).

Students move through four stages of development (see figure 3.4) to become self-regulated learners. From simple to complex, the stages are fluid and not always associated with the age of the learner but are more dependent on expected outcomes or performances. The process of developing self-regulation for learning is initially interactive and gradually shifts from expectations or needs of external support and guidance to a more proactive internal drive. Eventually, the learner achieves the capability to routinely apply the strategies of the ABCs toward ever successful outcomes.

Stage One: Modeling and Observing

Students need to see others using self-regulation to manage thinking, feelings, and behaviors. In some cases, students coming from disenfranchised backgrounds do not have role models at home using effective self-regulation strategies. The parents and other adults in their lives may not be modeling for the child-positive strategies for developing self-regulation. In fact, the adults may be modeling ineffective strategies, which may show up in the classroom. As teachers observe these students' lack of effective strategies or use of ineffective strategies, we may be misidentifying the root issue. We may be blaming the victims by saying "they aren't motivated," "they won't stay on task," "they are lazy," and so on. But in reality, they may not know how to manage learning, their feelings, and the use of appropriate behaviors attuned to the situation. At this stage we need to model positive strategies toward self-regulation, such as how to filter out distractions, work at something for an amount of time, reward ourselves for accomplishing a task, and reflect when we didn't achieve our goal.

Stage Two: Copying and Doing

Once students have role models for self-regulation, they need to begin using the strategies and be held accountable for the use of those strategies. A strategy is a conscious action, meaning that I know when to use a strategy and that I'm aware that I'm using it. This is a step that many teachers forget to emphasize in learning. Whether we are teaching strategies in math, reading, science, or self-regulation, we need to constantly reinforce with our students the strategies that we use. We also should be checking in with the students to find out what strategies they are using to solve problems, manage behaviors, stay on task, and so forth. Our job at this stage is to state out loud the strategies we use to be self-regulated, have kids copy our strategies, reinforce those strategies, and then request that the students do the strategies as they have learned them.

Stage Three: Practice and Refinement

Now that the students have amassed some strategies for being regulated, we should be providing experiences where they are required to use them. Situations should be academic, affective in nature, and include behavioral management. What this means is that we have to put students in learning situations that include emotions and will take some time to solve. For example, when investigating the pilgrim's coming to the "new world," ask kids to think about how people felt being crowded on the small boat for the eight months it took as they crossed the Atlantic Ocean. Ask students to think about what is was like going from one home to a new uncharted place. Try to link the pilgrim's experience to the students' experiences. Ask when they felt like they were leaving one secure place and going to an uncharted place. How might it feel to be with people they don't know for eight months? Have you ever been in a situation where you were in a small space with people you don't know very well? How have you learned to deal with people who are not like you? Linking the curriculum to feelings and how we manage those feelings is a very effective way to have students practice and refine their self-regulation.

Stage Four: Independence and Application

At this stage students should independently be putting to use the strategies of self-regulation. This skilled level means they have made the strategies a part of who they are and can do them without being asked or coached. Students at this level will need constant support and encouragement about their use of the strategies. An idea at this stage is to use reflection tools, such as a journal, diary, or blog, to document their personal learning development. We want to keep students focused on goals and what it takes to achieve those goals. "Effort is the key to success" (Dweck, 2006, 44).

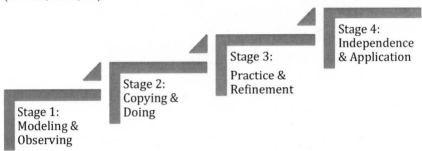

Figure 3.4.   Stages of Developing Self-Regulation for Learning.

PHASES OF LEARNING

Well-regulated students also employ strategies for engaging in tasks. Zimmerman, Bonner, and Kovach (1996) suggest that there are four phases to efficiently engaging in learning tasks (figure 3.5). The learner must (1) commit to doing well, (2) determine what he or she will do to do well, (3) monitor his or her process toward doing well, and (4) reflect on how well he or she did and what needs to be changed next time.

Phase 1: How Well Will I Do?

In the beginning phase of learning, the student needs to reflect on past performances and prior knowledge experiences to set forward into learning. For struggling students this initial stage may set them on the path to failure, because they can't recall positive past performances or prior successes in order to know what to think about (cognitive), how to act (behavioral), or how good it feels (affective) to be accomplished. This phase is considered the most important stage in learning—getting the student to ground him- or herself confidently.

What is necessary at this point is to foster the learner's confidence in learning. Begin by helping students identify their emotional state. How one feels about a learning situation determines the level of attention one will pay to the information. Get kids to feel good about the experience. This is not to suggest the "touchy-feely" kind of feel good—but about building a positive learning environment where all students are respected and encouraged to do their best. The teacher is a supporter of intellectual risk-taking, curiosity, and hard work.

Teachers need to help students develop a sense of positive self-belief and self-esteem. An effective strategy is visualization. Students either lie

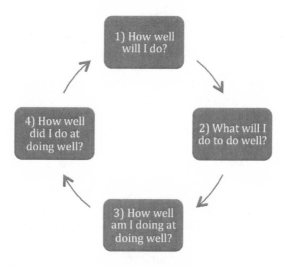

Figure 3.5. Phases of Learning (graphic based on work by Zimmerman, Bonner, and Kovach, 1996).

on the floor or sit comfortably at their desks with their eyes closed. Using a soothing voice, the teacher asks students to picture in their mind a peaceful, calming place. This place can be their bedroom, the fort they built as a child, or a movie theater. Then ask them to get in touch with how they feel when they are in this peaceful place. Have them "capture" that feeling and hold on to it as an example of success. Now ask them to think of a time when they were excited about their performance or when they accomplished something that was at first difficult. Again, ask them to capture that feeling of success and remember it. Have the students open their eyes and recall the feelings of calm and success. Say, "Those are the feelings you will have when you successfully complete this task."

More ideas for fostering confidence is through:

- Setting and maintaining acceptable learning behaviors in the classroom.
- Using a nonconfrontational style with your students—don't get into power struggles!
- Using affirmative language rather than punitive language ("Jamal is really focused on the task at hand!" rather than "Sarah, stay on task.").
- Giving students time to destress—play fun games or tell jokes after a difficult task, activity, or test.
- Refusing to engage in public arguments—don't allow students to "get your goat." If a student has a disagreement with you, take the student aside to debate and discuss it.

Another essential aspect of building students' confidence is through developing habits of thinking. Craft time in your class day to embed thinking activities where students develop the abilities to think independently.

To assist learners in developing a greater sense of confidence, build, activate, or teach the prior knowledge practices or experiences the students will need for the upcoming activities. Some students come to class without having a great deal of authentic experiences (such as having visited a museum, theater, zoo, or travels out of town). These students need enriched experiences to attach new material, such as fieldtrips to places they have never been; viewing of movies, videos, or websites that prep them for the upcoming units of study; play with manipulatives or artifacts of the study; having books or stories read to them that pique their interests, and so on. Building background knowledge can have an important effect on future learning.

Some kids may have had prior experiences with the topic but have "forgotten" what they were exposed to then. These kids need refreshers of past experiences. Show examples of prior products they created that used the strategies or skills necessary for the upcoming study; provide websites or YouTube videos of examples of what they have done in the past or refresh their memories by talking through the experiences they have had and discuss how those will link to the new learning.

For students to fully engage in learning tasks they must initially have confidence in their abilities and capacities to pursue new learning. All too often teachers ignore this crucial step in learning. We must first have confident learners before we can get successful learners.

Phase 2: What Will I Do to Do Well?

Once students have a sense of confidence that they can forecast their level of success in a learning task, we then need to help them set and manage goals toward that success. Phase 2 is about deciding what I will do to do well in the learning task. One of the best ways to assist students in this process is through having them set SMART goals. SMART goals are:

Specific: focusing the target on something you want to improve upon;
Measurable: being able to measure your success;
Assignable: listing the steps, materials, and resources you will need to reach your goal;
Relevant: making sure that the goal is within your reach with the resources you have; and
Time-bound: setting a time line for reaching your goal.

Once the goal has been SMARTed, teachers should teach students how to manage and achieve the goal. Students need to learn how to avoid distraction. Twenty-first-century kids have more than their share of distractors, from cell phones to websites, to tweets, to Instagram (and the list goes on). So we need to teach them specific tips for how to do homework by avoiding the perils of distractors. Below are listed seven tips for avoiding distraction:

1. Set time limits for work—no more than fifteen to twenty minutes of continuous work without a break.
2. Take breaks that are physical in nature—make sure they are no more than two minutes in duration and that you are doing something that is physical—jumping jacks, pushups, dancing.
3. If you play music, make sure that it is peaceful and without words. Our brains have a difficult time processing multiple bits of information. Music with words forces our brain to multitask, which is a very inefficient learning process.
4. Ensure that you have appropriate lighting for the work you are doing. If you are asked to read for homework, the more direct the lighting the better. Sunlight is the best!
5. Study in a cleared space. Get rid of clutter and disorganization—move it off to the side so that your brain can focus on the task at hand rather than the mess around your feet.
6. Plan to reward yourself when you finish your homework time. Whether it be spending an additional five minutes on the computer or eating your favorite cookie, we need to praise ourselves for putting effort forward. Even if you didn't complete the work, you stuck to the study period.
7. Take a moment to reflect on what worked and what didn't work while you were working. Write down what you will do again or not do again next time. Post those ideas in your work space as reminders.

Phase 3: How Well Am I at Doing Well?

Phase three of engaging in tasks requires students to monitor their progress toward achievement. The use of formative assessments is an excellent way to move students from the desire for extrinsic rewards (grades/certificates/trophies/pizza parties) toward intrinsic desire to achieve. As you are aware, formative feedback is the feedback provided to the learner throughout the learning process. The most beneficial type of formative feedback is descriptive feedback. This type of feedback goes beyond saying "good job" or "work harder!"

Descriptive feedback is:

- Ongoing throughout the learning process
- Provided to the learner in a timely manner
- Explicitly focused on skill development and understanding

- Articulated to the progress toward the goal
- Specific to the task or performance
- Incremental (never giving too much at once or too little to make sense)
- Praising the effort over the achievement to develop a growth mind-set

Phase 4: How Well Did I Do at Doing Well?

The final phase of this model is the reflective stage. This is when the summative assessments (the final product or end point in the learning) is used to help the student contemplate the effectiveness of his or her learning strategies and behaviors as well as define their feelings of success.

Reflection can also be accomplished through questions that stimulate metacognition, such as:

- What was I thinking throughout the learning process?
- How clearly did I understand what was expected of me during the lessons?
- In what ways did I use self-talk positively or negatively?
- Why would my teacher ask me to consider different points of view?

Other methods for reflection can be through:

- Logs or journals
- Portfolios of work (both good and poor quality)
- Group conversations (from large to small groups)
- Coaching sessions with the teacher (the teacher sits with two to three students and allows the student to talk about their learning process and the teacher offers advice toward improvement)

Finally, consider using promotes to get students to reflect more in the growth mindset, such as:

- Write about one thing you learned today.
- Tell a partner about a mistake you made today that taught you something about yourself or made you laugh.
- Sketch something you worked hard at today.
- Share with your table mates one thing that you were proud of in your learning today.
- Blog about something you would change about your learning to-day.
- Tweet me one specific goal you will set for yourself tomorrow.

When students are able to focus themselves on believing in themselves to do well; can identify what strategies, skills, and resources they will need to be successful; are able to monitor their progress toward the goal; and can reflect on what they did cognitively, behaviorally, and affectively postproduction, they are more likely to be successful in future learning endeavors.

It is critical for our students to learn, practice, and apply appropriate self-regulation strategies for them to attain success in the increasingly complex world of the twenty-first century. To solve all the problems and achieve all the wonders of their futures, our students will need to maintain focus in spite of increasing distractions of technology and learn to be both collaborative and independent. We must prepare to embed the direct instruction, practice, and application of managing affects, behavior, and cognition (Cash, 2016). Figure 3.6 provides a matrix to assist teachers and schools to integrate the stages of self-regulation for learning through the phases of engaging in learning. This useful tool can narrow down the approaches we can take to ensure our students' college and career readiness.

Stages of Self-Regulation	Development (Modeling & Observing)	Intervention (Copy & Do)	Support (Practice & Refinement)	Autonomy (Application & Independence)
Phases of Engaging in Learning				
Fostering Confidence	Teacher creates a learning environment that makes all students feel confident to take intellectual and creative risks.	Teachers provide opportunities to stretch intellectually and creatively. Students learn about theirs and others strengths and limitations.	Students put into practice learning behaviors that employ creative and critical thinking. Teacher supports students with building, activating or teaching prior knowledge.	Students independently put to practice thinking skills and habits of productive behaviors. Teacher is available as counsel.
Goal Setting	Teacher models how to set goals. Students fill in graphic organizer with teacher	Teacher provides students with graphic organizer on goal setting. Teacher checks all students' work on graphic organizer	Students complete graphic organizer or are allowed to craft their own goal chart. Teacher checks for clarity.	Student sets goal independent of teacher. Student seeks out assist when necessary.
Monitoring the Goal	Teacher models how to monitor goal attainment. Teacher uses pre-assessments to assist students in recognizing strengths & limitations.	Teacher provides immediate descriptive feedback to support students. Students monitor their goals based on formative assessments created by the teacher.	Students use daily practice to guide them in their goal monitoring. Students may also confer with peers or teacher to measure progress toward the goal.	Students use all forms of feedback (assessments, discussions, coaching opportunities) to monitor their goal progress. The teacher is available when requested.
Reflecting on the Goal	Teacher provides summative assessment review as a measure of goal attainment.	Teacher allows time for students to discuss and reflect on their learning. Students document their ideas in a reflection log or similar.	Students ask questions of self and/or peers regarding the learning process. Teacher may provide conversation starters. Teacher assists students in gather materials to quantify and qualify their learning	Students document their learning in the format that fits best. Based on the goal attainment students begin to set plans for future successes. The teacher acts as an advisor.

Figure 3.6.   Integrating the Stages of Self-Regulation for Learning through the Phases of Engaging in Learning.

REFERENCES AND RESOURCES

Bandura, A. (1977). "Self-efficacy: Toward a unifying theory of behavioral change." *Psychological Review*, *84*(2): 191.

Boekaerts, M., and Cascallar, E. (2006). "How far have we moved toward the integration of theory and practice in self-regulation?" *Educational Psychology Review*, *18*(3): 199–210.

Cash, R. M. (2011). *Advancing Differentiation: Thinking and Learning for the 21st Century.* Minneapolis: Free Spirit Publishing.

Cash, R. M. (2016). *Self-Regulation in the Classroom: Helping Students Learn How to Learn.* Minneapolis: Free Spirit Publishing.

Cohen, G. L., Garcia, J., Apfel, N., and Master, A. (2006). "Reducing the racial achievement gap: A social-psychological intervention." *Science, 313*(5791): 1307–1310.

Damasio, A. R. (1995). "Review: Toward a neurobiology of emotion and feeling: Operational concepts and hypotheses." *Neuroscientist, 1*(1): 19–25.

de Sousa, R. "Emotion." In *The Stanford Encyclopedia of Philosophy (Spring 2014 Edition),* Edward N. Zalta, ed. Retrieved from http://plato.stanford.edu/archives/spr2014/entries/emotion/.

Dweck, C. (2006). *Mindset: The New Psychology of Success.* New York: Random House.

Eccles, J. S., and Wigfield, A. (2002). "Motivational beliefs, values, and goals." *Annual Review of Psychology, 53*(1): 109–132.

Emmet, D. M. (1949). *The Nature of Metaphysical Thinking.* London: Macmillan.

English, H. B., and English, A. C. (1958). *A Comprehensive Dictionary of Psychological and Psychoanalytical Terms: A Guide to Usage.* New York: Longmans Green.

Freire, Paulo. (1985). "Reading the world and reading the word: An interview with Paulo Freire." *Language Arts 62*(1), 15–21.

Lepper, M. R., Corpus, J. H., and Iyengar, S. S. (2005). "Intrinsic and extrinsic motivational orientations in the classroom: age differences and academic correlates." *Journal of Educational Psychology, 97*(2): 184.

Livingston, J. A. (2003). "Metacognition: An overview." Retrieved from files.eric.ed.gov/fulltext/ED474273.pdf.

Locke, E. A., and Latham, G. P. (1990). *A Theory of Goal Setting & Task Performance.* Englewood Cliffs, NJ: Prentice-Hall.

Pajares, F. (2002). "Overview of social cognitive theory and of self-efficacy." Retrieved from http://www.emory.edu/EDUCATION/mfp/eff.html.

Paris, S. G., and Paris, A. H. (2001). "Classroom applications of research on self-regulated learning." *Educational Psychologist, 36*(2): 89–101.

Schunk, D., and Zimmerman, B. J., eds. (2012). *Motivation and Self-Regulated Learning: Theory, Research and Application.* New York: Routledge.

Tough, P. (2013). *How Children Succeed.* New York: Random House.

Vygotsky, L. (1987). "Zone of proximal development." In *Mind in Society: The Development of Higher Psychological Processes.* Cambridge: Harvard University Press, 52–91.

Wiggins, G. (2012). "Seven keys to effective feedback." *Educational Leadership, 70*(1): 10–16.

Zimmerman, B. J. (1989). "A social cognitive view of self-regulated academic learning." *Journal of Educational Psychology, 81*(3): 329.

Zimmerman, B. J. (2000). "Self-efficacy: An essential motive to learn." *Contemporary Educational Psychology, 25*(1): 82–91.

Zimmerman, B. J., Bonner, S., and Kovach, R. (1996). *Developing Self-Regulated Learners: Beyond Achievement to Self-Efficacy.* Washington, DC: American Psychological Association.

Zimmerman, B. J., and Kitsantas, A. (1999). "Acquiring writing revision skills: Shifting from process to outcome self-regulatory goals." *Journal of Educational Psychology, 91,* 1–10.

Zimmerman, B. J., and Kitsantas, A. (2005). "The hidden dimension of personal competence: self-regulated learning and practice." In *Handbook of Competence and Motivation,* C. S. Dweck and A. J. Elliott, eds. New York: Guilford.

Zimmerman, B. J., and Schunk, D. H. (2001). "Reflections on theories of self-regulated learning and academic achievement." In *Self-regulated Learning and Academic Achievement: Theoretical Perspectives,* B. J. Zimmerman and D. H. Schunk, eds. (2nd ed.) Mahwah, NJ: Erlbaum, 289–300.

Zimmerman, B. J., and Schunk, D. H. (2008). "An essential dimension of self-regulated learning." In *Motivation and Self-Regulated Learning: Theory, Research, and Applications*, B. J. Zimmerman and D. H. Schunk, eds. New York: Lawrence Erlbaum Associates, 1–30.

FOUR

Differentiated Instruction

A Framework for Learning Success

Melissa Dickson

This chapter will explore the ways in which differentiated instruction can increase the likelihood of student success in a standards-based classroom and how the strategies of differentiation can enable a teacher to reach and teach more learners. The habit of differentiation becomes the way we do the work in today's academically diverse and increasingly challenging classrooms. The habit of differentiation results in students enthusiastically engaged in learning, experiencing increasing levels of success, and gaining confidence in themselves as learners. We will explore the critical elements that distinguish authentic differentiation from indiscriminate teaching tips and tricks. Finally, we will examine the specific and practical instructional strategies that exemplify the habit of differentiation.

What is Differentiated Instruction?

The concepts and beliefs behind differentiated instruction are broad and cover so many different facets that explaining it to a new teacher is sometimes challenging. Although there are a lot of great definitions out there, I think I like Rick Wormeli's definition in his book, *Fair Isn't Always Equal* (2006), the best. He says:

> Differentiated instruction is doing what's fair for students. It's a collection of best practices strategically employed to maximize students' learning at every turn, including giving them the tools to handle anything that is undifferentiated. It requires us to do different things for different students some, or a lot, of the time in order for them to learn

when the general classroom approach does not meet students' needs. It is not individualized instruction, though that may happen from time to time as warranted. It's whatever works to advance the students. It's highly effective teaching.

I've never yet met the teacher who intentionally chooses to be ineffective. Every teacher I've ever worked with has wanted their students to succeed. The challenge has always been finding the right tools and strategies to make it happen and employing these tools and strategies strategically and often enough to make it a habit.

What is a Standards-Based Classroom?

Common Core State Standards were developed as a state-led effort in 2009 to ensure that all students, regardless of where they live, are graduating high school prepared for college, career, and life. The standards are informed by:

- The best state standards already in existence;
- The experience of teachers, content experts, states, and leading thinkers; and
- Feedback from the public.

But, long before Common Core State Standards came along, teachers were given the task of teaching their students to master specific standards in order to prepare them to leave the classroom and successfully navigate the real world. Traditionally, those standards were taught, practiced, and assessed in a "one-size-fits-all" fashion. Unfortunately, students have always differed in the way they think and learn, what they find interesting, and their academic readiness for the content standards. When I reflect on Rick Wormeli's definition of differentiated instruction, I realize that there have always been some highly effective teachers who broke away from the concept of one-size-fits-all instruction, where teachers taught and covered the *standards*, and moved to a more differentiated approach where teachers taught the *students*, using the best methods of instruction, to successfully master the standards. Those were usually the teachers that all the students wanted to have and the classes that students would try to fit into their schedules. How did those teachers know what to do? What made them different from the other teachers? I think the key was that they were authentic in their practices of differentiation.

What are the Elements of Authentic Differentiation?

Diane Heacox states that there are twelve elements to authentic differentiation in her book, *Making Differentiation a Habit: How to Ensure Success in Academically Diverse Classrooms* (2009). Detailed explanations and examples of each of the twelve can be found in Diane's book, as well as in many of the chapters of this book. These elements, with a brief explanation of how differentiation fits into them, are:

1. *Integrate strategies for differentiation and RTI into your classroom practices.* Response to Intervention (RTI) is a framework designed to identify struggling students before they fail and provide immediate, explicit, targeted instruction to close their gaps and catch them up with their peers. RTI *cannot* work without differentiation. Tier-one Teachers provide engaging, differentiating instruction to their students. A tier-one teacher must show evidence of differentiation before a student can be considered for tier two. Only if a student is unsuccessful in a highly engaged, differentiated classroom can they be considered for tier two. The same holds true for moving a student from tier two to tier three. The premise behind RTI is that all students can learn when provided research-based best methods for instruction that differentiates to meet their needs. The implication is that all teachers must differentiate.

2. *Identify learning goals, or KUDo's* (what your students need to Know, Understand, and be able to Do). Your KUDo's are what the students must learn. Differentiation is what we do to enable them to learn. Keep in mind that "standards in most states and provinces are the 'floor' not the 'ceiling' for learning goals" (Heacox, 2009). We must ensure that all students meet the standards, but we can always provide more depth and complexity for students once they demonstrate mastery.

3. *Examine your professional practices in light of your students' needs.* Teachers are just like the students that we teach. Some of us are further along on the differentiated continuum that others. Differentiation, just like learning, is a journey, not a destination. Know where you are and set realistic, reasonable goals for yourself as a teacher. Just as you want your students to continue to grow and advance each school year; you want the same growth for yourself as a teacher.

4. *Apply practical, doable, and valid assessment strategies.* Analyze the data you gather from pre-assessment, formative, and summative assessments to differentiate for your students. These don't have to be lengthy paper-pencil assessments, but they do need to give you enough information to make informed decisions about who you teach, what you teach, and how you teach. They should also inform you if changes are needed to increase your students' level of understanding. Every teacher has their own favorites. I personally like checklists, exit tickets, and rubrics. Talk with other teachers in your building in order to gather new ideas.

5. *Create differentiated learning plans.* The little square boxes in the old lesson plan books don't allow an effective teacher to purposefully plan for their instruction. There are many forms available to teachers. Choose the one that best meets your needs, but be sure it includes a place for the following:

- Your standard / KUDO's;
- Your pre-assessment data results;
- Your method to "hook" the students and get them invested in the learning;
- How they will be grouped for the initial learning, what methodology you will use, and how you will check for understanding;
- How they will be grouped to apply and practice the learning, how you will check for understanding, and what changes you might make based on your findings;
- How students will independently demonstrate their understanding and your criteria for success;
- Your method of closure for the day; and
- Your next steps for tomorrow based on the results from today.

6. *Use choice opportunities to motivate student learning.* Offer "controlled choice" activities. Anything that you have already taught once is fair game for a controlled choice activity. Some of my favorites are cooperative learning structures, tic-tac-toe activities, and cubes because they require very little preparation but yield great results.

7. *Prescribe tiered assignments and use flexible grouping as necessary and appropriate.* I find that I can differentiate for interest and learning profiles fairly easily by flexibly grouping the students and allowing for choice in content and product. The greatest challenge seems to be the wide range of readiness in classrooms today. For that reason, I usually design my tiered assignments with readiness in mind. The key here is to ensure that the content standard remains the same, while the cognitive depth and complexity changes. I challenge the students to look at the same standard through "different lenses" and then share their learning. This way, each student is matched at the appropriate cognitive level, yet is able to view the standard in different ways.

8. *Maintain flexibility in your planning and teaching.* While your content might be the same, your students are different every single year. So you will never be able to have laminated lesson plans or even the exact same lesson two years in a row. A highly effective differentiating teacher isn't afraid to make a change in the day's lesson. No matter how much planning you put into the lesson, sometimes, it just isn't working. Be flexible enough to change. I remember posting a note on my desk that read, "Flexibility is the key in the classroom and the key in life!"

9. *Develop student responsibility and independence.* We've all heard the saying that "You can't teach a class you can't manage." Differentiating teachers understand that good classroom management doesn't mean controlling or dictating the students. The teacher and students, together, establish routines and rituals that allow the class to be as student-centered as possible. Materials and resources are close at hand for students and they know what to do during their small-group or independent learning stations so the teacher is free to work with small groups of students for enrichment or re-teaching. Students understand their roles in their groups and facilitate their own learning and that of their teammates. They know what to do if they finish early. I remember a substitute once telling me that the students entered the room, got started working, and it wasn't until she called them together to check for absences, that the students realized that I wasn't there and they had a substitute for the day. After which, they gave her the name of three students she could go to if she had any questions.

10. *Use ethical grading practices.* This is a sticky area for all teachers, not just those who differentiate. Because grading reflects teachers' personal philosophy, it provides a great deal of debate on campuses. Teachers can teach and students can learn without the need for grades. Some questions that teachers need to discuss are: Why do we grade? What is the purpose of grades? How accurate are the grades reflecting the students' academic knowledge for the standards? Do we dilute the validity of grades? What about effort, attendance, and behavior? What about zeroes? If we view grades as an accurate report to parents and students about the students' learning progress in relation to the standards, then we only need to reflect on the learning goals and record it on the report card. But what about the students' work habits, attitudes, and behavior? How is that information shared with parents? These are lifelong skills argue teachers, and parents need to be aware. Many schools are choosing to conduct book studies using Rick Wormeli's book, *Fair Isn't Always Equal* (2006), and using it as a springboard for discussion and changes in grading practices.

11. *Differentiate instruction for gifted students with their particular and specific learning differences in mind.* Just when you've gotten good at differentiating for the diverse ranges in your classroom, in walks a gifted student with completely different needs. These students are far more likely to advance to other grade-level curriculum, work on independent learning contracts, and will need substantially more rigor, depth, and complexity in their thinking to be successful in their learning. Teachers working with gifted learners should seek guidance from the national standards for gifted education.

Many of the books listed as resources in this chapter support gifted learners, as well.

12. *Commit to a leadership framework for differentiated classrooms in your school.* Leaders no longer have to be the administrators, although our administrators certainly lead by example. But we can develop teacher leaders and coaches that model lessons and help us to move forward in our differentiation journey. We can form Professional Learning Communities (PLCs) to further our knowledge and skills as educators. The challenge is to take stock of where we are currently as a school or grade-level and set goals for the changes we would like to see. Remember the goals need to be realistic and relevant and include the action steps needed to move us toward our goal. Just as the students in our classroom are at different levels of readiness, so are our teachers. We must encourage and support our teachers as they embrace changing practices and mindsets.

HOW IS DIFFERENTIATION A FRAMEWORK FOR EFFECTIVE INSTRUCTION?

Teachers, today, are facing more and more diverse classrooms and are recognizing a need to be more effective, and thus differentiate their instruction. So, how do teachers move away from an "I know I taught it" mindset to "I know they got it" mindset? Carol Dweck, a leading researcher in the field of motivation and professor of psychology at Stanford University, suggests in her book, *Mindset: The New Psychology of Success* (2006), that those who are more successful in life possess a growth mindset over a fixed mindset. Teachers must be willing to examine their current practices and replace ineffective instruction and strategies for those research-based practices that are more effective, and they have to implement these strategies in a routine manner that becomes simply the way they teach. Teachers who are authentic and consistent in their practice of differentiated instruction have the following characteristics in common:

- They know their students, their content, and establish an environment that values learning growth, acceptance, and respect.
- They pre-assess to determine what to teach, who to teach, and how to teach.
- They use student-centered, best-practice methods for instruction and practice.
- They use formative assessments to make changes in the pacing of their instruction, their flexible groups, their enrichments or interventions, their practice activities or assignments.

- They analyze their summative data to determine both the level of student mastery and the effectiveness of their instruction.

So, how do teachers actually do this? You must first start with your standards and then use the data you have about each student to effectively plan your instruction. Because none of us want to waste valuable instruction time teaching something that a student already knows, we gather pre-assessment data to help us plan what we teach, who we teach, and how we teach. We instruct in the most efficient, effective way possible using the data that we have on our students learning modalities and interests and then use our formative assessment data to determine if we need to make changes in the pacing of our instruction, our student groups, our activities and assignments, or our interventions and enrichments. Finally, we use our summative assessments to determine the level of mastery and the effectiveness of our instruction.

Gathering Pre-Assessment Data to Determine What to Teach, Who to Teach, and How to Teach

Some of the best teachers I know are "students of their students." They take the time to differentiate for a variety of learning profiles and readiness levels. Our learning profile is simply how we learn best, and our readiness levels relate to our knowledge of the content. Teachers can find out about their students through observation, questioning, or a variety of assessments and inventories offered online. Carol Ann Tomlinson, in her book, *How to Differentiate Instruction in Mixed-Ability Classrooms* (2001), provides tips for teachers about how to plan lessons based on the learning profiles of your students. Some information that is worth collecting about your students, prior to teaching, as well as some questions to guide you are listed below:

- Learning Style: Are they visual, auditory, or kinesthetic learners? Do they like noise or quiet? Do they work best alone or in a group? Do they prefer lots of light or a darker area? Are they affected by the temperature of the room?
- Cognitive Style: Are they concrete or abstract learners? Are they part-to-whole or whole-to-part learners? Do they prefer a collaborative or competitive situation? Are they more inductive or deductive in their reasoning?
- Intelligence Preferences: How is their brain "wired" for learning? Are they verbal linguistic, logical mathematical, visual spatial, bodily kinesthetic, musical rhythmic, interpersonal, intrapersonal, or naturalists according to Howard Gardner's multiple intelligences?
- Culture and Gender: Does their culture or gender affect the way they learn, what they value or how they interact with one another?

- Interests: What do they like to do outside of the classroom? Can I use their interests to help them see the relevance in the lesson?
- Readiness: How ready are they for the content? Will I need to enrich for some students? Will I need to provide scaffolding for some students to reach the standard?

While you may not have the time to pre-assess their readiness for every standard that you teach, effective teachers recognize that some units of instruction contain critical standards that students must master. Pre-assessing allows you to determine whether you will teach whole-group or small-group, whether you need to compact or tier for some students, and determine the best method for your instruction. For example, if my pre-assessment showed that seven students needed instruction for a specific skill or standard, and that all seven were musical rhythmic, then I would plan to have the key details of the lesson put into a rhythmic framework during my instruction, as well as allowing them to use it in their practice and in demonstrating mastery of the skill. Of course, I am the teacher, so I could ignore the information and teach everyone the same thing in the same way. If I choose to do that, then I have to take responsibility for the possible problems that might arise. There is a possibility that some students might be bored or frustrated and act out, or a parent might complain that I am giving material that is too easy or too hard for their child, and they would be correct. The decisions I make based on my pre-assessment data are completely my own, and I must be accountable for the consequences of my decisions.

By giving a pre-assessment and analyzing the data, I was able to determine whether my data would allow me to differentiate the content (what I would teach and who I would teach), the process (how I would teach it and how they would practice it), and the product (how they would demonstrate their learning). This helps me recognize which standards might need more time, which students might need more instruction, and whether or not I might need to create additional practice materials or develop some independent studies for students. Taking the time upfront to pre-assess is actually making my planning for instruction more effective!

Combining the Science and Art of Teaching

The Common Core State Standards (CCSS) Web site states, "Teachers know best about what works in the classroom. That is why these standards establish what students need to learn but do not dictate how teachers should teach. Instead, schools and teachers will decide how best to help students reach the standards," (www.corestandards.org). Researcher William Sander and his colleagues have stated:

The results of this study will document that the most important factor affecting student learning is the teacher. In addition, the results show wide variation in effectiveness among teachers. The immediate and clear implication of this finding is that seemingly more can be done to improve education by improving the effectiveness of teachers than by any other single factor. Effective teachers appear to be effective with students of all achievement levels, regardless of the level of heterogeneity in their classrooms. If the teacher is ineffective, students under the teacher's tutelage will show inadequate progress academically regardless of how similar or different they are regarding their academic achievement. (Wright, Horn, and Sander, 1997)

The authors of the book *Classroom Instruction that Works* took the research and theory and translated it into classroom practice (Marzano, Pickering, and Pollack, 2001). They present each instructional strategy and the research behind it in the hopes that "Teachers can use these strategies to guide classroom practice in a way as to maximize the possibility of enhancing student achievement." These broad teaching strategies that have positive effects on student learning are:

- Identifying similarities and differences
- Summarizing and note-taking
- Reinforcing effort and providing recognition
- Homework and practice
- Nonlinguistic representations
- Cooperative learning
- Setting objectives and providing feedback
- Generating and testing hypotheses
- Questions, cues and advance organizers

While the authors provide statistical effect sizes and show how these strategies translate into percentile gains for students, they also recognize that "no instructional strategy works equally well in all situations" and that "teachers should rely on their knowledge of their students, their subject matter, and their situation to identify the most appropriate strategies." So, while science may give us research and information, it is the masterful teacher who is able to combine the science of teaching with the art of teaching to produce lessons that are recalled long past the test date.

BEST PRACTICES FOR EFFECTIVE DIFFERENTIATED INSTRUCTION

Way back in the day, when I was a student, it made sense for teachers to start on page one and work their way through the textbook. We had no knowledge about how the brain took in, processed, stored, or retrieved information. Today's teacher has a wealth of information and research about the brain and learning, thanks to Eric Jensen's *Teaching with the Brain in Mind* (2005) and David Sousa's *How the Brain Learns* (2011). With that much research, it seems silly to consider teaching using the ineffective methods we used in the past. At some point in our training to become teachers, most of us take an educational psychology course and study Lev Vygotsky (1987) and the Zone of Proximal Development (ZPD). The effective teacher is able to match instruction to the students' ZPD which allows their brain to be "slightly stressed" encouraging them to persevere in order to learn. In all my years of teaching, I have never had a class in which all students, all of the time, had the same ZPD. Recognizing this allows us to understand why Rick Wormeli's definition for differentiation included doing "different things for different students some, or a lot, of the time in order for them to learn." So what are some common ways that teachers differentiate for different learners in their classroom?

Differentiating Content to Address Students' Needs

Effective teachers recognize that the students entering their classroom each year vary in what they are interested in, how they acquire and retain information, and their readiness for the content that will be covered; and they plan accordingly. The effective teacher understands that gifted students "have more neural connectors in their prefrontal cortex than do typical learners . . . which will require that they use more of their brain to sort, categorize, and generalize abstract information" (Heacox and Cash, 2014). At the same time, "kids with learning difficulties really *cannot* learn in traditional ways" (Winebrenner, 2006). In addition, the National Clearinghouse for Bilingual Education said in 1999, "In the last decade, the total student enrollment in public schools increased by only 14 percent, while the number of English learners grew 70 percent and is projected to grow even more." The diverse needs found in inclusive classrooms today cannot be met without the use of differentiation. While we cannot change the standards that our students learn, we can make adjustments in what we teach and how we teach to make the content more relevant, interesting, and accessible for our students. Some ways that teachers differentiate the content for their students are listed below:

- Resource materials at varying readability levels
- Audio and video recordings
- Peer and adult mentors
- Keyed concepts and highlighted vocabulary
- Ideas presented through both auditory and visual means including graphic organizers and flip charts
- Use of varied manipulatives and resources
- Anticipation guides
- Charts and models
- Multimedia presentations including slideshow presentations

- Use of interest centers for additional exploration
- Use of events and interests in students' lives as examples in content areas
- Use of diversity regarding race, gender, cultures
- Use of multiple intelligences and learning styles, especially considering auditory, visual, and kinesthetic modes
- Compacting or providing independent learning contracts

Differentiating the Process to Address Student's Needs

"In the educational context, processing may be referred to as 'the consolidation, transformation and internalization of information by the learner' (Caine, Caine, and Crowell, 1994). It can be the path to understanding, insights, depth, and utility and, as a byproduct, the path to memory" (Jensen and Nickelsen, 2008). Processing is where learning takes place. Quality processing activities will engage students at high levels of thinking and will produce deeper understanding of key concepts and skills. Some ways that teachers differentiate the process for their students are listed below:

- Use leveled or tiered activities (same content, but different levels of difficulty or complexity)
- Use a variety of reflection models (cubing, interactive notebooks, learning logs)
- Provide interest centers
- Hands-on materials
- Vary pacing according to students' readiness
- Literature circles and debates as cooperative activities
- Allow choice in strategies for processing and for expressing the results of processing
- Allow for working alone, in partners, triads, and small groups

Allowing students to work in cooperative learning groups can "help develop cognitive abilities, improve working memory and everyday decision-making ability and improve emotional intelligence status and self-esteem" (Jensen and Nickelsen, 2008). Flexible grouping can easily be achieved in the classroom by grouping and regrouping your students based on the outcome you hope to achieve. As stated above, *cooperative grouping* enhances both academic and social skills. *Ability grouping* allows for rapid growth and achievement, which will allow the teacher to enrich and advance the gifted students, provide for instruction and practice for the students on level, and close achievement gaps for struggling students. *Interest groups* are sure to increase motivation and help students see the relevance for the content, while *learning profile groups* will increase the effectiveness of the learning and retention of the information since they will have acquired the learning in their strongest modality.

Differentiating the Product

As students process, independently or in teams, the teacher is constantly checking to see if the instruction and practice is appropriate. This constant checking is what is referred to as formative assessment and it can be as simple as "thumbs up-thumbs down," what you see as you observe the students working, or as complex as a written essay explaining the learning. "Formative assessment, when used effectively, can significantly improve student achievement and raise teacher quality" (Moss and Brookhart, 2009). Formative assessment allows the teacher and students to see what concepts and skills have been mastered and what learning problems still exist. Just as teachers can differentiate the content and process for their students, they can also differentiate the products their students create to demonstrate understanding of the content. Teachers give specific feedback to advance their students toward the instructional goal. "The feedback is intended to help students reflect on their own learning and adjust their strategies as needed in order to meet or exceed the standards and achieve deeper understanding of the important concepts" (Burke, 2010). The goals or criteria for the learning should never be a secret to the students and they should always be directing students toward the instructional and curricular standards. Some ways that teachers differentiate the process for their students are listed below:

- Layered or tiered product choices
- Model, use, and encourage student use of technology within products and presentations
- Provide product choices that range in choices from all multiple intelligences, options for gender, culture, and race
- Analogies, diagrams, demonstrations, presentations, open-ended response, on-demand writing, portfolios
- Use student-designed rubrics to showcase criteria and levels of knowledge and understanding (with teacher input and guidance)

Regardless of what formative assessment you use, the purpose and key to formative assessment lies in what the teacher does with the results. Formative assessment is meant to be analyzed immediately. It "Gives teachers information about what their students already know (or don't know) so they can change, modify or extend the instructional activities in which students are engaged. Teachers can use this information to make adjustments to their instruction as they teach and can differentiate instruction accordingly. It is assessment *for* learning rather than assessment *of* learning" (Coil, 2004). Of course, the teacher can decide whether to allow the day's assessments to remain formative (not graded) or to make them summative by entering a grade in the gradebook. If all students have been successful, you can simply enter the grade and move on to the next lesson. If not, then the assessment remains formative and changes are made to tomorrow's lesson. Sometimes, the teacher must move on, even if the students haven't yet met mastery of the content. In this case, you may have to enter the grade, continue to work with the students, and make changes in the grade at a later date. Some students may not master a standard at the end of the first quarter when your grades are due, but might demonstrate mastery by the end of the third quarter due to your spectacular re-teaching efforts. If so, record the new grade so that it is figured in the end-of-course results.

Theory to Practice—What's In It for Me?

By knowing my standards (what my students have to know, understand, and be able to do) and knowing my students (their interests, learning modalities, and readiness for the content), I am able to plan effective instruction and practice that takes students from where they are to where they need to, or are able to, go. So, sometimes, I've compacted the lesson for my high-fliers and allowed them to work on some independent studies. Other times, I've tiered the assignments to allow each group of students to examine the standard through the appropriate cognitive degrees of complexity. I've used flexible grouping to increase engagement and motivation while building both academic and social skills in a manner that supports retention. I've collected formative assessment data that has allowed me to determine whether to change my pacing, my grouping, my method of instruction, or my activities and practice. And, I've been able to give my students specific, targeted feedback to advance them to mastery, and beyond. I've created an environment that celebrates diversity and perseverance and grit, allowing the students to be more independent learners and me to facilitate their learning in whatever way they need. I've given them the freedom to choose how they will demonstrate their understanding and level of mastery. Granted, I had to put a lot of thought into my planning, but the students are working harder than I am. Now, that's working smarter, not harder!

CONCLUSION

Regardless of whether the standards we need to teach are Common Core State Standards or our own State Standards, our job as educators is to prepare today's students for a life outside of our classroom. They must be able to communicate and exhibit people skills. They have to be able to navigate their way through rapidly changing technology. It's difficult to know what you need to teach your students when you consider the fact that many of the jobs and careers today didn't even exist a decade ago. At the same time, many of the today's digital students, while being masters of technology, lack the skills needed to effectively communicate with their peers and persons of authority. Students must practice self-reliance and be accountable for their decisions if they plan to survive in today's work force. They will face problems in their jobs, as well as relationships, and must have the tools to problem-solve, think and reason critically, and collaborate. Today's classrooms are more diverse than ever before and the truly effective teacher has learned to differentiate and take the students from where they are, to where they need to go, and beyond. I am not a person who is extremely attentive to details or mechanically inclined. I, therefore, am grateful to the teachers who educated my surgeon, who operates on my body and the mechanic who works on my car and keeps it running. I want them both to stay up-to-date with current research and changes that will keep both me and my car in working order. Just as I expect them to continue growing in their field, I need to continue growing in mine. Teachers show their students every day what it means to be a life-long learner. They teach us to strive and persevere and continue to improve. They give us the opportunity, every day in their classrooms, to practice the skills that we will use for a life-time. They celebrate our achievements and when we fail, they help us to pick up the fragmented pieces of our learning, turn them over and over, examining and analyzing them until we see a pattern begin to emerge; they help us make modifications and changes until we reach success. Just as there is no one-size-fits-all student, teacher, or classroom, there is no one-size-fits-all way to differentiate. Everything will depend on the prior knowledge, interests, and abilities that the students and the teacher bring to the learning situation. It is the perfect blend between the science and the art of teaching. It is highly effective teaching.

REFERENCES AND RESOURCES

Bender, W. N. (2008). *Differentiating Instruction for Students with Learning Disabilities: Best Practices for General and Special Educators.* Thousand Oaks, CA: Corwin Press.

Burke, K. (2010). *Balanced Assessment: From Formative to Summative.* Bloomington, IN: Solution Tree Press.

Caine, G., Caine, R., and Crowell, S. (1994). *Mindshifts: A Brain-Based Process for Restructuring Schools and Renewing Education.* Tucson, AZ: Zephyr.

Cash, R. M. (2010). *Advancing Differentiation: Thinking and learning for the 21st Century.* Minneapolis, MN: Free Spirit Publishing, Inc.

Cohen, G. L., Garcia, J., Apfel, N., and Master, A. (2006). "Reducing the racial achievement gap: A social-psychological intervention." *Science* (5791): 1307–10.

Coil, C. (2004). *Standards-Based Activities and Assessments for the Differentiated Classroom.* Marion, IL: Pieces of Learning.

Dweck, C. (2006). *Mindset: The New Psychology of Success.* New York: Random House.

Heacox, D. (2009). *Making Differentiation a Habit: How to Ensure Success in Academically Diverse Classrooms.* Minneapolis, MN: Free Spirit Publishing.

Heacox, D., and Cash, R. M. (2014). *Differentiation for Gifted Learners: Going Beyond the Basics.* Minneapolis, MN: Free Spirit Publishing.

Herrell, A. L., and Jordan, M. (2012). *50 Strategies for Teaching English Language Learners.* Boston, MA: Pearson Publishing.

Jensen, E. (2005). *Teaching with the Brain in Mind*. Alexandria, VA: ASCD.

Jensen, E., and Nickelsen, L. (2013). *Bringing the Common Core to Life in K-8 Classrooms*. Bloomington, IN: Solution Tree.

Jensen, E., and Nickelsen, L. (2008). *Deeper Learning: 7 Powerful Strategies for In-Depth and Longer-Lasting Learning*. Thousand Oaks, CA: Corwin Press.

Lang, J. M. (2012, June 3). "The benefits of making it harder to learn." *The Chronicle of Higher Education*. Retrieved from chronicle.com/article/The-Benefits-of-Making-It/132056/.

Marzano, R. J., Pickering, D., and Pollock, J. E. (2001). *Classroom Instruction that Works: Research-Based Strategies for Increasing Student Achievement*. Alexandria, VA: ASCD.

McKnight, Katherine S. (2010). *The Teacher's Big Book of Graphic Organizers*. San Francisco: Jossey-Bass.

Moss, C. M. and Brookhart, S. M. (2009). *Advancing Formative Assessment in Every Classroom*. Alexandria, VA: ASCD.

National Clearinghouse for Bilingual Education. (1999). *K-12 and LEP Enrollment Trends*. Retrieved from www.ncbe.gwu.edu/ncbepubs/reports/state-data/index.htm.

NGA Center for Best Practices. (2005). *Reading to Achieve: A Governor's Guide to Adolescent Literacy*. Washington, DC: Author.

Rock, M., Gregg, M., Ellis, E., and Gable, R. A. (2008). "REACH: A framework for differentiating classroom instruction." *Preventing School Failure, 52*(2): 31–47.

Schunk, D., and Zimmerman, B. J. eds. (2012). *Motivation and Self-Regulated Learning: Theory, Research and Application*. New York: Routledge.

Sousa, D. A. (2011). *How the Brain Learns*. Thousand Oaks, CA: Corwin Press.

Tomlinson, C. A. (2001). *How to Differentiate Instruction in Mixed-Ability Classrooms*. Alexandria, VA: ASCD.

Vygotsky, L. (1987). "Zone of proximal development." *Mind in Society: The Development of Higher Psychological Processes*: 52–91.

Wiggins, G. (2012). "Seven keys to effective feedback." *Educational Leadership, 701*: 10–16.

Winebrenner, S. (2006). *Teaching Kids with Learning Difficulties in the Regular Classroom: Ways to Challenge and Motivate Struggling Students to Achieve Proficiency with Required Standards*. Minneapolis, MN: Free Spirit Publishing.

Wormeli, R. (2006). *Fair Isn't Always Equal: Assessing and Grading in the Differentiated Classroom*. Portland, ME: Stenhouse Publishers.

Wright, P., Horn, S., and Sanders, W. (1997). "Teacher and classroom context effects on student achievement: Implications for teacher evaluation." *Journal of Personnel Evaluation in Education, 11*: 57–67.

FIVE

Reading, the Foundation for *All* Learning

Katherine S. McKnight

Twenty-first-century life requires strong reading comprehension skills. As students grow into their roles as adult citizens, this need will become more and more apparent. In fact, regardless of whether a school has adopted the Common Core State Standard (CCSS) or a state-specific set of standards, a teacher's greatest goal is to help all their students develop these literacy skills.

We commonly hear that reading opens the door to all other content-area learning. Before we delve into ways to improve students' reading skills, it's helpful to discuss how linguists typically define the relationship between reading, writing, listening, and speaking.

Receptive language refers to language that we absorb, process, and understand. Reading and listening are the linguistic means by which we receive information. We generally receive information via reading and listening. *Expressive language* refers to language that we generate and produce. Writing and speaking are the linguistic means by which we express information. In spite of our technological advances, this is not going to change.

In their positions statement, the National Council of Teachers of English (NCTE) "Definition of 21st Century Literacies" states:

> Literacy has always been a collection of cultural and communicative practices shared among members of particular groups. As society and technology change, so does literacy. Because technology has increased the intensity and complexity of literate environments, the 21st century demands that a literate person possess a wide range of abilities and

competencies, many literacies. These literacies are multiple, dynamic, and malleable. As in the past, they are inextricably linked with particular histories, life possibilities, and social trajectories of individuals and groups. Active, successful participants in this 21st century global society must be able to

1. Develop proficiency and fluency with the tools of technology;
2. Build intentional cross-cultural connections and relationships with others so to pose and solve problems collaboratively and strengthen independent thought;
3. Design and share information for global communities to meet a variety of purposes;
4. Manage, analyze, and synthesize multiple streams of simultaneous information;
5. Create, critique, analyze, and evaluate multimedia texts;
6. Attend to the ethical responsibilities required by these complex environments.[1]

The Information Age has created an even greater demand on reading. All students, whether career or college bound, are going to need sophisticated reading skills in order to comprehend the overwhelming amount of written material that is expected to come their way. Evidence indicates that more information will be presented as written text in the twenty-first century than at any time in the past. It may be transmitted digitally rather than printed on paper, but tomorrow's citizens can expect to be bombarded by a great deal of text. As Frances E. Jensen, a renowned professor of neurology at the Harvard School of Medicine, said in an interview with Debra Bradley Ruder:

> It's truly a brave new world. Our brains, evolutionarily, have never been subjected to the amount of cognitive input that's coming at us. You can't close down the world. All you can do is educate kids to help them manage this.[2]

WHERE TO START

Whether your state is using CCSS or individual standards, the frameworks are strikingly similar. Since the CCSS has presented their reading framework with cited research-based evidence, we will use this as the focus for discussion. The CCSS for reading consist of ten anchor standards and their grade-level/grade-band articulations. These anchor standards are exactly the same for all K–12 students. In other words, all students are on a journey toward the same big goals. The anchor standards are articulated differently for students of different grade levels, but essentially students are simply at different points on the same journey.

The first three anchor standards in the reading strand are concerned with key ideas and details. A student is expected to be able to:

1. Read closely to determine what the text says explicitly and to make logical inferences from it; cite specific textual evidence when writing or speaking to support conclusions drawn from the text.
2. Determine central ideas or themes of a text and analyze their development; summarize the key supporting details and ideas.
3. Analyze how and why individuals, events, and ideas develop and interact over the course of a text.

The next three anchor standards in the reading strand are concerned with craft and structure. A student is expected to be able to:

4. Interpret words and phrases as they are used in a text, including determining technical, connotative, and figurative meanings, and analyze how specific word choices shape meaning or tone.
5. Analyze the structure of texts, including how specific sentences, paragraphs, and larger portions of the text (e.g., a section, chapter, scene, or stanza) relate to each other and the whole.
6. Assess how point of view or purpose shapes the content and style of a text.

The next three anchor standards in the reading strand are concerned with the integration of knowledge and ideas. A student is expected to:

7. Integrate and evaluate content presented in diverse media and formats, including visually and quantitatively, as well as in words.
8. Delineate and evaluate the argument and specific claims in a text, including the validity of the reasoning as well as the relevance and sufficiency of the evidence.
9. Analyze how two or more texts address similar themes or topics in order to build knowledge or to compare the approaches the authors take.

The final anchor standard in the reading strand is concerned with range of reading and level of text complexity. A student is expected to:

10. Read and comprehend complex literary and informational texts independently and proficiently.[3]

These ten standards can seem overwhelming for content-area teachers who aren't familiar with reading development. While every goal and every articulation in the entire CCSS reading strand is important, classroom teachers and curriculum directors have to start implementation somewhere. I find that it is most valuable to start by focusing on the following three anchor standard goals:

Reading Anchor Standard 1

(A student is expected to be able to) Read closely to determine what the text says explicitly and to make logical inferences from it; cite specific textual evidence when writing or speaking to support conclusions drawn from the text.

Reading Anchor Standard 2

(A student is expected to be able to) Determine central ideas or themes of a text and analyze their development; summarize the key supporting details and ideas.

Reading Anchor Standard 8

(A student is expected to be able to) Delineate and evaluate the argument and specific claims in a text, including the validity of the reasoning as well as the relevance and sufficiency of the evidence.[4]

To clarify, while it's impossible to isolate any standard or standards as more important than the others, schools who are in the process of incorporating new reading standards would do well to begin with these. These three reading standards also represent a good starting point for content-area teachers who are just beginning to incorporate literacy education in their classrooms. Those teachers who are using state-specific standards should look for the closest corresponding standards. Just as good teaching happens no matter what standards are being aimed for, close readers with highly attuned comprehension stills can come from any state!

Likewise, it's valuable to remember that reading doesn't exist in a vacuum. Balanced literacy means students learn to recognize spoken and written words, interpret subtext, analyze story plotlines, form written letters, increase vocabulary, and support arguments—all at the same time. We read about what we hear and we write about what we say. The Common Core State Standards are not just a simple list of requirements. They represent *a path* toward balanced and integrated literacy. This path goes through every classroom—not just the reading class or literature class. From a literacy standpoint, a middle school student's reading of the *ITTF Official Table Tennis Rules and Regulations* in physical education class, *Anne of Green Gables* in literature class, and primary source material like voting instruction posters in history class, all serve the same purpose. They're practice. Once a student has mastered the basic decoding skills, mastering literacy is all about pages read. The more pages read, the more skillful the reader becomes. And when all students read quantities of level-appropriate material every day, the achievement gap closes.

DIFFERENTIATION AND TEXT COMPLEXITY

The relationship between text complexity and comprehension growth is one of the key features of the Common Core State Standards. This is what the CCSS document itself has to say about it:

The Reading standards place equal emphasis on the sophistication of what students read and the skill with which they read. Standard 10 defines a grade-by-grade "staircase" of increasing text complexity that rises from beginning reading to the college and career readiness level. Whatever they are reading, students must also show a steadily growing ability to discern more from and make fuller use of text, including making an increasing number of connections among ideas and between texts, considering a wider range of textual evidence, and becoming more sensitive to inconsistencies, ambiguities, and poor reasoning in texts.[5]

In other words, students have to read appropriately complex texts. As they continue their K–12 academic journey, students' comprehension skills are expected to grow. We've heard that students need to read more. And they have to read appropriately challenging material. That all seems pretty straightforward, doesn't it?

In an ideal world, we'd just assign our grade-six students a wide variety of grade-six level texts. The next year they'd be assigned grade-seven texts. And so it would continue until they all finished grade twelve reading grade-twelve level texts.

But of course not all students in a classroom read at the same level, and they certainly don't all read at "grade level." In fact, students don't even all learn the same way. It's not unusual for a mixed ability classroom to include visual, kinesthetic, and auditory learners of varied interests. How can they all be expected to show enthusiasm for the same reading texts? The short answer is: they can't.

Offering a selection of varied and engaging texts on each topic has proven to be more successful in motivating students than using traditional textbooks or basal readers. Trade books, online texts, magazines, and the like also provide a more authentic reading experience. They're what real readers in the real world would read. This authentic experience allows students to take ownership of their literacy development. Students who choose their material don't just learn how to read, *they learn to enjoy reading*.

How do teachers decide what is appropriately challenging? The Common Core State Standards offers a three-part model for measuring text complexity (see figure 5.1).[6] As you can see, there are three equally important parts or aspects of text complexity: quantitative, qualitative, and reader and task consideration.

Quantitative aspects of text complexity would be very time consuming for a human reader to efficiently evaluate. Examples of quantitative aspects include: word length and frequency, sentence length, and text cohesion. They are typically measured by computer software. Most of us are familiar with the Flesch–Kincaid Grade Level measurements. This system typically measures word length and sentence length and assumes that longer words and longer sentences are more difficult to read than shorter

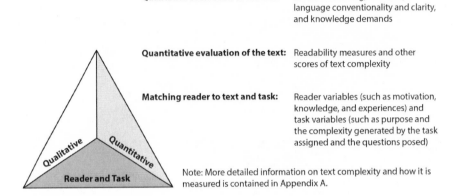

Qualitative evaluation of the text: Levels of meaning, structure, language conventionality and clarity, and knowledge demands

Quantitative evaluation of the text: Readability measures and other scores of text complexity

Matching reader to text and task: Reader variables (such as motivation, knowledge, and experiences) and task variables (such as purpose and the complexity generated by the task assigned and the questions posed)

Note: More detailed information on text complexity and how it is measured is contained in Appendix A.

Figure 5.1.   Measuring Text Complexity: Three Factors.

ones. Essentially, the program counts the number of words in a sentence, the number of syllables in each word, and assigns a numeric value. The lower the number, the higher the text's "readability." There are other, similar quantitative evaluation systems like the Dale–Chall formula, and the Lexile Framework for Reading. All of these quantitative evaluation systems measure things that would be labor-intensive to measure using human power. They are a useful shorthand way to determine "readability" of a text and align it with a grade level.

Not all content-area teachers are familiar with Flesch–Kincaid, but most curriculum directors and reading teachers have known about it for decades. Flesch–Kincaid scoring is bundled in with many word processing programs, so you may have encountered the concept there. Have you ever checked the "readability statistics" of a document? Or, like me, have you ever had it pop-up unintentionally after running spell-check? That's an example of Flesch–Kincaid in action. If you have a word processing program (like Microsoft Word, for example) you might want to take some time to play with it. Try increasing the readability of your document by replacing longer, polysyllabic words with smaller, one-syllable words. Or try replacing complex sentences with simple, shorter sentences. You'll be able to see both the value and the limitations of quantitative measurements.

Some educators, for good or ill, get stuck here and think that checking the Flesch–Kincaid Grade Level measurement or finding a text's Lexile score is the only thing that the Common Core State Standards considers when asking teachers to determine the appropriateness of texts. It's not. Look at the figure of the three-part model again. There are two more aspects to consider.

Qualitative measures, unlike quantitative measures, are the aspects of written material that can be best determined by an attentive human reader. Qualitative measurements include things like level of meaning (in literary texts), and purpose (in informational texts). Literary texts can have a single level of meaning or multiple levels of meaning. Informational text can have an explicitly stated purpose or a hidden and obscure purpose. Structure can be simple, with events arranged in chronological order, or it can be complex with events or steps arranged out of chronological order. Graphics can be simple supplements to the text or they can be complex and essential to understanding the text. The tone of the text itself can be conversational or highly academic. A trained human reader is required to make these distinctions. A computer program would be unlikely to reliably and consistently pick up on the subtleties.

In short, there is no substitute for an experienced teacher reading a text and asking themselves, "Never mind the word count and the length of the sentences, how easy is it to understand this text *really*?"

Reader and Task Consideration is a determination of the appropriateness of a piece of text for a particular student. It is the aspect of text complexity that is not just concerned with the text itself. Instead, it requires the teacher to look at the student for cues about his or her motivation, prior knowledge, and life experience.

The following checklist will help teachers determine Reader and Task Consideration:

Looking at my student's reading skills:

- Does the reader have the necessary inferencing skills to make connections that may not be explicit in this text?
- Does the reader have the necessary visualization skills to picture what is being described in the text?
- Does the reader have the active questioning stance necessary to explore the ideas in the text?
- Does the reader have sufficient comprehension strategies to actively read this text?
- Does this text support the development of inferencing skills, visualization skills, active questioning, and comprehension strategies in the reader?

Looking at my student's motivation and level of engagement:

- Is the reader interested in the specific content of this text?
- Is the student motivated to actively engage with this text?

Not only is this checklist useful for determining appropriate levels of text complexity, it can be used as a sort of "diagnostic tool" as well. Many content area teachers are likely to know that individual students aren't able to comprehend certain material, but they've never tried to determine what exactly is preventing the student from understanding a particular text. This checklist can help.

For example, imagine a student who is able to read a description of plant cell anatomy, but doesn't seem to be able to grasp the concept; she can't describe what she's read in her own words. It's almost as if she recites the words without meaning. Consider that this is a student who has repeatedly demonstrated her ability to grasp other more complex concepts. Her biology teacher would like to help her, but he isn't sure what exactly is going on.

Looking at this checklist, the teacher might be inspired to think that the student lacks the necessary visualization skills to picture what is being described in the text. The student could be encouraged to stop after each sentence and draw what she's just read about. Or the teacher might consider offering this student a text that is more visually stimulating, one that is accompanied by illustrations maybe, while she continues to develop her skills.

Having a variety of texts is a critical component of a classroom that aims to support literacy development in all students. It also represents a change from the textbook-based curricula and lesson plans that many schools and departments have come to depend on. It requires time, commitment, and inter-department cooperation. There are sources for varied texts, but teachers are capable of doing much of the text selection themselves. For example, preparing a classroom offering a variety of texts might look something like this:

A grade-ten consumer science class is learning to compare various nutrition guidelines and explore the correlation between diet and disease. In an effort to support her students' literacy development, the teacher searches for a wide variety of texts. She uses a combination of school and public resources.

- The school librarian points her to a Web site where she and her students can find downloadable copies of state nutrition guidelines. The teacher explores independently and finds a few Web sites with short, downloadable articles that might interest her students. The teacher plans to cut and paste sample paragraphs from each one into a word processing program so she can accurately determine their Flesch–Kincaid (quantitative) value.
- A well-known history museum offers an article comparing the contemporary American diet to the traditional diets of other cultures. The American history teacher loans her a magazine article that compares the diet of a eighteenth century British sailor, a Civil War soldier, a World War II soldier, a NASA astronaut in the 1960s, and a contemporary member of the U.S. armed services. Some of her students are planning military careers so they might find this inter-

esting. But the writing style is fairly advanced. In fact, when she cuts and pastes a few paragraphs from the Web site into her word processing program she sees that part of it is written at the eleventh-grade level. The article includes some fairly big words and some of the sentences are complex. But the material is organized very well and it seems like something her students might like. She decides to print up some copies anyway.

- One of the biology teachers recommends that she print a page from a natural history museum Web site that compares the nutritional needs of humans with those of other primates. This article seems to be written at or slightly below grade level. It includes entertaining graphics. The class includes some reluctant readers and the teacher knows they love animals. So this article is a particularly welcome addition.
- Yesterday the local newspaper ran an article about nutrition guidelines and a proposed change in the school lunch program. The newspaper is written at a level significantly below grade level. But the teacher notices that the article's focus seems to switch from federal guidelines to state guidelines to decisions made by municipal authority. This might be a little hard for some students to follow. Even so, she collects a few copies of the newspaper articles from her fellow teachers.

Armed with this wide variety of relevant reading material, geared toward the varied interests of her students, this consumer science teacher would now be ready for class.

IN THE SCHOOLS

There are two common fears about reading and the new standards. One is that the new standards will require schools to adjust their focus so that the amount of time spent on developing reading skills, specifically the reading of literature, will be reduced. The other is that content-area teachers will now be expected to take over the responsibility for teaching students how to read, thus making English Language Arts (ELA) teachers obsolete. Let's address these one at a time.

First, in almost every case, schools will see no reduction in the amount of literature that students read. Instead, they will see students read an increased amount of informational text. This means there will be an increase in the *overall* amount of reading. Because, as I said earlier in this chapter, after students master decoding skills, reading comprehension is all about practice. The number of pages read is expected to increase significantly, but not at the expense of literature. This emphasis on interdisciplinary literacy is described in the Common Core State Standards document:

Part of the motivation behind the interdisciplinary approach to literacy promulgated by the Standards is extensive research establishing the need for college and career ready students to be proficient in reading complex informational text independently in a variety of content areas. Most of the required reading in college and workforce training programs is informational in structure and challenging in content; postsecondary education programs typically provide students with both a higher volume of such reading than is generally required in K–12 schools and comparatively little scaffolding.[7]

In other words, teachers in all content areas will be expected to ask themselves, "Can students read well enough to explore my discipline?" And they will be empowered to enable students to do just that.

Second, there is an element of truth to the fact that content-area teachers are now going to be expected to teach and reinforce the development of reading skills. But hasn't that been true for a long time? For as long as most of us can remember, content-area teachers have scheduled classroom discussions about assigned readings and found that many students weren't able to comprehend the material well enough to participate. They then had to take it upon themselves to instruct the students in the necessary steps toward comprehensive reading in their specific discipline. Imagine if they didn't have to flounder when that happened. Or better yet, imagine if they were able to address the comprehension struggle before it happened. Wouldn't it be better for these teachers to have a tool belt loaded with literacy development tools ready to go whenever they were needed? Furthermore, imagine that students and their parents actually knew the reading goals for each and every class. That's what the Common Core State Standards and some of the state-specific standards are going for. This does not mean that ELA teachers will be obsolete. Literature will continue to be valued as much as any other content. Indeed, the opportunity for students to examine an author's use of expressive and symbolic language is unlikely to be found in texts in other disciplines.

The new standards may highlight the difficulties teachers face, but they're not creating them. The good news is that, in almost every case, schools are up to the challenge. Administrators, communities, and school boards realize that when all teachers in a school district work together to improve student reading—using common language and working toward common goals—students will benefit. And when administrators and teachers share a common language to discuss these challenges, it will be easier to share resources and ideas.

IN THE CLASSROOM

In an attempt to help students achieve this goal of college and career readiness, the classroom dynamic is already starting to change. The

Gradual Release of Responsibility (GRR) model, as described by Pearson and Gallagher (1983), has become more relevant than ever. This learning model can most easily be described as one in which the teacher gradually releases control and responsibility for learning back to the learner. In education circles, this is frequently summed up as the, "I do, we do, you do" progression.

It's slightly more complicated than that, though. Those of us who actually use the model and have seen it successfully employed in the classroom realize that the progression is more: "I do you watch, we do together, you do I help, you do I watch." In lesson-plan construction the actual steps are sometimes described thusly:

1. Demonstration
2. Shared demonstration
3. Guided practice
4. Independent practice

The guided instruction, mentoring, modeling, prompting, and interactive instruction that teachers provide during steps two and three are commonly known as "scaffolding." During scaffolding, the instructor breaks a complex skill down into manageable chunks and focuses on these one at a time. The skills are sequenced in such a way that they build on each other and eventually result in comprehension and mastery:

> The hope in the model is that every student gets to the point where she is able to accept total responsibility for the task, including the responsibility for determining whether or not she is applying the strategy appropriately (i.e., self-monitoring).[8]

Regardless of how it's described, gradual release of responsibility means that as students become more adept at a particular skill set, the teacher relinquishes his or her place at the center of the classroom. Instead, the students are given freedom to achieve their individual goals, first in peer groups under the watchful eye of the teacher, and finally as independent learners. And while the new standards do not identify any specific strategy or curriculum as a means to meet expectations, there are some models that are very effective in meeting these new demands.

Centers-Based Learning

Whether you call them Literacy Centers, Reading Centers, or Learning Centers, the centers strategy provides an organic method for gradually releasing learning responsibility to the students. The classroom procedure grows naturally out of the gradual release of responsibility model.

As used in K–3 classrooms, centers have proven to be a valuable instructional strategy for building literacy skills with differentiated instructional support.[9] Now educators are beginning to see that centers can be equally effective in middle schools, high schools, and even at the collegiate level.

Evidence shows that when adolescents work in a center, whether they're participating in a shared demonstration or shared practice with peers, they become more engaged.[10] Students with special needs often report that they feel safer in small peer groups. And all students reveal that it's easier to focus in small groups rather than as part of a full class activity. Teachers find that learning centers enable them to cover more content and skill development in the same amount of class time. Plus, it's easy to give individual instruction to students who need it! And learning centers allow teachers to give students the individual attention that is so difficult to manage in a traditional classroom setting.

Essentially, learning centers are *stations* at which students work as members of small groups. The teacher designs each station for one clearly articulated activity. During a classroom learning centers activity, students rotate through all stations and perform various tasks all centered on one topic, theme, or text. The centers model is flexible and can be adapted to almost any classroom and any grade level.

The most effective learning centers start with a "mini lesson" delivered by the teacher. This lesson represents a teacher demonstration— or "I do" activity where students can see a short lesson, observe a model or gold standard of a particular skill, or review a previously mastered skill.

For the purposes of reading skill development, reading centers might include small-group or individual applications of any of the reading strategies we've already discussed. An example of a well-structured learning center might include the following stations:

- *Vocabulary*: At this center, students are provided with an activity where they can manipulate and work with words.
- *Reading*: Students encounter a specific text or group of texts to read at this center. They can read silently, read together, or work on a reading strategy like Survey, Question, Read (SQR) at this station.
- *Visualization*: At this station students can work on translating written text into graphic organizers, storyboards, or history trails.
- *Listening/viewing center*: Using videos, audio recordings, and other media-based materials at this station encourages students to compare how the same content can be delivered through written word, spoken word, and visual representation.

I've found it helpful to place written instructions at each station. Ideally, the teacher gives a brief overview of the instructions for each station at the beginning of the class period, and students have the option of confirming the instructions by reading them before beginning the activity. This has the added benefit of incorporating even more reading practice into the activity. There is no one right way to provide these written instructions. I've seen teachers hang signs on the wall at each station, tape handwritten instructions on top of each table, and display all instructions on the chalkboard or via the overhead projector for easy reference. Experiment until you find something that works in your situation.

Learning center activities work best when the groups, or teams, consist of three to five students each. Large groups have difficulty staying focused. They chatter, fall prey to distractions, and find it difficult to complete tasks. While there might be occasions when a teacher wants students to work individually or in pairs, most of the time that makes the activity too unwieldy. It's difficult to keep track of so many small teams and teachers can't identify students who might need extra help. In short, trying to run a classroom learning center activity with student groups that are too large or too small results in frustration. Many teachers who are convinced that learning centers don't work have discovered this small adjustment makes all the difference!

Timing is one of the trickiest parts of creating and running a learning center. There is no right or wrong, but most teachers have found it best to devote ten to fifteen minutes for each station. Then, because it's sometimes impossible to balance the time requirements, consider ending with a makeup station. Once students have completed their circuit of all the stations, allow five or ten minutes for them to revise or finish any center work. Unlike the other stations, students can do makeup station work anywhere. It's common to ask students to stay in their last position to complete the makeup station work unless there's a need to move (to relisten to a recording or reexamine a map, for example).

Learning centers are a great way to incorporate reading skill development into any classroom. Literacy centers can easily be combined with timeline manipulation, primary source examination, and map reading in a social studies class, for example. Simulated scoring activities, physical skill practice, reading official game rules, and analyzing sports reporting can be combined in a physical education class. The possibilities are almost endless.

Text Circles

Essentially, text circles in the classroom work very much like adult book clubs. That is why they are often lauded as a means to provide students with "authentic" reading experiences. They can be used in the ELA classroom to explore literature or in the content-area classroom to examine a range of written material about a specific topic. For example, this strategy could be used in a social studies class when the students are studying a variety of primary source documents. Regardless of how they are used, the text center reading strategy always has a few consistent elements:

- Students choose their own reading materials. It's important to offer a wide variety of texts on the specific content, topic, or theme.
- The class is divided into small groups (usually three to five students per group) based on text choice. This is important: grouping is by text choice rather than by ability, reading level, or other tracking.
- Reading groups meet on a regular schedule.
- Teacher-led mini-lessons are scheduled before and after text circle meetings. These usually represent the demonstration or shared demonstration elements of the GRR model. Teacher support Web sites abound with examples of these short, practical mini-lessons that can easily be applied in the ELA or content-area classroom. Or teachers can see Daniels and Steineke's excellent book *Mini-lessons for Literature Circles* (2004) to get started. [11]
- Student-led small group discussions about the text represent the guided practice stage of the GRR model. The teacher does not lead these text discussions, but instead acts as a facilitator, fellow reader, and observer. The students' personal responses, connections, and questions serve as discussion starting points.
- When texts are completed, the groups share highlights of their reading through presentations, debates, reports, reviews, or other activities. The independence demonstrated in this final stage of a completed text circle illustrates the final step in the GRR instructional model. Students themselves are empowered to "teach" what they've learned to members of other student groups.
- Teacher observations combined with student self-evaluation throughout all text circle steps provide enough information to form assessment.

To clarify, the teacher's mini-lessons can include any of the reading strategies discussed earlier in this chapter in addition to strategies for teamwork and overcoming obstacles.

Teachers who use text circles notice that the classroom develops a spirit of collaboration. [12] It's not unusual to detect playfulness as students share thoughts, work together, and accept responsibility for their own learning. The change can be astounding. That is why many teachers choose to use text circles regularly. Of course the number of text circles depends on each school's schedule, but many teachers do at least ten per year. New groups are formed around new reading choices as soon as one circle is completed, and the cycle begins anew.

It's important to emphasize the value of student-centered discussion instead of teacher-centered discussion. Remember, students in charge of their own learning read because they enjoy it. Students who enjoy reading become lifelong learners—and that's the ultimate goal!

Fix It Up Strategies

Many teachers combine gradual release of responsibility with an introduction to Fix It Up strategies. These Fix It Up strategies give students tools to use when they're stuck on a particularly difficult or troublesome text and the teacher isn't around. Fix It Up strategies can be printed and hung on any classroom wall as a poster. Or they can be given as a printed handout to students with the instructions that the Fix It Up hints can be referred to throughout the school year. This strategy is particularly useful when it's used school-wide, in content areas as well as ELA classrooms.

A Fix It Up reading strategies chart typically looks something like this:

Are you stuck? Try doing these tricks before you give up!

- Get a sense of the text before reading—scan for clues.
- Guess what will happen.
- Decide why you are reading.
- Create a mental picture.
- Think of what you already know about the topic.
- Develop logical guesses based on the text and your own experiences.

EFFECTIVE READING COMPREHENSION STRATEGIES

There are many effective strategies and activities that help develop reading comprehension. Some of the most popular are listed below. These activities are suitable for literature class, content area classes, and as support activities for independent reading. Most of them can be incorporated into learning centers or used as stand-alone activities. The goal of all reading comprehension strategies, however, is to provide students with the tools they'll need to read complex text in high school, college, and in the working world beyond.

Before-reading strategies are especially effective in supporting struggling readers as they "unpack" particularly challenging texts. Designed to draw out students' prior knowledge (or schema), these pre-reading activities can help individuals make personal connections with the text. Also, previewing new information allows students to predict what the text is about. This further supports comprehension and creates a sense of ownership of material—something that is particularly important to reluctant readers.

ABC Brainstorm

This strategy helps students to organize their thoughts about a topic or text prior to reading and studying the new information. The student scans the text, looking for words or terms that begin with the letters A, B, C, and so on. The student records those words in alphabetical order. Then they go back and actually read the same text. While they read, they attempt to uncover the meaning of their words. The list of words, created before actual reading, serves as a guide for exploration. This activity helps the student focus on discovering the meaning of the full text.

Anticipation Guide

An anticipation guide previews the key information, themes and ideas that will be presented in a text. Contemplating the questions in the anticipation guide gives students an opportunity to draw on their prior knowledge and experiences. It piques their interest and encourages them to recognize how their personal points of view can influence their opinions about a text. The anticipation guide strategy can be used as a full class, small group, paired, or individual activity:

1. To create an anticipation guide, the teacher comes up with a list of statements about the text. For a piece of fiction, the statements should be potentially controversial thematic statements that relate to the text's key ideas. If the text is informational, the teacher should come up with interesting or compelling ideas about the text.
2. Ask the students to rate their level of agreement with each statement and to write a short rationale for their opinion.
3. After reading the actual text, students are encouraged to review their original answers and decide if they want to change them based on what they've learned from their reading.

SQR

This three-step (Survey, Question, Read) strategy encourages readers to predict what they will encounter in a particular text before they read it. Then it requires them to follow up their predictions with a during-reading question answering strategy:

1. Survey: Students should survey the chapter prior to reading. Prompt the students to look at the heading and subheadings and to skim the introduction and conclusion.
2. Question: Once students have identified the headings in the text, instruct them to change the statement headings into questions.
3. Read: At this point, students read the text and answer the questions that they created in step 2.

During-reading strategies encourage students to become more active and engaged readers. Struggling readers benefit from strategies that prompt them to make connections, monitor their understanding, and keep focused on the text. The intention of during-reading strategies is for student readers to eventually make these behaviors a natural and automatic part of independent reading.

Assessing the Author

One way for a student reader to attempt to understand a difficult passage is to guess what the author was trying to do and decide if he or she reached that goal. Encourage students to write answers to the following "author assessment" questions:

1. What is the author trying to say in this passage? (What is the main message or purpose?)
2. Are the author's ideas clear and well expressed?
3. What did the author assume you (the reader) already knew before you started reading this passage?
4. Are the author's points consistent with what he or she has already said?

Stop and Writes

In a Stop and Write activity, the student decides independently when to stop and record his or her thought about a text. Generally a two-column graphic organizer is used. The reader records facts and details from the text in the left column. In the right hand column, the reader records personal connections, predictions, and questions about the text.

Think Alouds/Sticky Notes

In a Think Aloud, the teacher narrates his or her own thought process while reading a text. By sharing this ongoing internal monologue the teacher shows students how to develop their own close reading skills. This is a perfect example of the first step in the Gradual Release of Responsibility model. As student gain experience with Think Alouds, they can begin using the Sticky Note variation themselves. In the Sticky Note variation, students can practice using the same strategy independently stopping as often as necessary while reading to record questions, personal insights, or connections on sticky notes. Instead of sharing their comments aloud, as the teacher did during Think Aloud, the students post their sticky notes at relevant spots in the printed text.

After-reading strategies direct students to think reflectively about what they have read. As they consider particular elements of the text, they explore deeper levels of meaning. These post-reading strategies prompt students to extend the meaning of the text by going beyond the literal meanings and considering inferences, summarize what they have learned from the text, and develop final conclusions about the author's message and their personal connections to the text.

Question-Answer Relationship

The Question-Answer Relationship, or QAR, is an outstanding strategy for developing close reading skills. In this strategy, students develop questions after they have read an assigned text. There are four types of questions. In most cases, students are asked to write at least one question of each type. Other students in the class can then be invited to answer the questions:

- Right There Question—The answer is in the text and is easy to find.
- Think and Search Question—The answer is in the text, but students may have to look at several different sentences and make inferences from what they've read.
- Author and You Question—The answer is not in the text. However, readers may have some background knowledge that will help them to answer the question.
- On Your Own Question—The answer is not in the text. This kind of question requires a high level of comprehension because students must first analyze what they've read and then synthesize the information in order to represent the information in a unique and personal way.

Sequence, Cycle, and List Graphic Organizers

Graphic organizers use visual images and words, they are especially effective learning tools for a wide variety of learners: English language learners, visual learners, and students with special needs, for example. Graphic organizers are visual representations of information and concepts. So, for many students, the graphic organizer is a more innate structure for processing information rather than recording information exclusively in words.[13] Sequence, cycle, and list graphic organizers help students recognize a text's organization scheme and anticipate the author's claims.

Story Trails/Sequence Trails

This strategy offers a structure for students to identify key events from a narrative informational text, especially one that involves sequential steps. Technical instructions and explanations of scientific method applications are often presented in this kind of narrative format. Once the students have identified the key events in the text, they are asked to arrange them in chronological order and create a visual representation of each event. The teacher can also prompt the students to answer the question, "Why do you think this event is important?" This represents metacognitive questioning which prompts students to analyze, synthesize, and then explain or represent each event. This is a high level of comprehension.

There are even *combined before-, during-, and after-reading* activities that reinforce the skills learned in the above strategies. These combined activities encourage student readers to be active readers and engage with the text every step of the way.

DRTA (Directed Reading and Thinking Activity)

Students use a pre-printed three-column graphic organizer or they can create their own. Instruct them to fill in the column for a text passage, article, story, or essay:

- Column 1—Preview before you read: In the first column, write what you think the text is going to be about before you read it. What clues do you see? What questions do you have for the author?
- Column 2—Take notes while you read: In the second column, take notes while you read the text. What are the author's main points? Does the text answer your questions?
- Column 3—Review after you read: In what ways did the text answer your questions? In what ways was the text what you expected it to be? In what ways did the text surprise you?

READING FOR ALL LEARNERS

Because reading is an essential element of college and career readiness for all students, educators in all areas need to incorporate literacy education into the classroom. This requires flexible literacy instruction. And while the Common Core standards don't endorse any particular teaching technique or style, many schools are exploring powerful new methods of employing the gradual release of responsibility model. Using strategies that accommodate learners of different styles—visual and kinesthetic, as well as verbal—challenging texts are being put within the reach of all learners.

A strong reading program is also critical to student achievement beyond school. In his article for AdLit, "The Scope of the Adolescent Literacy Crisis," Rafael Heller describes this urgent need:

> The literacy skills of the typical American teenager haven't improved since the 1970s, but the *demand* for literacy skills has increased dramatically.[14]

A generation ago, the economy was a lot more forgiving to young people who couldn't read and write very well, or who left high school without a diploma. Today, it is next to impossible to find a decent entry-level job without at least a two-year college degree. And once they do land a job, workers are finding it increasingly difficult to climb the career ladder unless they have the ability to communicate effectively, both in person and in writing. Even in industries such as manufacturing and transportation, where a strong back used to count for more than a clear memo, employees must be able to read and write with competence. . . . Simply put, if the middle and high schools continue to churn out large numbers of students who lack the ability to read critically, write clearly, and communicate effectively, then the labor market will soon be flooded with young people who have little to offer employers and who cannot handle the jobs that are available.

Clearly literacy—and reading in particular—is the single most valuable skill for opening doors to educational opportunities throughout life. It requires the effort of every educator in every classroom.

NOTES

1. "The NCTE Definition of 21st Century Literacies." (2008, February 15). *NCTE Comprehensive News*. National Council of Teachers of English. Retrieved from www.ncte.org/positions/statements/21stcentdefinition.

2. Ruder, D. B. (2008, September 1). "The Teen Brain." *Harvard Magazine*. Retrieved from harvardmagazine.com/2008/09/the-teen-brain.html.

3. National Governors Association Center for Best Practices and Council of Chief State School Officers. (2010). *Common Core State Standards (ELA)*. National Governors Association Center for Best Practices and Council of Chief State School Officers, Washington, DC: 10.

4. National Governors Association Center for Best Practices and Council of Chief State School Officers. (2010). *Common Core State Standards (ELA)*, National Governors Association Center for Best Practices and Council of Chief State School Officers, Washington, DC: 10.

5. National Governors Association Center for Best Practices and Council of Chief State School Officers. (2010). *Common Core State Standards (ELA)*. National Governors Association Center for Best Practices and Council of Chief State School Officers, Washington, DC: 8.

6. National Governors Association Center for Best Practices and Council of Chief State School Officers. (2010). *Common Core State Standards (Appendix A)*. National Governors Association Center for Best Practices and Council of Chief State School Officers. Washington, DC: 4.

7. National Governors Association Center for Best Practices and Council of Chief State School Officers. (2010). *Common Core State Standards (ELA)*. National Governors Association Center for Best Practices and Council of Chief State School Officers. Washington, DC: 4.

8. Pearson, P. D., and Gallagher, M. C. (1983, October). "The Instruction of Reading Comprehension." University of Illinois, National Institute of Education. Washington, DC: 35.

9. Doyle, Terry. (2011). *Learner-Centered Teaching: Putting the Research on Learning into Practice*. Sterling, VA: Stylus Publishing.

10. McKnight, K. S. (2014). "Chapter 6." In *Common Core Literacy for ELA, History/Social Studies, and the Humanities: Strategies to Deepen Content Knowledge (Grades 6-12)*. San Francisco, CA: Jossey-Bass.

11. Daniels, H., and Steineke, N. (2004). *Mini-lessons for Literature Circles*. Portsmouth, NH: Heinemann.

12. Pitton, D. E. (2005). "Lit Circles, Collaboration and Student Interest." *Academic Exchange Quarterly* 9.4: 87.

13. Fountas, I. C., and Pinnell, G. S. (2001) *Guiding Readers and Writers, Grades 3–6: Teaching Comprehension, Genre, and Content Literacy* (first ed.). Portsmouth, NH: Heinemann.

14. Heller, P. (n.d.). "The Scope of the Adolescent Literacy Crisis." *AdLit.org*. Retrieved from www.adlit.org/adlit_101/scope_of_the_adolescent_literacy_crisis/.

SIX

The CERCA Framework for Career and College Readiness

Eileen Murphy

SHIFTING TOWARD CRITICAL LITERACY ACROSS THE GLOBE

Think back over the past three or four days of your professional and personal life. How many times did you have to make an evidence-based argument, or a CERCA? In other words how many times did you have to make a *claim*, support it with *evidence*, explain your *reasoning* clearly, address a *counterargument*, and use language that appealed to your *audience* given the occasion and the purpose?

The critical literacy skills required to make an effective argument, what we call a CERCA, are the most important skills we can have in our personal, academic, and professional lives. For a civil society, it is essential that we empower everyone with these skills.

For our students to survive, get ahead, and even just stay out of trouble, they need to be able to read critically, evaluate and synthesize information from many different media, and express their thoughts effectively in many mediums, especially online writing in a world where job applications, banking, and even health care require these skills. They need critical literacy skills and a deep reservoir of language to learn, think, and express themselves.

Given the centrality of these skills in all aspects of our lives, it is not surprising then that Aristotle and others were devoted to this instruction. These skills make up the core of new academic standards around the globe as well. Aside from the discrete skills focused on particular content, such as grammar rules or the study of particular authors or texts, most

91

new literacy standards, globally, focus on one's ability to comprehend a wide range of media and synthesize one's thinking into an argument, expressing one's critical viewpoint about a topic or text in a written, spoken, or multimedia product. Therefore, our classroom instruction needs to support these goals. It is a big shift, but absolutely necessary for our students.

WHY STUDENTS NEED THIS SHIFT TO HAPPEN

Beyond the fact that educators are supporting students as they strive to achieve on new standards and assessments, the frequent, in-class practice of these very skills has had the most dramatic impact on student achievement on assessments of college and career readiness skills such as the ACT and, therefore, are best practices. One sample study that indicates the power of the practice of argumentation and writing in increasing a student's likelihood to be career and college ready came out of the University of Chicago (ccsr.uchicago.edu/sites/default/files/publications/ACTReport08.pdf).

Researchers there found that writing across subjects five or more times per month compared to less than five times per month had the single greatest impact on student achievement. In addition to writing, the other practices that led to higher scores included discussion, debate, and practices such as peer editing and other collaborative activities. These practices are the keys to success in all subjects. Students who engage in the practice of argumentation across subjects simply do better.

Only a fraction of American students have successfully acquired these skills. Despite the fact that the United States spends more on education than most other countries in the world, nationally we haven't had any significant impact on the outcomes of the average seventeen-year-old since we first started measuring ourselves with National Assessments of Educational Progress (NAEP) in 1971.

It surprises a lot of people, for example, to learn that only 40 percent of U.S. students who enter college actually complete an associate's degree or better (NCES, 2013). It also surprises people to learn that, since the 1970s we have fallen from first to thirteenth globally in our high school completion rates, according to the latest data, despite decades of school reform efforts. Today, when over 70 percent of jobs in the United States will require some post-secondary education, it is imperative that we prepare our students with the skills they need to have a shot at a decent job.

Luckily, right now, we are all focused on the goal of equitable career and college readiness on scale. And, the majority of state standards are finally focused on explicitly teaching these particular skills.

THE CHALLENGES OF MAKING THE SHIFT TO FOCUSING ON CRITICAL LITERACY

Focusing on critical literacy is an enormous challenge for many complex reasons.

It's Hard Work

Not only is this hard work for teachers, but it is difficult for students to learn these new skills. Remember also that our own workforce of over three million teachers didn't have this instructional focus when they were students. When we introduced new standards and assessments, we did not factor in new time for teachers to learn, so new standards have contributed to the already difficult workload for most teachers.

Some Legacy Instruction Does Not Mirror the Demands of Current Career and College Readiness

In the past, state assessments and college placement exams focused on content that could be objectively assessed with multiple-choice assessments, and we started leaning more and more toward this kind of automation and moving away from assessing student writing. We, therefore, focused less and less on using writing both as an in-class assessment tool and an instructional strategy.

Furthermore, our instructional technology often supported automating every task of a teacher and, therefore, hardly ever involved the teacher, whose job, in many ways, is to create the context in which it is meaningful to put forth effort. The technology lived in the computer lab, where students read comprehension passages and where dashboards and in-app rewards were expected to make up for any gaps in student motivation. While there were great successes in the field of gamified learning, including *Oregon Trail* and *SimCity*, the effective practice of writing, discussion, and debate-oriented tasks have not been well represented in technology.

We need technology that recognizes the important role that both teachers and other thinking humans, including collaborative peers, need to play in this learning dynamic. Again, when we consider the human behaviors that research indicates are critical in developing these skills, we have to move away from the idea of individuals working quietly with computers. We need technology to support teaching and learning that mirrors the demands of a complex world where collaboration and debate are key skills and where technology is an important tool. We must also work to close the digital learning gap by making access to the digital tools equitable.

CONTENT KNOWLEDGE CANNOT BE UNBUNDLED FROM
CRITICAL LITERACY SKILL INSTRUCTION

As we transition into focusing on critical literacy skill development, after decades of classroom instruction being focused, instead, on larger units of knowledge based on content—understanding the artistry of a novel, the politics behind the Revolutionary War, or the steps in photosynthesis, for example—teachers, students, and parents all feel the tension between content knowledge and the critical literacy skills in more acute ways.

As we make this shift, we have to be careful that we don't throw the baby out with the bath water. We still need units of in-depth study in particular content areas. We simply can't stop having great discussions about the *Outsiders, Black Boy*, or Jane Austen, send kids to computer labs to read random informational texts, and expect that we're going to raise the achievement levels of students across the country. Instruction in critical literacy in any discipline requires significant teacher content knowledge, deep units of study, and active intellectual engagement by students.

It is impossible to move to higher order thinking skills development if we skim across the surface of lots of topics. Without building background knowledge, we can't move beyond comprehension. Critical thinking requires sustained active mental effort, which requires engagement, both of which depend upon that background knowledge that comes from deeper units of study.

Critical literacy instruction also requires an explicit, as opposed to an implicit, focus on imparting the language of a discipline. Students, after all, will need the language to express their own thinking with those disciplinary words.

In short, idea-based learning that is intellectually and personally engaging to students along with explicit contemporary literacy skill instruction both belong in classrooms and need to be supported by both technology and thinking humans, including both teachers and peers.

Therefore, technology that supports this type of learning must account for all of those factors: coherent content that deepens knowledge about a subject, explicit skill and language instruction in each discipline, and the knowledge that teacher users and collaborative students will have something to do with creating the context for motivating learning. Feedback from thinking humans is required.

Why Is Critical Literacy Instruction a School's Job, Not Just a Teacher's Job?

I will discuss the evolution of the literacy framework called CERCA, which was developed in classrooms with real teachers and real students and in schools with real principals.

Having worked as a high school English teacher and a college-level developmental composition instructor, as well as an AP English teacher and department chair, I had already developed a number of writing frameworks that yielded results on a smaller scale. After working with colleagues and professional developers across a large urban school system as the director of curriculum and instruction in Chicago Public Schools' Autonomous Schools Office, I became convinced of a few things that evolved into the larger CERCA framework and eventually a technology to support personalized learning:

1. The Five Essentials work of the team at the University of Chicago's Consortium on School Research and common sense tells us learning must be at the center of schools. Ambitious instruction simply has to be the focal point of a school for student outcomes to be continuously improved. Building level leaders have to take ownership of literacy instruction for students to achieve maximum outcomes in all subjects. If a principal doesn't own an initiative, it is unlikely that it will be owned by the team.

2. Collaboration across teams is essential for maximizing student outcomes. Teaching students complex critical literacy skills takes a village. One reading or writing teacher alone each year can't do it. It is simply too difficult to take on alone, because it requires deep content knowledge across subjects. It is also unrealistically labor intensive to provide rich feedback to young writers on a frequent basis if only one teacher is carrying out that work, especially if teachers continue to have 140 students, as I did for fifteen years.

3. A focus on critical reading, argumentation (the process), and argumentative writing (the product) makes sense to teachers across subjects and, therefore, doesn't feel like a weird add-on. Teacher buy-in for any school-wide effort is essential but also more difficult to achieve as one moves into instruction across subjects, so the universal value of critical thinking in content areas makes a great focus for collaborative work.

4. A simple, common language that anyone can understand is not something that is nice to have; it is a must-have for collaboration to take place in the village's effort to teach these skills. In a sea of jargon left by various products and approaches, students and teachers find it impossible to connect ideas, which has prevented us from making anything else work (more on this to come). We have spent too much of our extremely limited time teaching teachers about the language of various learning systems, rather than spending time increasing the discipline-specific skills and content knowledge teachers bring to the teaching of content. The other problem is that parents are often left out of the club with jargon, which also doesn't translate well to the real world. It is difficult for

students to make the connection between school work and life outside of school, which is essential in terms of the student valuing
what we ask them to do in school, as Carol Dweck and Deanna
Kuhn (2008) found in their research.

5. Deep content knowledge in a discipline is essential to literacy instruction in that discipline. The two should not be considered separate. Literacy instruction is about reading and writing, but the
secondary definition of the term is knowledge and competence, so
it applies to every single subject including math. Simply put, a
teacher has to know their subject really well to teach critical literacy skills in that subject. Experts training novices or apprentices
need to be able to rely on their own ability to understand content in
a variety of mental models in order to explain things in a variety of
ways for diverse learners. We need to invest in teacher knowledge.

6. Machines cannot take the place of thinking humans who create a
context in which it is meaningful to put forth effort, but they can
certainly make life easier for said humans.

Using these principles, I developed a framework after fifteen years of
classroom practice and several years at the central office. While there, I
was tasked with helping to improve instruction, with a specific focus on
individual student growth, along with rolling out the Common Core
State Standards. Here is a brief description of the evidence-based argumentation framework we used at one time. Keep in mind that teachers
were being held accountable for achievement on one set of assessments
and were being asked to prepare for others, while also juggling the implementation of data-driven and differentiated instruction. The CERCA
Framework was our simple solution to a variety of complex problems.

The CERCA framework has worked to drive outcomes on paper and
continues to drive those outcomes on a greater scale via technology.

WHAT IS THE CERCA FRAMEWORK?

The CERCA framework is a flexible critical thinking and literacy framework that empowers entire school teams to improve student growth
across disciplines by engaging students.

Any framework for teaching and learning has to account for the three
core aspects of teaching and learning. What does a student need to know
and be able to do (curriculum)? How can we facilitate that learning (instruction)? How will we know if students have learned it (assessment)?
The CERCA framework facilitates teachers in aligning curriculum, instruction, and assessment within and across classes, subjects, and grade
levels.

To be ready for the workplace or college, not to mention civic life,
students need to know how to read critically, analyze content in various

mediums, synthesize information, collaborate/listen, problem-solve, and convey their thinking in a variety of mediums. Whether they are speaking, writing, or increasingly today, creating visualizations and multimedia productions, the critical thinking skills required to perform these tasks remain the same as when Aristotle was teaching them two thousand years ago.

Curriculum: What Students Need to Know and Be Able To Do

We really can't predict everything students will need to know and be able to do, so the content we're teaching will vary. However, the skills for critical literacy will remain the same across grade levels, subject areas, and disciplines, and from one career to another. Regardless of what else we teach, the meta-language of claim, evidence, reasoning, counterargument, and audience (CERCA) is the foundation of a working language that can be used to teach any curriculum.

To achieve competence in each discipline, students have to have the skills, knowledge, *and* language to demonstrate proficiency in a content area. The language to express one's understanding of a poem's basic action versus the language required to write a poetry explication are very different. The language required to provide a short answer to what happened in a science experiment is very different from the language required to write an analysis of another scientist's argument. Therefore, disciplinary or academic language instruction must be part of any critical literacy curriculum.

We are all ALLs (academic language learners) in that sense and many of the strategies from teaching English as a second language apply.

INSTRUCTION: HOW THE CERCA FRAMEWORK CAN BE USED TO FACILITATE THIS LEARNING

CERCA can be a lens for reading, a process for facilitating learning, and a framework for building one's own arguments.

Try, for example, reading Shakespeare's argument, "My mistress's eyes are nothing like the sun" in Sonnet 130 through the lens of the CERCA framework. Examine an advertisement, a published scientific research report, or an image of Rosie the Riveter who proudly proclaims "We Can Do It" (figure 6.1). In any of these examples, you will find that the framework for reading the text works to promote close analytical reading. The goal is to move students from what a text says, to understanding what it means, and analyzing why it matters.

CERCA as a Framework for Critical Reading

Claim: What is the author's/designer's/artist's claim? In other words, what argument is the author making?

Evidence and Reasoning: How does the selection and arrangement of details help to convey that argument?

Counterargument: How, if at all, are counterarguments addressed?

Audience: What words and images has the author chosen to convey their point of view and why?

CERCA as a Process for Facilitating Critical Thinking and Collaboration

While arguments are products students produce and teachers assess, the process of argumentation is the way we can facilitate a student's active engagement in learning. Let's take the Rosie the Riveter image.

Here is the typical response a student gives in response to the question, "what is the claim of this image?"

> Student: "It's saying that women are strong, and they can do anything that men can do."

Figure 6.1. Rosie the Riveter.

It is a perfectly reasonable claim, and in many settings, we would nod our heads in agreement and move on. In fact, outside of work life and college life, many of our claims are accepted without question. If there is no controversy, no reason to engage in a counterargument, "ya know" is all we have to say, and we move on.

Students are pretty good at making claims. We all are.

But in career and professional settings, we are asked to present more than a claim. We have to back it up with evidence. Going back to the Rosie the Riveter example, if we ask students to find evidence to support their claim, one student will notice the lipstick and the hairstyle, while another will notice the woman pointing to her muscles. Yet another will point to the text, "We Can Do It," that sits atop the larger than life image of Rosie.

Again, students are pretty good at pointing to evidence that supports their claims. Now they aren't always spot-on, but they are can find evidence. Explaining how that evidence supports the claim, on the other hand—well, not so much.

If we push students further to answer the other questions the framework presents, the results are very different. Suddenly the metacognitive processes and disciplinary language demands kick in. When students move beyond "what does it say," into "what does it mean," and "what does it matter," they have to convey their thinking in words. The deep conceptual understanding of content and discipline-specific language demands require an intellectual confidence and a level of vocabulary that both come only with practice, and that practice needs to be out loud just as often as it is in writing.

If we begin shaping learning experiences with the end goal of creating controversy and preparing students to express their critical thinking about a topic, we realize what will be required to explain. For example, if we ask students why the author chose to show Rosie's large muscle in the foreground along with manicured nails, and curled hair wrapped in a fashionable handkerchief, they need to have the language to describe those images. They will also need the background knowledge to be able to contrast the work clothes represented by the blue shirt with the narrow-wasted, well-groomed woman who would have been familiar to anyone shopping for bracelets or home appliances in magazines of the time.

So, while the framework provides a routine process, great critical literacy instruction requires preparing deeper units and explicit language instruction. We will dive more into how the framework can help there as well later.

HOW THE PROCESS OF ARGUMENTATION SUPPORTS MORE EFFECTIVE GROWTH THROUGH DIFFERENTIATION

Five Reasons Why High Reading Levels Aren't a Deal Breaker for Students

Whether it is a quantitative score assigned to a reading, a grade-level label, or even a sticker on the spine of a book at the library, it is now commonplace to quantify texts in terms of how difficult they are in order to gauge how well a student will be able to understand them. But is it appropriate to judge students' ability based on one number or standard?

The complexity of a text involves dimensions beyond the quantitative and even the qualitative factors used to determine different reading standards and levels, so it's important to look holistically at original texts to determine whether or not students can tackle them. When it comes to critical literacy, as compared to making information accessible, rewriting and revising texts to make them fit a certain grade level or standard may not be the most effective approach. Building critical literacy skills is simply different from making knowledge on a given topic accessible.

One of the reasons the debate-oriented framework is useful is it keeps all students engaged in rigorous tasks, but also because differentiated readings are an asset for the whole community of learners. Using different levels of authentic texts based on the same topic provides all students with the appropriate level of challenge while also providing the learning community with different points of view.

Here are five things to keep in mind when selecting texts for students who may struggle below grade level in reading.

1. Kids are capable of reading anything when they have the background knowledge, vocabulary, and interest.

Take this example from a blog about the computer game *Minecraft* (APP Lincoln Students, 2014):

> While ranged attacks will be easier for you, melee attacks will deal more damage per attack; an effective tactic is to wait for it to charge, sidestep its attack, and then whack it with your Sword.

This sentence (and the text it's pulled from) is written at a fairly high level, requiring specific vocabulary knowledge and the ability to decipher complex sentences. But can you understand it? Maybe not, if you don't have the background knowledge and vocabulary that very young players of this video game have.

Many third graders—kids familiar with the world of *Minecraft* and melee attacks—do an excellent job of interpreting this text. That is why student background knowledge and interest are so critical to determining just how far kids can go with difficult texts. As we prepare texts to fuel debate and written arguments, we're thinking about what students will need to be successful, and that goes far beyond algorithms, as the Rosie and *Minecraft* examples show. They will need depth of knowledge in a particular topic.

2. Algorithms can't capture the complexity of ideas.

Take this *New York Times* excerpt (Liptak, 2014):

> WASHINGTON—The Supreme Court ruled on Monday that requiring family-owned corporations to pay for insurance coverage for contraception under the Affordable Care Act violated a federal law protecting religious freedom. It was, a dissent said, "a decision of startling breadth."

While the syntax and word choice is by no means simple, the true complexity of this text lies in the conceptual knowledge behind the statement. The reader must have some background knowledge of the Supreme Court, the rules regarding publicly versus privately traded companies, contraception, the Affordable Care Act, and multiple other issues relating to current events and politics.

Knowledge demands go well beyond vocabulary. Simplifying language or shortening sentence length can't make up for missing knowledge that enables students to make meaning rather than simply decode. This example shows that no matter how accessible the text is from a vocabulary or syntax standpoint, we still need to create context for a reading to help students truly create meaning. The process of debate does just that and increases the amount of background knowledge floating in the classroom.

If we provide teachers with texts that allow each group of learners at different levels of readiness the opportunity to fill in background knowledge for the group, while practicing their own critical reading skills, we set the whole class up for success.

3. Building comfort with complexity and gaining confidence in taking on new challenges is critical, and it takes years to achieve.

Words really can't be separated from meaning. Great poetry, historical speeches, Shakespearean plays, and complex arguments in science are only a few examples of texts that cannot be rewritten without fundamentally changing the meaning of them. All students deserve exposure to the language, syntax, and genres of the most highly educated, most powerful people in the world. Otherwise, they will never be equipped with the skills necessary to cross the moat that separates so many students from those centers of power.

Introducing them to difficult texts in the safe environment of a classroom helps them build the critical literacy muscles and build the knowledge base required to meet the demands in content areas at higher levels.

When you search a key word on the Internet, a million complex texts appear before you. Standardized tests, college textbooks, and even the *New York Times* will not adjust to the reader. The reader must adjust to the texts to achieve success in many aspects of their lives—and that means becoming comfortable with unknowns and making sense of harder texts on one's own. To build confidence and persist, students need small victories that remind them that they can do this hard thing, because they have done it before.

The CERCA framework's collaborative approach to instruction helps students engage shoulder to shoulder in a productive struggle with complex texts and the process of debate, which motivates students in their intrinsic desire to win the assent of their peers.

4. Learning in a social setting motivates and engages students, so unique, accessible, and complex texts on the same topic engage students in meaningful collaboration.

Great teachers use peer engagement as a key to learning. New standards, assessments, and research over decades prove that discussion, debate, and written argumentation are the key to college and career readiness. Collaboration is the reason behind why and how we jigsaw our text sets together. We want both the top-performing and lowest-performing students in a class to benefit from their peers; to feel equally motivated to read critically; to form compelling arguments; and to teach each other about topics. With this collaborative approach to exploring a topic, everyone is exposed to the topic at a deeper, multidimensional level (Applebee, 2003).

Text sets made up of different levels of accessibility enable differentiation without sacrificing rigor. In fact, they increase rigor by adding depth and complexity to any subject.

5. If students practice reading harder things, they get better at reading hard things.

The cumulative effect of reading—the effort made over time—matters. We need to put complex texts in front of students on a regular basis, so they can practice reading comprehension, critical thinking, and argumentation in ways that hone these skills for future success in college and their careers. In short, we need to enable success on the hard things kids will face without us, not just enable success on the things we are doing with them.

In order to engage and develop all students, teachers must provide texts that challenge the students' individual reading levels. Students should be given the opportunity to work through their own articles, create their own arguments, and share them with one another without relying on teachers and peers to do all the heavy lifting on new topics or complex texts.

Let's challenge our students with engaging texts and lessons that develop their critical thinking skills and encourage them to engage with their peers, develop their own arguments and opinions, and challenge themselves to get through difficult reading.

How Does CERCA Work as a Discussion, Debate, and Writing Framework?

Challenging students to include all of the key components of arguments is one way in `which the framework can help students develop the habits of mind, intellectual values, and genre awareness they need to be effective.

Also, since it applies across subjects, CERCA makes a great framework for collecting a simple set of data points that can help teams calibrate expectations and see trends in student needs and achievements for personalized learning plans.

An effective argument, whether it is a paragraph long or book length, contains a claim, reasons, and evidence that support the claim, reasoning that links the evidence back to the claim or reason supporting the claim, a counterargument, and audience-appropriate language. How we arrange them varies, but the core components are always the same. It is that simple.

Also, because we have a basic set of components that can apply across subjects, we can provide stems or sentence frames that equip students with the language they'll need to use to make arguments.

In addition to supporting academic language development, these stems also provide a scaled-down process for thinking through a single aspect of one's argument.

Let's see the framework in action using the following examples, again based on Rosie the Riveter:

Claim: What is the author's/designer's/artist's claim? In other words, what argument is the author making?
"The poster is making the argument that _____."
Evidence and Reasoning: "How does the selection and arrangement of details help to convey that argument?"
To answer that question the student might use a stem such as, "The designers chose to portray the woman as having _____ in order to suggest that _____."
Counterargument: "How, if at all, are counterarguments addressed?"
The designers were obviously addressing the counterargument that _____ when they chose to portray _____.
Audience: "What words and images has the author chosen to convey their point of view and why?"

The choice of the (word/image of)_____ suggests that the designers wanted viewers to _____.

The CERCA framework, as a process, provides a systematic approach to
thinking critically. In a classroom, it provides a social and collaborative
process for evidence-based reading, writing, listening, and speaking that
engages students at all levels of readiness in rigorous cognitive tasks.

When students have an opportunity to engage in the process collaboratively, engagement is high because the task is social. Pairing students
and using small group collaborations prior to large group discussion and
writing yields even greater results, because students have a wider variety
of evidence to pull from, more exposure to various expressions of inferential thinking, and multiple perspectives to draw from in their final
argument.

Assessment: How Can CERCAs Be Used to Assess Student Learning?

Students ultimately make arguments about their learning in the form
of written arguments, presentations, discussion, and debates, or multimedia presentations. The product of the learning shows that students know
their content and possess the communication skills they need in the discipline to convey their point of view effectively. When there are deficits in
the content knowledge, or their ability to convey it effectively, teachers
can identify the gaps readily and provide additional feedback and instruction to improve student learning. The CERCA, as a student product,
can take the form of a paragraph, a poetry recitation, an infographic, a
magazine article, an entrepreneur's pitch deck, or a formal academic
paper. Regardless of the medium, students and peers can evaluate student writing by asking the same questions of the student as we asked of
the authors of the texts they read. See below:

Claim: What is the author's/designer's/artist's claim? In other words,
what argument is the author making?
Evidence and Reasoning: How does the selection and arrangement of
details help to convey that argument? What examples of the reasoning, explicit or implicit, does the author use to connect that
evidence back to the reasons and claims they have presented? Do
they organize and express the argument clearly and effectively?
Counterargument: How, if at all, are counterarguments addressed?
Audience: What words and/or images has the author chosen to convey
their point of view and why? How effective was the expression?

In the case of certain genres, we would also add components to a
rubric to measure progression and achievement in other categories. For
example, we would require a category for conclusions and grammar/

conventions in formal academic writing or a category for visual clarity in a multimedia presentation.

WHY THE CERCA FRAMEWORK BENEFITS STUDENTS

Students benefit from the simple coherency on several levels. First of all, by having the teams use the same words to describe their practice, we can eliminate some of the cognitive overload that comes from just learning "how to do school" when every teacher is teaching students their own working vocabulary for teaching and learning.

The mere time savings that comes from using a common language across grade levels and subjects to describe aspects of reading and writing means additional instructional minutes that teachers can use to teach content rather than teaching each teacher's own working language for instruction and grading.

With the common language, common rubrics are also possible. These lead to common data that can reveal patterns over time and can easily be correlated to a variety of other formative, summative, and standardized assessments.

WHY THE CERCA FRAMEWORK BENEFITS TEACHERS

Teachers benefit from the CERCA framework because, with the shared language and common practices across teams, teachers reinforce each other's work. They have a clear working vocabulary for discussing student work, as well as a shared focus in instructional strategies, which often means sharing materials more easily. In other words, I don't have to teach "my kids" "your language" to borrow something you developed.

What about Math?

For decades we have all been hearing about the importance of literacy across disciplines.

One of the challenges of actually implementing writing across the curriculum for any literacy strategy across disciplines is that it often fails to take into account the inextricable relationship between content in a discipline. When math teachers were asked to adopt some forms of writing, for example, they often felt that they were losing mathematical instruction time in order to serve the writing gods.

However, the CERCA framework is readily accepted by mathematicians who, like Karim Ani, ask students to make arguments about real-world applications in math. For example, Ani, who developed *Mathalicious* (Mathalicious.com), asks what the fairest way is to determine the winner in the "Biggest Loser" or how our eating habits would change if menus at fast food restaurants were presented in terms of how much exercise it would take to burn off the calories each item contained. Mathematical practices developed by the National Council of Teachers of Mathematics (NCTM) and built into new standards show that writing mathematical arguments is a process for learning math and a student product that can be used to assess mathematical learning.

A deep conceptual understanding and a specialized language is required for critical literacy in each discipline. Even in English classes, which are different from reading classes, there is content that must be taught in order for a student to develop the skills required to be literate in the discipline of English. It is impossible to teach a list of vocabulary related to literature, for example, have students comprehend a poem, and automatically be able to put two and two together to describe how they constructed the meaning of the poem in the language of literature. As Robert Pinsky underscores in the *Sounds of Poetry* (1998) and Robert Scholes notes in *The Crafty Reader* (2001), one cannot identify a metaphor and describe how that metaphor relates to the larger meaning of a poem simply because they know the definition of a metaphor. In many cases, they have to consciously apply these literary devices as writers to be able to truly identify and describe them well as readers and critics.

To have evidence of this level of literacy in the content areas, students need the following three components: (1) basic comprehension skills in the content area (knowledge), (2) the analytical skills required to be able to understand the way features of text work (discipline-specific awareness of content area texts), and (3) the language to describe the features of that text in an argument.

We therefore cannot separate content instruction from literacy skills, yet in order to successfully collaborate as a team around student growth, we need a framework for collaboration that allows us to revere both.

If we believe that strategies become skills when they are automated, then practice that leads to automation is what is required. The practice of the CERCA framework and careful attention to the development of discipline-specific language across disciplines provides an efficient set of instructional strategies and assessment tools that leads to reinforcement across subjects, and facilitates collaboration across the team.

HOW DOES THE CERCA FRAMEWORK HELP SUPPORT THE WORK OF INSTRUCTIONAL LEADERS?

A critical voice in instructional design has to be the principal of the school (Bryk et al., 2010). For school leaders and district level instructional leaders, the common language of the framework, classroom practices, rubrics, and resulting data provide insight and coherency in an instructional plan.

In an era of technology and big data, I often hear school leaders express their desire to connect all the instructional technology into one dashboard. While standards-based assessments built into new instructional technologies do make it easier than ever before to build a coherent picture of a student's progress and provide meaningful insights into their performance, dashboards don't solve one of the larger issues that undermines the effectiveness of each technology—incoherency in the content connections and pedagogies. When teachers can't make strong connections at the content/topic level or the pedagogical level, they find it challenging to make instructional sense of multiple resources.

Sewing a bunch of literacy programs that build skills together on a dashboard doesn't help teachers and students make much sense of their overall learning experience and doesn't meet the requirement of building depth of knowledge. I liken the experience to sitting on a couch next to an adult with a remote control in their hand flipping through channels.

Without depth, we can't get to rigor. Teachers, especially as we move up the grade-level ladder, need to weave content together, not just data, so the framework's flexibility to work in any content area and any subject allows leaders to provide both the necessary autonomy to support ownership of great instruction and standardization to support team efforts.

When teams share common languages in common practice, teachers also generate data that can bring important insight to school leaders. Using common CERCA rubrics, for example, teachers can examine student work collaboratively and then be able to calibrate expectations across teams (McEntee et al., 2003). This practice is the best professional development for literacy instructors, especially for teachers who may not have experienced a significant amount of training on evaluating student writing and providing feedback to students. *Professional learning communities that are teaming up based on the strategic inquiry model* (Scharff Panero and Talbert, 2013) are able to gather student data, determine student learning objectives (Lachlan-Haché, Cushing, and Bivona, 2012), and work as a team to deliver the necessary instruction to help students move onto their next achievement.

These practices also yield results on all sorts of standardized tests. See examples of some of our own case studies showing the impact of the framework on student achievement: thinkcerca.com/results/.

THE FRAMEWORK AND STUDENT MOTIVATION

Aside from taking needless anxiety and translations out of the mix, there is another reason why the framework is effective in improving student outcomes. It improves student motivation. As Dick Clark points out, there is evidence that students learn in many different ways, but when their learning is guided, they learn more effectively (Clark, Kirschner, and Sweller, 2012).

Let's face it—when a student is faced with writing an essay, it is daunting. The clarity of the discrete steps required for success in the task, the predictability of what it will actually be like to carry out those steps or how long it might take, and the joy of completion that one might experience with other assignments are sort of undermined by the very nature of writing. It is a fuzzy business. After all, students don't know what they think until they begin writing. And we can't really tell a student what to think; therefore we can't tell them what to put on the paper. Because, ultimately, that is what writing is—an expression of one's thinking. Making thinking visible for others is difficult, unpredictable work. Furthermore, like many academic endeavors, great effort doesn't always equal great success. It is tough!

While no particular answers are hidden in the framework, the process itself is definable and reliable. It takes some of the unpredictability out of the process and presents students with markers of achievement. Making a claim, developing a reason to support it, finding a single piece of evidence. Each one of these steps in the process of critical thinking provides a little completionist joy to help students mark progress.

Getting Started

As teachers, we also have the option of helping students over the "getting started" hump. We can, for example, provide students with the claim and the evidence, allowing them to complete the writing by providing reasoning. As Alan Kazdin points out, we can help students be successful by placing them in a step in the process in which they can be successful (Rotella and Kadzin, 2009).

Persistence

So what do we do when students hit a roadblock? How does the framework help students persist? Again, it isn't magical, but the familiarity of the routine involved with the framework helps takes the novelty out of the process, which provides students with some level of confidence that there is a way to approach the work that has been successful in the past, for oneself or for others, which increases a student's perception of self-efficacy. Parents, teachers, and other supporters can also take advantage of the simple framework as they help move students forward.

The step-by-step approach and familiarity also eliminate the cognitive overload that students can experience when they are faced with tasks that involve a lot of extraneous processing (what does this teacher want me to do?) at the same time their working memory is grappling with new content (what is this about?) and making it fit into existing models in their working memory.

Sustained Mental Effort

There is enough cognitive demand involved in making an argument in any subject, so why complicate it with all sorts of new jargon? The process itself is a cognitive process that requires sustained mental effort. Of course it just isn't as simple as filling out a worksheet or a form; the task always requires sustained mental effort. Rereading a text, consciously thinking about one's thinking about evidence, and formulating the words to express those notions cannot be done without active mental engagement. In short, it influences a student to engage in thinking. Again, in collaborative implementations, the engagement is even greater, as Matthew Leiberman points out in his book *Social* (2013) and Richard Elmore of Harvard's Graduate School of Education suggests in his work on how to improve the Instructional Core.

CONCLUSION

It is imperative that we make the shift toward focusing on precise tactical problems in learning if we are going to tackle what seems like an intractable literacy problem in our nation based on NAEP scores over time where we have had almost no impact on overall reading outcomes in decades.

We have plenty of research that shows that when we align to standards, work as a team, monitor progress, and provide teachers with the time to respond to specific academic needs, we can change outcomes dramatically (Rosenkrantz et al., 2014). (See appendix A for a graph depicting the importance of strong teacher cooperation relationships.)

We know we can change outcomes dramatically when a school focuses its attention on ambitious instruction, and when teachers orient themselves around addressing specific academic skills, monitoring progress, and re-teaching as needed to help students learn.

The CERCA framework enables all of these practices.

APPENDIX A

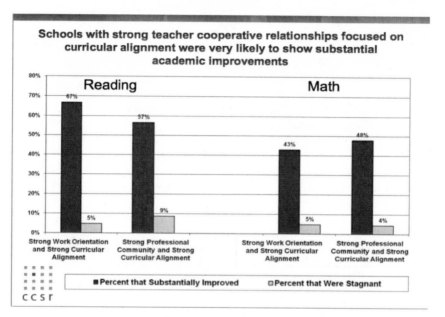

Figure 6.2. The Importance of Strong Teacher Cooperation Relationships.

REFERENCES AND RESOURCES

Applebee, A. N., Langer, J. A., Nystrand, M., and Gamoran, A. (2003). "Discussion-based approaches to developing understanding: Classroom instruction and student performance in middle and high school English." *American Educational Research Journal 40*: 685–730.

APP Lincoln Students. (2014, May 21). "Minecraft Guide." *SeaDragon Press*. Retrieved from seadragonpressdotcom.wordpress.com/2014/05/21/minecraft-guide/.

Bryk, A. et al. (2010). *Organizing Schools for Improvement: Lessons from Chicago*. Chicago, IL: University of Chicago Press.

Clark, R. E., Kirschner, P. A., and Sweller, J. (2012). "Putting students on the path to learning: The case for fully guided instruction." *American Educator*: 6–11. Retrieved from www.aft.org/sites/default/files/periodicals/Clark.pdf.

Ferguson, R. F., Schwartz, R., and Symonds, W. C. (2011). *Pathways to Prosperity: Meeting the Challenge of Preparing Young Americans for the 21st Century*. Cambridge: Harvard University Graduate School of Education. Retrieved from gse.harvard.edu/sites/default/files//documents/Pathways_to_Prosperity_Feb2011-1.pdf.

Kuhn, D. (2008). *Education for Thinking*. Cambridge, MA: Harvard University Press.

Lachlan-Haché, L., Cushing, E., and Bivona, L. (2012). *Student Learning Objectives as Measures of Educator Effectiveness: The Basics*. Washington, DC: American Institute for Research. Retrieved from educatortalent.org/inc/docs/SLOs_Measures_of_Educator_Effectiveness.pdf.

Lieberman, M. D. (2013). *Social: Why Our Brains Are Wired to Connect*. New York: Random House.

Liptak, A. (2014, July 1). "Supreme Court Rejects Contraceptives Mandate for Some Corporations." *New York Times* Retrieved from www.nytimes.com/2014/07/01/us/hobby-lobby-case-supreme-court-contraception.html?_r=0.

McEntee, G. H. et al. (2003). *At the Heart of Teaching: A Guide to Reflective Practice*. New York: Teachers College Press.

National Center for Education Statistics (NCES). (2013). *The Nation's Report Card: Trends in Academic Progress 2012*. NCES 2013 no. 456. Washington, DC: Institute of Education Services: U.S. Department of Education. Retrieved from nces.ed.gov/nationsreportcard/subject/publications/main2012/pdf/2013456.pdf.

Pinsky, R. (1998). *The Sounds of Poetry: A Brief Guide*. New York: Farrar, Straus and Giroux.

Rosenkranz, T., et al. (2014). *Free to Fail Or On-Track to College: Why Grades Drop When Students Enter High School And What Adults Can Do About It*. Chicago: University of Chicago Consortium on Chicago School Research.

Rotella, C., and Kadzin, A. E. (2009). *The Kazdin Method for Parenting the Defiant Child*. Boston: Mariner Books.

Scharff Panero, N., and Talbert, J. E. (2013). *Strategic Inquiry: Starting Small For Big Results in Education*. Cambridge, MA: Harvard Education Press.

Scholes, R. (2001). *The Crafty Reader*. New Haven, CT: Yale University Press.

SEVEN

High-Leverage Practices in Math Education That Bolster Academic Achievement

Michael Troop

Education today is much different than it was even fifteen years ago. With the increasing focus on college and career readiness standards, school districts across the United States are making adjustments to their curricula to meet these new expectations. English/language arts, math, and science content-area teachers are now in a position to create curricula that focus on big ideas within their content area and develop students' problem-solving skills through real-world scenarios.

In this chapter, I will introduce high-leverage practices that will support efforts to raise academic achievement for students. To do this, I will focus on how to use the College and Career Readiness standard to plan for effective instruction. I will also identify specific instructional strategies you can use to engage your students in meaningful learning.

The changing landscape in education across the United States is forcing schools and teachers to rethink their paradigm in education. The central focus of this chapter is on how math teachers can change their approach to teaching by using high-leverage practices that can bolster student academic achievement. The chapter will focus on three major sections:

1. College and career readiness standards and why they are important.
2. Big ideas and lesson planning.

3. High-leverage practice approach that will bolster academic performance of students in mathematics.

COLLEGE AND CAREER READINESS STANDARDS

In mathematics, a focus on big ideas means that teachers are now able to cover content deeper than ever before and build student conceptual understanding of specific topics. Another benefit of the new standards is that they are built in a way that helps students seamlessly construct learning of these big ideas coherently across grade levels as opposed to the old model where the topics in mathematics were covered broadly and were disconnected from year-to-year. Lastly, the new standards emphasize academic rigor; whereby, students build conceptual understanding of key concepts at each grade level, are able to expeditiously and accurately calculate "core functions," and apply big idea concepts across disciplines. In essence, these standards provide the framework for higher-order thinking development.

What also makes the new standards unique is that each grade level was carefully crafted to provide the infrastructure for all other future concepts. With that in mind, it is just as important for teachers to review previous years' standards as it is for them to review the standards at their grade level and beyond. This gives the educator the big picture and helps the teacher connect the concepts and ideas into their own narrative.

Wiggins and McTighe (2012) recommend that teachers unpack the new college and career readiness standards into four basic categories:

1. Long-term transfer goals that identify what students should know, understand, and be able to do. An example of this could be to have students use mathematical reasoning to solve novel problems.
2. Overarching understandings that outline the specific skill sets students will need to develop in order to apply their learnings to novel situations or contexts.
3. Essential questions that focus on deeper understanding of the big ideas. These questions are very broad in nature and should be consistent throughout a unit of study. Hence, they should not change from lesson to lesson.
4. Cornerstone tasks that support learning via applying the knowledge and skills developed over time (performance indicators). Keep in mind that the standards are designed so that students construct knowledge and meaning across grade levels (e.g., spiraling the standards).

Using the above method for unpacking the standards as recommended by Wiggins and McTighe (2012), teachers build a roadmap for teaching content in a rigorous, yet meaningful way for students. I would argue that the college and career readiness standards coupled with valid and reliable assessment structures provide teachers with the foundation necessary to develop a rich and rigorous curriculum that will bolster their efforts to close the achievement gap and improve teaching and learning overall.

BIG IDEAS AND PLANNING

Now that we have outlined the importance of and utility of the College and Career Readiness Standards, we can shift our focus onto high-leverage practices in planning for high-impact and engaging lessons. Problem solving and mathematical reasoning are key tenants of the new standards. That being said, it is not only important to teach "the basics" of mathematics, it is fundamentally important for math teachers to plan deliberately around conceptual understandings. One way to do this is by using the backward design framework. Developed by Wiggins and McTighe (2005), the idea behind it is simple; teachers plan a lesson with the end in mind. That is, teachers begin planning by first thinking about the student outcomes and key understandings for a particular unit of study. In order to do that, the teacher needs to understand the big ideas associated with each unit they are teaching.

When I teach preservice educators how to plan, I teach them how to approach their lesson with a good understanding of where they want their students to end up by the end of their unit. An example of a lesson planning template I use when utilizing the backward design framework is in figure 7.1.

In order to implement high-leverage teaching practices in mathematics, it is imperative that teachers plan very carefully. The template in figure 7.1 uses a three-part model approach to planning. In part one of the model, pre-planning, teachers are expected to begin their planning using with the standards for mathematics, College and Career Readiness Standards, and National Council of Teachers of Mathematics (NCTM) process standards. Two very important questions should be considered at this stage: What are you teaching? Why are you teaching it?

From here, teachers then unpack the standards in order to identify the big ideas and essential questions for the unit. A big idea is defined as a disciplinary core concept or principle that enables students to comprehensively acquire the knowledge necessary for transfer of learning to take place (Salmon and Kelly, 2015). A few examples of big ideas in mathematics include statistics and probability, ratios and proportions, and counting and cardinality.

Lesson:	Teacher:	Course:	Date:
STEP ONE: Pre-Planning			

Standards addressed			
Essential Question(s)			
Big Ideas			
Objectives	**Content**	What students will *know and understand* - - -	
	Skills	What students will *be able to do* - - -	
Relevance	Why do students need this knowledge and skills right now? How are these objectives preparing students to use mathematics to think critically and solve problems?		
Assessment/Checking for Understanding	What tools will I use to see if students have understood the content and can apply the skills?		

STEP TWO: The Lesson	
How are you teaching it? How do you know the students know and understand concepts? How do you provide opportunities for students to assess their own learning?	
Warm-up/catalyst	How will ideas be introduced and linked to prior knowledge?
Instructional Activities	What instructional strategies and resources might I use to help students perform well?
Multiple Means Representation	How do you ensure that all students have access to the information presented?

Multiple Means of Engagement	How do you provide multiple pathways for students to learn the material through multiple entry points, activity settings, and choices for interacting with the content? (Listening, talking, interacting with physical models, web search, etc.)	
Multiple Means of Expression	How will students express and/or demonstrate what they have learned? (Tests, tiered assessments, oral exams, building a model, making a video,	
Closing	How will the lesson end and bridge to learning for the future? How will you assess whether the students reached the objectives set for the lesson?	

STEP THREE: Set-Up

What do students need to be prepared for the lesson?

Posted for students to see on board	**Objectives**	Students will be able to . . .
	Warm-up/Catalyst	
	Agenda	
	Homework	

Figure 7.1.   Backward Design Lesson Plan Template.

Since big ideas are broad, they give way to a deeper understanding of domain specific concepts by allowing teachers and students to make connections they would not otherwise see. To illustrate this, we will look at statistics as our big idea. There are various components that contribute to student understanding of statistics. For example, students will explore statistical measure and displays, scatter plot diagrams, and data analysis to name a few. It is important for the teacher to understand how each of these concepts relates to the others in order to present the information in a meaningful way to their students. Instead of looking at statistical measure or scatter plot diagrams as completely separate concepts, we can see how they are concepts that together bring about meaning in a broader but much deeper way. By building student capacity to develop connections between concepts, teachers are preparing their students to take a problem-solving approach to real-world problems using mathematics as their tool.

In my previous example, I explained that when a teacher begins their planning by identifying big ideas for a particular unit, it gives them an opportunity to approach lesson planning from a big picture lens. The question is, how do we pick the right big ideas and then how do we create a narrative that makes sense for our students? After all, without an accurate narrative, students will not be able to make connections needed to transfer learning and develop key understandings of the material.

The College and Career Readiness Standards were developed through research on how students learn. There is a focus on big ideas throughout the standards. The biggest challenge for teachers, however, is how to make connections between the big ideas and concepts within them. One way to do this is through the process of concept mapping. Using concept mapping to plan for instruction is key to developing the adaptive expertise needed to improve teaching and learning. Salmon and Kelly (2015) state:

> Adaptive experts adopt a learning orientation to their work to continually learn from what they do and then use that learning to improve their practice. [They] intentionally investigate the adequacy of their own knowledge for teaching particular subject areas and seek new ways to extend their knowledge bases for teaching. (3)

Concept mapping provides two very important solutions to planning: (1) it serves as a metacognitive tool that helps teachers think about their own approach to the big ideas identified with the standards and addressed in the lesson. This is helpful because teachers will see what gaps they may have within the content they are teaching, which will allow them to build their content capacity if needed; and (2) it helps educators teach the big ideas by making connections between concepts more explicit. This helps teachers create their story, or narrative, in a way that makes sense. In many cases, teachers do not make their thinking to students about the core ideas explicit. In turn, this leads to a series of disjointed ideas and fragmented learning for the student.

Concept mapping is an important part of the pre-planning process because it helps educators make the big ideas identified in the College and Career Readiness Standards as well as their thinking about those big ideas more explicit. Once this has been done, teachers will be in a better position to develop essential questions for the unit.

Now that we have a better understanding of how the big ideas relate to the new standards, we can move into developing essential questions for mathematics instruction. Essential questions are part of the backwards design process developed by Wiggins and McTighe (2005). As with the standards, and the big ideas, essential questions are broad by nature and are used to structure the big ideas. You can see that there is a theme here. Broad is good during parts of the planning process because it helps teachers develop a roadmap for a unit of study. As mentioned before, in order to know where you are taking your students, you need to know the endpoint first. Also, in order for a teacher to plan effective instruction based on the standards, they need to understand how the big ideas relate.

Let's look at an example of an essential question in mathematics. We can use the topic of statistics as I mentioned earlier in the chapter. An example of an essential question in statistics might be, "How can mathematical modeling and representations be used to communicate?" As you can see from this example, the question is broad in nature and can be used throughout an entire unit of study. There are several types of models and representations in mathematics. For instance, financial advisors focus on models that help predict financial growth. Scientists use models to explain pandemics, climate change, and weather patterns to name a few. By approaching a unit of study using essential questions, the teacher has created context for the unit—a direction for students and a way of thinking conceptually about the unit of study.

Once a teacher has developed their essential questions and big ideas using concept mapping, they will be in a much better position to create learning objectives. As you can see in figure 7.1, objectives are made after we have determined our direction for the unit. Further, we break down our objectives into content we want our students to understand and the skills we want to develop. These objectives come from the College and Career Readiness standards. And unlike the essential questions and big ideas, they are much more specific. Another major characteristic of objectives is that they need to be measurable. To make objectives measurable we typically use action verbs when stating them.

A College and Career Readiness Standard for high school algebra on creating equations looks like this:

> CCSS.MATH.CONTENT.HSA.CED.A.2. Create equations in two or more variables to represent relationships between quantities; graph equations on coordinate axes with labels and scales.

At first, a teacher needs to decide what students need to know, understand, and do in order to meet this particular standard. Refer to table 7.1 for an example of how one might delineate this. Keep in mind that this is not an exhaustive list, this is being used as an example. I would invite you to delineate this standard yourself as well.

As you can see, this is not an exhaustive list. However, even with this partial list, there are many topics to cover for this one standard. On average, I recommend covering no more than three to four topics in one particular lesson. That being said, if this were an exhaustive list, one would anticipate spending approximately four days on this particular

Table 7.1.   Example: What Students Need to Know, Understand, and Do.

Know	Understand	Do
• What is an equation • What is a rational number • Exponents • Inequalities • Linear and quadratic functions	• How an equation is used • How commutative, associative, and distributive properties can be used to add, subtract, and multiply complex numbers • Relationships between quantities	• Develop an equation • Solve an equation using exponents • Graph equations • Read and interpret graphs

standard. Using this method will help you pace your unit accurately, making it more manageable for you and your students.

Once you have broken down the standard into the content and skills you need to teach students, you can write your objectives for the lesson. One example of an objective might be: "By the end of this lesson, students will be able to accurately develop a graph of an equation." This objective is measurable in that you have specifically identified the skill you want your students to be able to do. If students are able to create a graph by convention and correctly graph an equation, they have met that objective for the day.

The last stage in the preplanning section is your assessments. Wiggins and McTighe (2005) recommend that the assessments for a particular lesson and unit should be developed prior to planning the instructional strategies. You should create both summative and formative assessments for your unit. Summative assessments are characterized as assessments of learning; that is, they should be given at the end of a lesson or unit. Formative assessments are characterized as assessments for learning. These assessments drive your instruction at any given moment and help you determine whether you need to slow down or speed up your lesson or tailor your instruction based on your students' needs. Therefore, formative assessments should be used daily and frequently throughout a lesson.

Although formative assessment should be used throughout the lesson, the most critical places to utilize this structure are at the beginning of the class and at the end. Over the years of visiting with teachers in their classrooms, I have seen inconsistency with this practice. Many are very good at developing warm-ups for the day. These are relatively short (three to five minute) snapshots of what students remember from the previous day, or to give a baseline of student readiness for the teacher.

One area that teachers typically lack in formative assessment is at the close of a class. To add context as to why this is important; students are bombarded with a lot of information hourly, daily, and weekly in school.

So many concepts and topics, with very little time to process the information that is thrown at them. Allowing time at the beginning (three to five minutes) and end of class (three to five minutes) for students to process what they learn is essential for retaining the information. It is also a way for students to create their own narrative of what they are learning. I like to call this beginning and ending formative assessment as the cycle for learning. Without this cycle for learning, students go into cognitive overload and begin to miss out on key information.

Most formative assessments in math are typically skill based; however, using a big idea approach you can develop more meaningful assessments for learning that measure student conceptual understanding. One particular strategy I like to use was highlighted by Saphier and Haley (1993a) called Paired Verbal Fluency, or PVF. In this strategy, students are paired together and asked to recall information from the previous lesson. The teacher identifies the topic and gives students a timeframe to complete their discussion.

When using PVF, there are three rounds and each round is timed. Round one lasts for forty-five seconds per student, round two lasts for thirty seconds per student and round three lasts for twenty seconds. As you can see, this is a very quick activity, lasting only a little over three minutes. During each round, partner A explains something they have learned to partner B. What I recommend is that students write responses down. That way, it is easier to participate in whole class discussion afterward. After partner A finishes their explanation, partner B has a turn. This goes on for three rounds with the understanding that partners cannot use the same explanation of concepts throughout the rounds.

Once students finish the three rounds, they review their notes and decide if there are things that they still do not understand or want the teacher to address in more detail. What I like about this strategy is that it provides teachers with the data they need to tailor the lesson for their students based on their needs. One note: due to the nature of this strategy, a teacher can use it at the beginning or the end of a lesson. Lastly, the time allotted for each round is a suggestion. As the teacher, you need to decide time ranges based on your students.

There are hundreds of formative assessments teachers can use. I identified one strategy as an example, but also to illustrate the utility of formative assessment. I would recommend that you search for a variety of strategies you can use as assessments for learning as this is out of the scope of this chapter. However, many of the strategies presented in this book can be used across all content areas; they specifically work well with mathematics.

In part two of the planning process—the lesson—teachers begin to think about how their essential questions and big ideas will be taught. Some useful questions to think about when approaching this section are:

- How are you teaching the concepts and skills to your students?
- How do you know the students know and understand concepts?
- How do you provide opportunities for students to assess their own learning?

As you refer to figure 7.2, you will see that there is reference to Universal Design for Learning. This framework was developed by the Center for Applied Special Technology, or CAST. This framework takes into account how students learn. That being said, it is important that we use this framework in our planning and implementation of that planning. In figure 7.2, I have identified specific questions that would guide your thinking when creating activities for multiple learner types.

For the final stage of planning, educators should focus on how they will make their expectations and specific learning explicit to the students. As I mentioned earlier, one important high-leverage practice for math teachers is to use the cycle for learning. This is where teachers give students an opportunity to show you what they know and understand from the previous lesson. It is also an opportunity for the teacher to explain to the students what they will be doing for that particular day and bridge previous learning to the new learnings. Refer to figure 7.3 as an example of how to do this for your class.

Previously, we spoke about how to create measurable learning objectives using the College and Career Readiness Standards. These objectives are used to guide the teacher in their instruction. However, in order to create context for the lesson, it is necessary to explain the objectives to the

STEP TWO: *The Lesson*	
Warm-up/catalyst	How will ideas be introduced and linked to prior knowledge?
Instructional Activities	What instructional strategies and resources might I use to help students perform well?
Multiple Means Representation	How do you ensure that all students have access to the information presented?
Multiple Means of Engagement	How do you provide multiple pathways for students to learn the material through multiple entry points, activity settings, and choices for interacting with the content? (Listening, talking, interacting with physical models, web search, etc.)
Multiple Means of Expression	How will students express and/or demonstrate what they have learned? (Tests, tiered assessments, oral exams, building a model, making a video,
Closing	How will the lesson end and bridge to learning for the future? How will you assess whether the students reached the objectives set for the lesson?

Figure 7.2. The Lesson.

	STEP THREE: Set-Up		
	What do students need to be prepared for the lesson?		
Posted for students to see on board	**Objectives**	I will be able to . . .	
	Warm-up/Catalyst		
	Agenda		
	Homework		

Figure 7.3.   Lesson Set-Up.

students, in student-friendly terms. I have seen this written as *I will be able to*, or IWBAT. An example of this might be, "By the end of class today, I will be able to create a scatter plot diagram using data." By explaining what students will be doing for the day, in student-friendly terms, a teacher can create context for the lesson. I think of it as a preview for what is to come.

Now that we have a better understanding of the importance of planning and the intricacies of the planning process, we can move into high-leverage pedagogical practices in mathematics education. The College and Career Readiness Standards should be used as a guide in structuring what students should learn in order to be prepared for the world outside of school. That being said, it is essential for educators to carefully plan opportunities for students where they can apply their learning of math content to real situations.

One of the more popular strategies for teaching students how to apply math to real situations is through scenarios or problem-based learning. This is a high-leverage practice that I encourage all teachers to use. However, in addition to using a problem-based learning approach, I propose a supplement to this practice. For the remainder of this chapter I am going to focus on three very important concepts related to high-leverage pedagogical practices in math: linking homework to specific projects students need to complete, creating a badging system based on expected student outcomes, and unique quarterly experiences.

I am going to begin with identifying high-leverage homework practices that will increase student engagement and provide them with the ability to apply their learning to contexts outside of the school setting, such as college or career. In typical classrooms I have observed, teachers typically follow the "I Do, We Do, You Do" model for teaching. That is, the teacher gives an example of how to solve a particular problem. The teacher shows students how to do it, then poses a problem that all students, or groups of students work on. After the teacher checks to be sure students understand the concepts, they are assigned individual problems. This is usually assigned for homework. Students work on multiple problems to practice what they learned in class.

We learned earlier that when we plan our lessons using the backward planning method, we use the standards to develop a set of outcomes we expect our students to achieve based on what we are teaching them. When I work with preservice, and in-service teachers, I hear time after time that students do not do their homework. Those teachers that do have students that complete homework consistently often wonder if the homework is really teaching students how to think.

What I have done over the years is change the way teachers approach homework. Homework is typically not tied to anything that matters outside of points and grades. And typically, homework does not account for a big part of a student's grade, diluting its importance in the eyes of students. When homework is tied to a quarterly project, however, it changes student perspective and helps students apply the big ideas in a meaningful way.

As teachers construct student outcomes and carefully plan their lesson and homework, they should think about how the topics link from one lesson to the next. This is where the concept mapping exercise discussed earlier in this chapter is useful. If teachers followed the backward planning model, whereby they know what students should understand and be able to do by the end of the unit, and they also know how the concepts they present to students link together, they can create homework assignments that are on pace with their lessons, but ultimately lead to an end of unit project (which is an assessment in and of itself). This takes problem-based learning to a whole new level. The teacher assigns a group project based on a real world problem. Each week, students are completing a homework assignment based on the information presented that week, which also helps them develop their project. This provides students with an opportunity to apply what they are learning and makes homework more meaningful.

Teachers can create other structures that reinforce the application of student learning to other contexts outside of the classroom. Building off of the idea that homework can be tied to an end of unit project or assessment, teachers can create what I call a badging system. A badging system is very similar to what is used in video games today. A gamer works through different levels in a game and, in the process, develops a certain set of skills or competencies at each level.

Take this paradigm and juxtapose it with a math class. A teacher that has carefully planned using the standards can develop a list of competencies needed to meet a particular standard, or set of standards. When students have met all of the competencies, they would earn a badge. Depending on grade level, these badges could look different of course. The teacher would need to consider their students' level of maturity, and such. These badges represent something very important. They are significant in that they illustrate to the student that they have earned and developed a set of skills in math that will help them to solve problems. Not all students will earn all of the badges. As with grades, not every student earns an A in class. The overall goal is to help students earn that "A," or that badge. However, it does not always work out that way.

At this point, I have discussed how to link homework to meaningful unit projects that can serve as assessments of student learning. I have also talked about creating a badging system whereby students earn a badge after they have developed specific competencies. Putting these two models together can create a very strong learning opportunity for students. I have suggested using unit projects as an assessment of learning. Since our assessments are designed to measure student learning of a specific set of outcomes, we can integrate the badging system seamlessly into this structure.

This can be set up as follows: In quarter 1, you have planned three units for the term. Each unit has a project whereby students are illustrating to the teacher their attainment of a specific set of outcomes or competencies. If students achieve each of the outcomes or competencies in a given unit, they earn a badge. If they achieve the competencies for all three units as measured by the end of unit project, they would earn three badges. The name of each badge should relate to the outcomes for that unit. Be creative! If one unit was on statistics and probability, the student that achieves all of the outcomes would earn the statistical analyst badge. This could be done for each quarter. You determine how many badges a student can earn as well as the outcomes needing to be achieved for each badge.

Once you have determined student outcomes, projects, and badges, you can then identify unique quarterly experiences. These quarterly experiences would be specific to careers in mathematics. The idea behind this is students that earn all of the badges for a specific set of units would have an opportunity to visit an organization where they can see how the competencies they learned in class translate to careers that use mathematics. A list of possible careers is in table 7.2.

Students that participate in the unique quarterly experiences should have very specific tasks for the trip. Ideas include shadowing and observing a member of that organization, taking a tour, or interviewing an employee, or set of employees. After the selected students visit the established organization, they would be required to present what they learned to their classmates. This is an important skill set that is emphasized in the College and Career Readiness Standards.

Although this skill set is emphasized in the ELA standards, specifically:

> CCSS.ELA-LITERACY.CCRA.SL.4. Present information, findings, and supporting evidence such that listeners can follow the line of reasoning and the organization, development, and style are appropriate to task, purpose, and audience.

This does not mean that a mathematics teacher should not incorporate this skill set in their classroom.

As one would imagine, this is something that would take time and effort to develop. Teachers need to consider a number of variables such as what organizations would be appropriate to establish a partnership? How willing would these organizations be to partner with a school? How many students can be brought to these establishments? Is the school supportive of field trips? These are all valid concerns. From my experience with this process, I have learned that many organizations are interested in partnering with schools to give students an opportunity to view a day in the life of. The challenge would be finding organizations within the area of the school.

The focus of this chapter was on how the College and Career Readiness Standards play a crucial role in math education. There was a major emphasis on the planning process and how to use the standards as a tool to create essential questions, big ideas, and measurable objectives. The remainder of the chapter focused on specific high-leverage pedagogical practices that increase academic achievement. Developing homework assignments that are attached to unit presentations makes the homework more meaningful to students. By using unit presentations as an assessment of specific competencies, teachers can use badges to keep track of student mastery of content and skills. Lastly, creating opportunities for students to experience how mathematics is used in various careers will help them apply their understanding.

Table 7.2. Careers in math.

Finance	Statistics	Computers	Teaching	Engineering	Mathematics
• Accountant	• Demographer	• Programmer	• Elementary	• Aeronautical	• Research
• Actuary Auditor	• Market Research	• Software	• Secondary	• Agricultural	• Mathematical
• Banker		Engineer	• University	• Architecture	Modeling
• Financial Advisor		• Systems Analyst		• Astronautical	• Operations
• Economist				• Biomedical	Research
				• Chemical	
				• Civil	
				• Electrical	
				• Industrial	
				• Mechanical	

REFERENCES AND RESOURCES

Keeley, P. (2008). *Science Formative Assessment: 75 Practical Strategies for Linking Assessment, Instruction, and Learning.* Thousand Oaks, CA: Corwin Press, NSTApress.

Salmon, D., and Kelly, M. (2015). *Using Concept Mapping to Foster Adaptive Expertise.* New York: Peter Lang.

Saphier, J., and Ann Haley, M. (1993a). *Activators: Activity Structures to Engage Students' Thinking Before Instruction.* Carlisle, MA: Research for Better Teaching.

Saphier, J., and Ann Haley, M. (1993b). *Summarizers: Activity Structures to Support Integration and Retention of New Learning.* Carlisle, MA: Research for Better Teaching.

Wiggins, G., and J. McTighe. (2005). *Understanding by Design* (second edition). Alexandria, VA: Pearson.

Wiggins, G., and J. McTighe. (2012). *Understanding by Design Framework.* Alexandria, VA: ASCD.

EIGHT

What Do the New Standards Mean for Students Who Receive Special Education Services?

Nicole Lambson and Brenna Sherwood

Historically students who receive special education services have not been held to the same standard of learning as the general population. Teachers of inclusion classes have watered down content or failed to push these students to high standards of learning. In today's era, we can no longer afford to allow this to happen. Although Common Core State Standards do not specifically address the needs of students with special needs, the standards have given teachers the power to adapt instructional practices through proven pedagogy and specific learning targets for college and career readiness. Many have felt the burden of working toward the goal of increasing test scores, not only within the special education subgroup, but all subgroups being assessed through an end-of-year, high-stakes assessment. As the new standards shift toward a focus on college and career-readiness, what should classroom instruction look like, particularly for our students with special needs?

Throughout this chapter, we hope to share some strategies as well as best practices that have led to success within our classrooms, all while moving our students who receive special education services to high levels of learning. We have narrowed our focus to five strategies and practices that had the most impact on our students with special needs and their growth within our content areas: active processing, self-monitoring progress, feedback, chunking, and multiple opportunities for success.

STRATEGY ONE: ACTIVE PROCESSING

David Sousa teaches us in *How the Brain Learns* about our "prime time" of learning and our ability to retain new information presented. As we plan learning activities it is imperative that we keep this cycle in mind, and engage students during the times in which their ability to retain information is at its greatest. These peaks are not times to call roll, play guessing games, or create a seating chart for the class. But, the time is critical for processing and providing students the information needed to succeed in the learning goal. Along the same lines, studies have shown we are able to pay attention to those speaking for our age plus one (in minutes), before requiring time to process. This means that a student who is in the seventh grade would be able to intake approximately thirteen minutes of new, direct instruction before needing time to process in order to retain the information and also stay on task for the remainder of the instructional time. As adults this processing break comes very naturally and we tend to stop listening of our own accord without any guidance or direction, turn to our neighbors, and have a quick conversation about the content. However, adolescent students are not always given that opportunity within a classroom setting. We have learned that structured processing activities, when used often and carried out in various ways, ensure the retention of information.

A few quick-and-painless activities are given below. Each is great in ensuring students are given the opportunity to "reboot" and process new information. All of these strategies require no prep work, and can be done on the fly within any type of lesson within any content area:

1. Numbered Heads Together:

    - Each group should have three to five students, but four is ideal.
    - The students in each group choose a number from one to four.
    - At the end of a question, you ask students to stand, huddle, and come up with a unanimous answer to the question.
    - Once the group has their answer, students sit back down in their seats.
    - Choose a number, and whichever student has that number shares the group's answer with the class.

2. Thirty-Second Expert:

    - Students choose a partner (this can be elbow, cross-room, same color hair, etc.).
    - Partners then stand back to back.
    - Taller become Teacher A and shorter Teacher B.
    - Teacher A has thirty seconds to tell Teacher B all they know about whatever subject you have given them to process.

- They start the conversation with "I am an expert in _____ because _____."
- Teacher B then repeats what they heard from Teacher A.
- Start retelling with, "According to you, you are an expert because you said _____."
- You then can have Teacher B add thirty seconds of information to Teacher A's remarks if you feel it is necessary or needed.

3. Clock Buddies:

- Each student draws a clock face with the numbers 12, 3, 6, and 9.
- They find partners to sign the numbers of the clock and they then become the partner for when you call out those numbers.
- You can go as far as intentionally partnering for a strategic purpose (low–high readers, interest based, behavior reinforcement, etc.) at specific numbers for collaboration as well.
- Reinforce ZERO tolerance for ugliness to other students who they may be partnered with.

4. Concept Charades:

- Students choose a partner (or can be assigned a partner or partnering technique).
- Each pair receives a vocabulary word or concept they are studying.
- Pairs must decide on a way to enact the word or concept with only their body.
- Could also be adapted into drawing instead of charades.
- Other pairs and teacher would have to guess what word or concept they are enacting.

5. Four Corners:

Version 1

- Students are posed a question.
- Each corner of the room is assigned an answer.
- Students must move to the corner of the room that they feel is the appropriate or correct answer.
- Could also be adapted into a full body point to the corner instead of moving there.

Version 2

- Students are assigned a corner.
- Students are then posed a question.
- Students are then shown the response that is paired with each corner.

- Student groups in the corner are asked to state whether their answer is the correct one or not and defend/justify their reasoning.

Version 3

- Students choose a corner (or are assigned a corner).
- In their corner student groups must respond to the specific prompt (could be reflection/closure question, clarifying question, defendable question, open-ended question, multiple choice question, etc.) found in their corner. May or may not be the same question for each corner.
- Groups share out their question and answer and defend or justify to the whole group their answer.

6. Stand and Huddle/Turn and Talk:

- Student groups are asked to stand and huddle (talk) about a question posed.
- Groups are then asked to share at random. (Could ask all groups to share if time permits.)

7. Cross-Town Partner:

- Students are given a question or topic for discussion.
- Students get up and find a partner that is not in their immediate area (across the room).
- Students spend thirty seconds to one minute discussing the question or topic.
- Student partners report (all or some at random).

8. Block Party:

- Students are given a question or topic for discussion.
- Students gather with three to four people near them to discuss the question or topic.
- Students spend a few minutes (or a deemed appropriate amount of time) discussing the question or topic.
- Student parties share (all or some at random).

As our district continues struggling with both reading scores and growth within our population receiving special education services, Katherine McKnight and her team were contracted to assist in implementing a targeted instructional strategy. The goal of this strategy would ultimately allow students the processing time needed to retain information, fit the criteria in which a teacher could capture student attention, and hit the retention primes for direct instruction. The goal: To create a center-based learning environment within a middle school classroom, while meeting the increased rigor of Common Core and allowing a varie-

ty of processing activities, teacher-led intervention/enrichment groups, and quick formative assessments. With Dr. McKnight's Three-Phase Process, we were able to slowly lead teachers and students to an instructional practice that proved to encourage student learning through self-evaluation,
self-reflection, and the ability to self-adjust within a fifty-five- or ninety-minute class period. The goal of this process: to allow students the needed processing time, in a variety of ways, to ensure retention and deep understanding of content material.

Literacy Based Instructional Phases for Center Based Learning: Farmington Municipal Schools, Farmington, New Mexico

Phase One

Goal: Change Physical Environment
FMI Protocols: Engagement, Classroom Management, New Knowledge
Create physical environments that are conducive to the balanced literacy model and twenty-first-century learning. Teachers will focus on the physical environment of the classroom:

1. Seating arrangements that support flexible grouping (Cash, 2010; Heacox, 2009).
2. Purposeful movement that reflects current research in brain based learning (Gurian, 2010; Jensen, 1998; Medina, 2014).
3. Chunking of instruction that supports current research in adolescent learning (Gurian, 2010; Jensen, 2009; Marzano, 2007; Marzano and Pickering, 2013; Medina, 2014).
4. Written, explicit directions that encourage student ability to self-regulate their learning (Cash, 2010; Hattie, 2011).

No center activities are required at this time, but become familiar with routines of center-based learning such as transitions, teacher talk, collaborative norms, student roles, and time.

Phase Two

Goal: Increase Cognitive Load (Marzano's Taxonomy of Cognitive Levels; Bloom's Taxonomy of Educational Objectives for Skills-Based Goals; John Hattie's *Visible Learning for Teachers: Maximizing Impact on Learning*)
FMI Protocols: Feedback, Deepen/Practice, Hypothesize and Test
Implement centers one to two times a week, adapting current lessons to meet the center framework and guidelines (McKnight, 2014):

1. Collaborative, centered activities that develop higher-order thinking skills that are aligned with Marzano's taxonomy (majority of activities represent the upper tier of taxonomy):

   The Common Core asks students to read stories and literature, as well as more complex texts that provide facts and background knowledge in areas such as science and social studies. Students will be challenged and asked questions that push them to refer back to what they've read. This stresses critical-thinking, problem-solving, and analytical skills that are required for success in college, career, and life. (CCSS, 2010)

This will be achieved through:

- A site-based instructional plan created to include the role of principal, instructional coaches, and classroom teachers.
- A support plan defining the expected outcomes, action steps, responsible person, timeline (including data monitoring), and progress measurement.
- The implementation of instructional strategies to support student competency in reading.
- Fostering student comprehension of increasingly complex texts.

Phase Three

Goal: Assessment and Feedback
FMI Protocols: Entire FMI Model of Instruction
Ensure that centers are incorporated two to three times a week and all activities fall within the analysis, synthesis, and evaluation levels of the taxonomy:

1. Formative assessment to adjust and enhance instruction that develops student learning (e.g., observational, checks for understanding, descriptive feedback) (Marzano, 2009; Wormeli, 2006).
2. Response to Intervention to address:

   a. gaps in learning,
   b. knowledge and skills that students need to be successful in tier one (Buffman, Mattos, and Weber, 2008).

3. Activities are designed to promote learning goal mastery as articulated in the Farmington Municipal Schools Proficiency Scales (*Farmington Model of Instruction*).
4. Descriptive feedback to foster student skill development mastery and content knowledge (Marzano, 2009).
5. Teacher-led center to address individual learning needs (i.e., interventions, differentiation, enrichment, formative assessment, and targeted skill development) (McKnight, 2014).

As center-based learning was implemented, an increase in student engagement, the use of best practices by teachers, and a decrease in negative classroom behaviors (specifically from struggling students) became a commonality among observed classrooms, specifically the resource classrooms. While using a scripted curriculum, one special education teacher, was able to chunk instruction, have movement, keep students engaged, and have pure learning through peer collaboration all while maintaining the integrity of her program. "All students can learn at high levels if given the appropriate tools, even with the increased complexity of common core," states Farmington Instructional Coaches. As students become an active part of their education, the ability for them to transform their ideas to those of independent learning and self-monitoring becomes routine.

STRATEGY TWO: SELF-MONITORING AND TRACKING PROGRESS

In the book *Fair Isn't Always Equal* by Rick Wormeli (2006), we learn the importance of student self-assessment and student progress monitoring. Wormeli states that a student's ability to self-assess is an important aspect of successful differentiation and provides invaluable feedback helping students reach their individual goals. The use of proficiency scales or rubrics allows students to monitor progress and identify needs for mastery, while self-adjusting and reflecting on tasks in order to meet the designated scores. The overall purpose of having such definite criteria for tracking is that it allows students to have a visual targeted goal that doesn't change, but shows exactly what is needed or required in order to obtain each level of success within its scoring. Providing a consistent target allows students to engage in conversations and activities that guide them to high levels of mastery.

Rubrics and proficiency scales are great tools for students to self-monitor and track progress. It is important to remember that the more criteria in which a student is scored, the more confusing it gets, and the less criteria in which a student is scored the more subjective the scoring becomes. When creating such a document, you must find the "sweet spot," allowing for specific requirements within each level and show the scaffold within each score. A quick graph, showing the goal, the actual score, and the improved score, is also a great visual for students when working within a unit of study (see figure 8.1).

Example Unit Student Tracking

Front of worksheet page

Topic: Energy

> **4** In addition to 3.0, can use the understanding of energy to explain the impact on your own life and the global economy.

> **3** In addition to 2.0, knows the earth processes that form renewable and non-renewable energy, know how they are extracted, know the risks and benefits of the production, understand the role of carbon chemistry, and know how a change in the flow of energy can impact an ecosystem.

Learning goal
Understand earth processes that form energy sources and how these energy sources impact daily life.

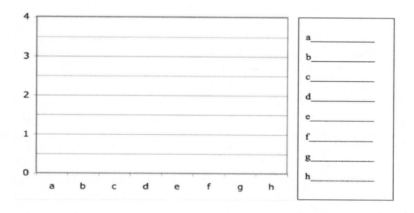

2 Knows renewable, non-renewable, energy production, and fossil fuels. Knows the difference between renewable and non-renewable. Know how New Mexico came to have energy. Know that carbon is a major component in energy sources and know how energy flows through an ecosystem.

1 Can ALL 2.0 items <u>with help,</u> or do most of the 2.0 items <u>by yourself.</u>

Back of worksheet page
Concept Checklist

2.0		Check once achieved		
A	Knows renewable energy.			
B	Knows non-renewable energy.			
C	Knows energy production.			
D	Knows fossil fuels.			
E	Knows the difference between renewable and non-renewable resources.			
F	Knows the geologic conditions that have resulted in energy resources available in New Mexico.			
G	That living organisms are made of a limited number of elements including carbon.			
H	How energy flows through ecosystems.			
3.0				

I	Understands the earth processes that form renewable and non-renewable energy resources.			
J	Understand how resources extraction is conducted for renewable and non-renewable resources.			
K	Understand the risks and benefits of energy production.			
L	Describe the widespread role of carbon in the chemistry of living systems.			
M	Understand how a change in the flow of energy can impact an ecosystem.			

Another useful tool for students to use when tracking specific goals are practice maps. Practice maps are visuals, showing direct correlation, between the tasks/assignments given and the overall goal they are trying to attain.

Learning Goals	P-1 Types of propaganda	P-2 Elements of an argument	P-3 Why can't I live on French Fries?	P-4 Formative assessment	P-5 Why do we need schools?	P-6 Debate	P-7 Argument Essay	P-8 Analyzing Texts
A. Draft an argument essay							x	
B. Develop a pre-write		x					x	
C. Compose a rough draft		x					x	
D. Revise written work for elements in specific text.							x	
E. Edit for grade appropriate grammar, mechanics, and							x	

spelling								
F. Publish a formal essay		x				x	x	
A. Identifying elements of argumentation	x	x	x	x	x	x	x	x
B. Word choice	x		x	x	x	x	x	x
C. Organization	x	x	x	x	x	x	x	x
D. Transitions		x	x	x	x	x	x	x
E. Point-of-view	x	x	x	x	x	x	x	x
F. Off-topic information		x	x	x	x	x	x	x

Figure 8.1. Example Student Unit Tracking.

We learn from Wormeli (2006) and Robert Marzano (2007) the importance of having an educational target related to the standards. Not only should there be a target, but the learning target should never move, and the pathway to that learning target should be transparent to students. Within our district, committees were created to analyze and synthesize the Common Core State Standards. These specific committees designed proficiency scales for all content-areas in grades six through eight, starting at a foundational level and progressing to complex understanding or the grade-level target.

STRATEGY THREE: FEEDBACK

In education, we are constantly looking for strategies that provide the most "bang for our buck," if you will. We want things that will be easy for us to implement and yet have a high yield impact on student learning within our classrooms. Feedback is one of those golden strategies and yet is often overlooked. Good feedback gives students information they need so they can understand where they are in their learning and what to do next—the cognitive factor. Once they feel they understand what to do and why, most students develop a feeling that they have control over their own learning—the motivational factor. This is what makes feedback such a powerful instructional strategy for students who receive special education services. Too often these students are identified as lacking in motivation. The counter is that they are instead lacking in a map or route for achieving success. In John Hattie's book *Visible Learning for Teachers* (2011), he synthesizes over eight hundred educational meta-studies and finds that feedback has an effect size on learning of 0.73. The hinge point of desired effect size is 0.4, making the effect size of feedback quite substantial and not to be overlooked or undervalued. This feedback is the map or route that all students, but especially special education students, need in order to achieve at high levels in the classroom.

Some people argue that giving grades is the feedback that students need and that taps into this highly lucrative strategy. This is a mistake. Time and again we have seen in our classrooms that giving descriptive feedback only is more influential and motivational than giving grades or a combination of letter grades and descriptive feedback. Students shut down and feel a sense of finality when grades are attached to assignments and tasks, even when paired with descriptive feedback. When it is only descriptive feedback, they feel like they still have a chance to improve, and not that this was "the final" shot at achievement. This is so important for our special needs population.

So what do we mean when we say "descriptive feedback"? Very simply, it is feedback that describes exactly what is seen, what is desirable, and what needs to be improved upon in a given task. There is no mistaking the value of giving feedback that is clear and concise, as this is where the most impact will be had. Doug Reeves, an assessment and grading researcher, states:

> The Class of 2013 grew up playing video games and received feedback that was immediate, specific, and brutal—they won or else died at the end of each game. For them, the purpose of feedback is not to calculate an average or score a final exam, but to inform them about how they can improve on their next attempt to rule the universe. (2013, 227)

It is with this mindset that we must approach the feedback we give to our students in order to most greatly impact their achievement and motivate them to higher levels. Giving descriptive feedback is a challenge at first. It is tempting to give generic feedback like "good job," "I like your introduction," "showing your work really helped," and such. This type of feedback does not give students the information necessary to improve their achievement. Students must have specific information from which to work and improve upon or celebrate. If the introduction of their paper is good, they need to know what specifically is good about it in order to put more of that into the rest of the paper or into the next one they write. If showing their work in math really helped, they need to know exactly where and why it helped. Two ways to frame giving effective descriptive feedback are the "Point and Describe" method and the "Goal, Status, and Plan" method. These can serve as a springboard as you begin to give descriptive feedback to students:

Point and Describe Method

- Point out what the student did.
- Describe the impact it had on their work.

Goal, Status, Plan Method

- Identify the goal of the assignment or task.
- Identify and describe where the student is in relation to the goal (their status).
- Identify and describe what needs to happen in order to close the gap between the goal and the student's status (the students' plan).

The path to giving feedback to students can begin as a rocky one at first, but we have seen in our classrooms and in studies like that of Hattie (2011) that feedback is a force to be reckoned with on student achievement and that makes the rocks at the beginning worth it. With consistency and relentlessness feedback becomes easier to give, students become more motivated to achieve, and that is what makes this strategy truly one that we can do easily with a great amount of "bang for our buck."

STRATEGY FOUR: CHUNKING

Question: How do you eat an elephant?
Answer: One bite at a time.

Chunking is a strategy that I love for several reasons. First, it is easy to do and takes minimal prep, something that all of us in education desire. Second, it has a huge impact on student learning, especially for students with special needs. There are several things that crack me up about educators and education in general; chunking discussions with other educators are one of those. As educators we all have to attend a certain number of professional functions, a staff meeting, training, webinar, seminar, or other such function. Rooms filled with educators that expect their students to sit and listen to them uninterrupted until given permission, are "off task": googling information they just heard about, talking to their neighbors about applications for that, and so on. Why is it that we do not apply our own learning techniques into our teaching but argue that they are a waste of time? As professionals, we create our own "chunks" of information. Once we have heard our fill, we stop and process the information in one way or another, regardless of whether or not the person leading our training or meeting has specified that time for such. Our students need the same opportunities. Chunking should be happening in many different phases of the classroom day or period, direct instruction, learning activities (regardless if paired, individual, or group), and even assessment, in order to maximize the learning that takes place in the classroom. Students however need a bit more direction in this than we do as professionals but that is not to say that it should not be done and cannot be done with minimal prep. Again, the rule of thumb is that a student can only pay attention for their numerical age plus one. This means that if you are teaching sixth grade and your students are around ten and eleven years old, then you will have their attention for ten to twelve minutes. This of course is not a hard and fast rule and it has been found that with students who receive special education services it is far safer to err on the side of less time than more.

This needs to be done in all aspects of the day, direct instruction, assignments and activities, assessment, and so forth. At the end of this chunk of time it is important to have kids process the information presented or being worked on. This can be done in many ways and several examples of processing activities are given earlier in this chapter, in the "Strategy One: Active Processing" section. The thing to remember is that kids need to be given direction and guidance on how that time looks. It is not just a time to stop the video, lecture, reading, game, or assignment, and have kids "talk" to one another undirected. This is a time to guide their talk to the information that they are learning and have it root in their brain for the long haul. This can be done by instructing and modeling what "teacher talk" looks like and putting into place accountability talk and accountability norms within the structure of the classroom and the processing time. Some examples of this type of accountability talk are sentence stems to show students how to begin their thoughts. Examples include:

I agree . . .
I disagree . . .
I want to add . . .
Could you explain . . .
Could you repeat . . .
I have a question about . . .
What I heard you say . . .
My evidence is . . .
I am confused about . . .
This reminds me of . . .

When this is done consistently, I have seen huge gains in achievement, motivation, interest, and focus. Yet, despite of all of those wonderful things the thing that struck me the most after using this strategy is that I was able to cover more material, with my students who receive special education services performing at higher levels than before by taking the time on the front end of instruction to give them multiple times and opportunities to stop and experience the material, instead of before when there would be (a) a large number of failing students or (b) I would have to go back and reteach huge amounts of material to all the students. This is why chunking is a favorite instructional strategy of mine, especially when paired with active processing strategies.

STRATEGY FIVE: MULTIPLE OPPORTUNITIES FOR SUCCESS

By now I'm sure that it is clear that our view of student success and opportunities for achievement may be different from those of others. We prefer to look at student learning like we approach coaching. One of our favorite movies is *Man on Fire* with Denzel Washington. There is a point in the movie where he is thrown into the role of swim coach. His charge, a girl named Peeta, is in a swim meet and does not win. On their drive home she says she is a slow swimmer. He disagrees and says that she is the fastest in the water and the slowest off the blocks. He inquires what she thinks she should do about that, to which she responds get faster off the blocks. And so the long process of practicing over and over and over and over again getting off the blocks faster begins. If Peeta were only given one chance to get off the blocks she would never have improved to the point where she could win, essentially stunting her achievement and pummeling her motivation to continue swimming. This is what we do to students in our classroom when we give them one shot to "show us what they've got." We even get frustrated that their motivation lacks more and more as these pummeling blows to their egos continue. It is human nature to lack motivation for something that feels hopeless. In order to change that, we must provide opportunities for students to become successful. That is not to say that there are not times when students must be assessed with "finality," but that students must know and have confidence that they will get plenty of coaching along to the way before those assessments happen.

So how do we do this? We evaluate our assessments, and make some decisions. We choose assignments that allow for lots of descriptive feedback, give formative assessments regularly enough that we can feel the ebb and flow of learning in our classroom, while also informing students of their progress along the way. We then give summative assessments that are not "tricks" or "surprises," but true indicators of learning, that students know are coming and feel empowered and confident that they are prepared for them.

No child enters school and wants to fail. It is the systems we have (or do not have) in place that place children into a defensive position in which they "want" to do poorly or give up. As the professional educators in this scenario, we must find the tools and strategies that will work in making sure that all of our students achieve at high levels. Multiple opportunities for success is one of the most motivating, realistic, and easy strategies to implement in order to make sure that this is more than just words, but is a reality for all our students who receive special education services.

ENSURING SUCCESS FOR LEARNERS WITH SPECIAL NEEDS IN AN ERA OF NEW STANDARDS

Ensuring the success of our students who receive special education services requires that we, as educators, provide the progression of learning, clear expectations, active processing time, time for self-monitoring, effective descriptive feedback, chunked instruction to meet learning needs, and multiple opportunities for success. Although the pathway may be rocky at times, the end result is worth it as we see successes within our classrooms, identify specific needs, and help our students reach their goals. Our ability to change a student's view on school comes from the small successes they are able to achieve in the classroom. As soon as a student feels defeated, all motivation to learn is lost and the ability to rekindle that fire becomes more difficult. We hold the ability to encourage, engage, and provide clearly articulated paths for students to follow in order to meet the demands of Common Core and get every student college and career ready. We are educators; we leave you with the encouraging words of Rita Pierson and hope that the strategies we have shared help you make a difference in your classroom as you tackle the shifts of common core and find your pathway to success:

> Teaching and learning should bring joy. How powerful would our world be if we had kids who were not afraid to take risks, who were not afraid to think, and who had a champion? Every child deserves a champion, an adult who will never give up on them, who understands the power of connection, and insists that they become the best that they can possibly be. Is this job tough? You betcha. Oh God, you betcha. But it is not impossible. We can do this. We're educators. We're born to make a difference. (Pierson, 2013)

REFERENCES AND RESOURCES

Bloom, B. S. (1956). *Taxonomy of educational objectives: The classification of educational goals.* New York: David McKay Company.

Buffman, A., M. Mattos, and C. Weber. (2008). *Pyramid Response to Intervention: RTI, Professional Learning Communities, and How to Respond When Kids Don't Learn.* Bloomington, IN: Solution Tree Press.

Cash, R. M. (2010). *Advancing Differentiation: Thinking and Learning for the 21st Century.* Free Spirit Publishing.

Gurian, M. (2010). *Boys and Girls Learn Differently! A Guide for Teachers and Parents,* second edition. San Francisco: Jossey-Bass.

Hattie, J. (2011). *Visible Learning for Teachers: Maximizing Impact on Learning* (first ed.). New York: Routledge.

Heacox, D. (2009). *Making Differentiation a Habit: How to Ensure Success in Academically Diverse Classrooms.* Minneapolis, MN: Free Spirit Publishing.

Jensen, E. (1998). *Teaching with the Brain in Mind.* Alexandria, VA: Association for Supervision and Curriculum Development.

Jensen, E. (2009). *Teaching with Poverty in Mind: What Being Poor Does to Kids' Brains and What Schools Can Do About It.* Alexandria, VA: Association for Supervision and Curriculum Development.

Marzano, R. J. (2007). *The Art and Science of Teaching: A Comprehensive Framework for Effective Instruction.* Alexandria, VA: Association for Supervision and Curriculum Development.

Marzano, R. J. (2009). *Formative Assessment and Standards-Based Grading: Classroom Strategies that Work.* Bloomington, IN: Marzano Research Laboratory.

Marzano, R. J., and D. J. Pickering. (2013). *The Highly Engaged Classroom.* Bloomington, IN: Marzano Research Laboratory.

McKnight, K. S. (2014). *Common Core Literacy for ELA, History/Social Studies, and the Humanities: Strategies to Deepen Content Knowledge.* San Francisco: John Wiley and Sons.

Medina, J. (2014). *Brain Rules: 12 Principals for Surviving and Thriving at Work, Home, and School,* second edition. Seattle, WA: Pear Press.

National Governors Association Center for Best Practices and Council of Chief State School Officers (NGA and CCSSO). (2010). *Common Core State Standards.* Washington, DC: Authors.

Pierson, R. (2013). "TED Talk: Every Kid Needs a Champion." Retrieved from www.ted.com/talks/rita_pierson_every_kid_needs_a_champion?language=en.

Reeves, D. B. (2013). *Elements of Grading* Bloomington, IN: Solution Tree, 227.

Sousa, D. A. (2011). *How the Brain Learns.* Thousand Oaks, CA: Corwin Press.

Wormeli, R. (2006). *Fair Isn't Always Equal: Assessing and Grading in the Differentiated Classroom.* Portland, ME: Stenhouse Publishers.

NINE

Higher-Order Thinking Skills for English Language Learners

Diane Arrington

Historically, teaching English Learners (ELs) has been like trying to put a puzzle together with some of the pieces missing or trying to solve a riddle without all the clues. Unfortunately, there is a long history in this country of schools and teachers struggling to educate and understand culturally and linguistically diverse (CLD) students in the classroom. This struggle is so evident that the commonly used terms English Proficient (LEP) and Language Minority Students (LMS) focus on the limitations of language learners instead of the strengths (Herrera and Murry, 2011). In response to the continued struggle for positive educational experiences for ELs, the U.S. Department of Education and the U.S. Department of Justice recently released a joint guidance reminding schools of their obligation "to ensure that EL students can participate meaningfully and equally in educational programs" (2015, 1).

One of the most discouraging trends in the United States has been the idea that ELs cannot process higher-order thinking skills in content until they are English proficient. Nowhere is this trend more evident than in the historical practice of providing English as a Second Language (ESL) services through a few, specific staff members who are kept separate from the regular education classroom. Under this type of structure, ELs were not integrated into the content, native English-speaking classrooms until they were considered "ready." Herrera and Murry explain, "Depending on school or state policy and resources availability, ELs were schooled in ESL or bilingual classes and were not a concern of the regular content or classroom teacher until they exited the language support program" (2011, 11).

Another negative, but pervasive, attitude schools use to address the needs of ELs is to argue that all students are treated the same, thus providing equality for all (Herrera and Murry, 2011). Unfortunately, "this viewpoint in effect denies the accommodations that would provide CLD students with meaningful instruction" (Herrera and Murry, 2011, 16).

Fortunately, the rigorous academic demands of the Common Core State Standards (CCSS), with its focus on skills and higher-order thinking, provide all students, including ELs, an opportunity to excel academically. As administrators, teachers, parents, and communities join together in an effort to find ways to help ELs meet the demands of the Common Core, there is an enormous opportunity for ELs to not only achieve academically, but to become part of content classrooms in a way that has not been seen before in U.S. schools.

OPPORTUNITIES IN THE COMMON CORE FOR ENGLISH LANGUAGE LEARNERS

Embedding expectations for ELs within the English language arts (ELA) and math standards is one of the most important contributions of the CCSS. The Common Core Addendum for English Language Learners states, "The National Governors Association Center for Best Practices and the Council of Chief State School Officers strongly believe that all students should be held to the same high expectations outlined in the Common Core State Standards" (Corestandards, 2015). Thanks to the CCSS, the days of putting ELs in an isolated classroom until they learn English are over.

Individual state standards attempted to provide equal access to the curriculum for all students, but the Common Core's focus on college and career readiness solidifies the goal of equality and makes it very difficult for teachers to sidestep the required higher-order thinking skills. Furthermore, TESOL International Association states, "Unlike previous reform efforts, the CCSS represent state education policy leaders working collectively to improve the educational attainment of all students" (2013, 3). Furthermore, "Because U.S. education is widely accepted to be a function of the individual states, this new policy holds more promise than others in the past" (TESOL International Association, 2013, 3). This means that administrators, schools, teachers, parents, and communities now have much more motivation to find ways to help ELs achieve academically.

Rigorous, grade-level goals in the domains of speaking, listening, reading, and writing embedded in the CCSS provide important opportunities for ELs. By addressing the four domains of language acquisition directly, the CCSS facilitate the use of additional English language proficiency development (ELPD) standards. ELPD standards are important for ELs, because they provide language use targets by language domain and language level. Using language domain and language level targets, teachers can create language proficiency objectives that coincide with and complement the content objectives (Echevarria, Vogt, and Short, 2010). Now teachers can create the essential language objectives ELs need in order to access the content objectives of the CCSS. Thus, teachers can focus on language and content in one classroom while using ELPD standards and the CCSS. Finally, language instruction and content instruction can coincide peacefully, side-by-side in the same classroom.

Another important opportunity embedded within the CCSS is the ability for ELs to demonstrate higher-order thinking while using imperfect English language. The CCSS acknowledge that, "Teachers should recognize that it is possible to achieve the standards for reading and literature, writing and research, language development and speaking and listening without manifesting native-like control of conventions and vocabulary" (Corestandards, 2015, Addendum for English Language Learners). This is powerful news for ELs! Language learners can now show mastery of the CCSS while using the expectations of ELPD standards. Instead of putting content on the back burner until an EL masters English proficiency, now teachers can use language ability targets contained in ELPD standards to guide their expectations of language acquisition during content instruction. If ELPD standards are carefully and critically utilized during content instruction, ELs can demonstrate content competency using the English language they have acquired; even if it is not "native-like" (Corestandards, 2015, Addendem for English Language Learners). The vision of equality anticipated by the U.S. Department of Education and the U S. Department of Justice can, more than ever before, become a reality.

Opportunities for ELs within the CCSS are not limited to ELA. The CCSS Addendum for English Language Learners argues, "Language is a resource for learning mathematics; it is not only a tool for communicating, but also a tool for thinking and reasoning mathematically" (Corestandards, 2015, Addendum for English Language Learners). Additionally, "All languages and language varieties . . . provide resources for mathematical thinking, reasoning, and communicating" (Corestandards, 2015, Addendum for English Language Learners). By acknowledging the use of language as a tool for learning math, the CCSS provide ELs with additional resources for accessing grade-level content while they acquire English. Just as racial segregation has become an offensive practice in society, the segregation of ELs from the content classroom is also becoming an unacceptable practice in schools.

The idea of language as a tool is embedded into more than just the math CCSS; it is actually one of the overarching concepts that prompted the creation of the CCSS. In order for all students, including ELs, to be ready for college and careers, they must be able to manipulate and apply language in precise and premeditated ways (Bunch, Kibler, and Pimentel, 2012). For example, students need to be able to use language for different purposes as determined by the required task. The CCSS encourage teachers and students to see language as a tool for accomplishing worthy, authentic tasks, not just for the perfect control of the English language (Bunch et al., 2012). So what does this mean for ELs? It means that ELs can now participate in the cognitive learning processes of difficult content instruction without having acquired complete proficiency in English. Bunch and colleagues explain, "ELs can no longer be envisioned as isolated from the context of meaningful and engaging academic work" (2012, 7).

Another essential component of using language as a tool is that language does not have to be perfect to be useful. This idea broadens the thought of how language can be used effectively for content instruction and opens the door for ELs to use their first language knowledge and skills as a "resource to help them locate, evaluate, and analyze information" (Bunch et al., 2012, 6). Long before the CCSS, language acquisition experts understood the value of using all language skills for the comprehension of complex content. Garcia and Kleifgen argue, "Effectively educating emergent bilinguals, even in programs that teach through the medium of English, must include and support the dynamic bilingual practices by which bilinguals construct knowledge and understandings" (2010, 43). Hopefully, administrators, teachers, and students who understand this important aspect of the CCSS will be able to see language as a tool and will allow students to use all their language tools, even their native language skills, as they attack the rigor of the CCSS.

In addition to changes in overall beliefs about language use, there have also been several key shifts for ELA and math under the CCSS. These shifts have the potential to raise academic achievement for ELs. For example, the shift to regular practice with complex texts through the application of a "staircase of increasing complexity" (Corestandards, 2015, Other Resources) assures that ELs will have access to complex texts. For ELs, who historically have been segregated from the regular education, content-heavy classroom, this shift ensures equal access to complex texts using a scaffolded system of exposure and practice. Scaffolding for ELs is essential. Echevarria and colleagues (2010) consider verbal and procedural scaffolding a fundamental feature of instruction for ELs. When teachers incorporate this shift with fidelity into their practice, ELs are given access to complex texts through a scaffolded system of exposure, which intrinsically incorporates best practices for ELs.

An increased focus on academic vocabulary is another ELA CCSS shift that opens opportunities for ELs. Freeman and Freeman (2009) argue, "Despite the different kinds of supports for ELLs in the early years, almost all of them develop conversational English" (19). However,

"The conversational English the students gain is deceptive, because they do not have the academic language needed to understand classroom instruction or to read and write well in English" (Freeman and Freeman, 2009, 19). Therefore, the increased focused on academic vocabulary introduced in its own strand within the CCSS is an enormous plus for ELs who require academic language in order to comprehend instruction.

Another key ELA shift within the CCSS is the focus on building content knowledge. As discussed previously, equal access to content is a serious issue for ELs. The CCSS's Key Shifts Resource Material states, "in grades 6–12, the standards for literacy in history/social studies, science and technical subjects ensure that students can independently build knowledge in these disciplines through reading and writing" (Corestandards, 2015). This statement defines the embedded idea that all students must be able to read and write using the appropriate academic vocabulary for the specific content area. Defining the academic language for content instruction is a tremendous advantage for ELs. Teachers of all content areas must now focus on language and content for all students, including ELs.

The key shifts in the math CCSS also have some benefits for ELs. The math CCSS ask teachers to focus instruction on the "major work of each grade" (Corestandards, 2015, Other Resources). This means that teachers must increase the time and energy spent on the essential topics, instead of "racing to cover many topics in a mile-wide, inch-deep curriculum" (Corestandards, 2015, Other Resources). Focusing deeply on fewer topics is a well-known strategy for ELs. Echevarria and colleagues (2010) state, "When considering pacing for ELs, it is also important to chunk information in smaller conceptual units and allot time for processing the material taught in the new language between the chunks" (165).

Another crucial idea within the math CCSS is the teaching of procedural knowledge. By adding this focus in writing to education standards, the CCSS emphasize a vital concept for language acquisition. Echevarria and colleagues (2010) conclude, "effective teachers incorporate instructional approaches that provide procedural scaffolding" (103). Again, the CCSS have incorporated an important component of English language acquisition theory and practice into its structure for all. Because this concept is now stated, ELs have a better chance of receiving the instruction they need.

The key shift of linking math topics and thinking from one grade level to the next is another valuable contribution the CCSS make for ELs. The CCSS are specifically designed to help students build on prior knowledge as they progress through the grades. This shift represents a practice that has been an essential part of instruction for ELs since the beginning of differentiated instruction for language learners. By explicitly incorporating math targets that build year after year, the CCSS address the scaffolding needs of ELs. Echevarria and colleagues (2010) state, "it is imperative that all teachers provide English learners with sufficient scaffolding" (116).

TURNING OPPORTUNITIES INTO REALITY

Knowing that opportunities exist under the CCSS for ELs is not enough. Because ELs require differentiated instruction, there are specific things teachers can do to help ELs turn these opportunities into reality. As discussed earlier, one of the important concepts of the CCSS is that language can be used as a tool and does not have to be implemented perfectly in order for higher-order thinking to take place. This does not mean, however, that teachers should stop focusing on English language instruction. So how do teachers know when to correct English language errors? Fairbairn and Jones-Vo (2010) suggest, "As in assessment, error correction during instruction should target only certain, level-appropriate aspects of language" (69). Levine and McCloskey (2009) argue, "Errors are sometimes an indication of language growth" (18). Additionally, "Public correction of errors is embarrassing to students" (Levine and McCloskey 2009, 18). Correcting every language error can be very overwhelming for ELs, but teachers can focus on the language objective from ELDP standards for the current lesson and provide corrections as needed for that objective in writing or through modeling correct language use. In this way, students receive the feedback for correct English language use in context and without humiliation, which helps ELs feel successful as they learn correct English.

There are other supplemental steps teachers can take to ensure EL success. The divisions of text complexity (Quantitative Measures, Qualitative Measures, and Reader and Task Measures) within the CCSS may seem perplexing at first, but there are strategies teachers can use to untangle the enigma. For example, teachers must take advantage of students' existing background knowledge and then use research-based strategies to help students develop new background knowledge (Echevarria et al. 2010). All students come to the classroom with vast personal experiences and differing academic levels. This is especially true for ELs. Teachers need to carefully consider the student's first language proficiency, English language proficiency, and culture as they plan lessons (TESOL International Association, 2013). Once teachers understand the cultural background, academic background, and linguistic background of their students, they can help students develop the necessary content background for understanding complex texts (TESOL International Association, 2013). Freeman and Freeman (2009) believe that without the necessary content background information, text can be extremely confusing for ELs.

Teaching students the purposes of different types of texts helps ELs develop appropriate content background knowledge (Bunch et al., 2012). Teachers can expose students to different text types and their purposes through more manageable texts in the students' first language, reading level, and interest level before moving on to more complex, difficult texts on the same topic (Bunch et al., 2012). Teachers can also help EL readers by introducing one or two characteristics of the text at a time instead of teaching all text features in one lesson on a single day (Bunch et al., 2012).

Think-alouds are another important method teachers can use to help students comprehend and manipulate complex texts. During think-alouds, teachers "model the thinking processes of proficient readers" by making predictions, helping the students infer, categorizing important information, and asking questions which facilitate higher-order thinking (Freeman and Freeman, 2009, 88). After completing the think-aloud activity, students are then supported in their independent attempts to utilize the same skills. The natural order of language acquisition moves from listening and speaking to reading and writing (Krashen 1982). Thus, think-alouds are important avenues for building on students' strong language skills before asking them to do the more difficult language skills of reading and writing.

Since ELs typically struggle in reading, and have usually struggled in reading for a significant amount of time, motivation can be an important factor for helping them deal with complex texts. The ELA shifts in the CCSS intentionally do not include a required reading list. This aspect of the CCSS is important for ELs who need to read a wide variety of texts, which also include the cultural components they are used to (Freeman and Freeman, 2009). This is just another example of how the CCSS incorporate established theory and practice for ELs. Allowing students to choose from among many interesting texts, which focus on students' personal lives, is an important strategy for helping ELs engage in reading (Freeman and Freeman, 2009). At the same time, this strategy validates personal choices and interests (Freeman and Freeman, 2009).

Collaboration is an important strategy for all students, but it is an essential and critical strategy for ELs attempting to meet the difficult reading demands of the CCSS. As early as the 1970s, Vygotsky (1978) proposed that language learning is the result of authentic social interaction. Herrera and Murry (2011) extend this theory by arguing that collaborative, academic group discussions help students improve concept understanding, negotiate meaning, and move from social language to academic language. Collaborative groups also create an environment where ELs can experiment with and practice new language in authentic, informal situations where anxiety and stress is reduced (Herrera and Murry, 2011). According to Herrera and Murry (2011), some important considerations for groupings of ELs might include: language level, interest level, available roles, and opportunities for positive interaction.

Academic vocabulary proposes another unique challenge for ELs. TESOL International Association (2013) suggests that teachers incorporate games that encourage students to make guesses about words they don't know. Additional academic vocabulary development strategies include explicitly teaching cognates, prefixes, suffixes, and multiple meanings in context (Freeman and Freeman, 2009).

Echevarria and colleagues (2010) remind teachers that academic vocabulary includes "content words," "process/function words," and "words and word parts that teach English structure" and that "English learners' vocabulary instruction must be accelerated because ELs are learning English later than their native-speaking peers" (61).

Conversation is the base or "cornerstone" of "literacy and learning" (Zwiers and Crawford, 2011, 7). Furthermore, since listening and speaking tend to be the first stages of language acquisition (Krashen, 1982) using conversations to begin literacy instruction makes sense. Thus, academic language and vocabulary development begins with authentic, academic conversations. Zwiers and Crawford (2011) argue, "Sadly, academic talk is most scarce where it is most needed—in classrooms with high numbers of linguistically and culturally diverse students" (8). In order to help students develop academic language, Zwiers and Crawford (2011) suggest reducing teacher talk and encouraging student academic conversations.

Since ELs have had very little exposure to academic English conversations, it's important to support and prepare them as they learn this new skill. Teachers can begin by having students participate in "structured interaction activities" (27) like "Stand and Converse" (Zwiers and Crawford, 2011, 28). This activity can be implemented by asking groups of students to stand in a circle and pass around a long string, which each student continues to hold as he or she contributes to a conversation, thus creating a conversation web (Zwiers and Crawford, 2011).

Once students have practiced conversation skills, they can move on to authentic academic conversations. Zwiers and Crawford (2011) remind teachers that academic conversations look different from social conversations and are identified by five basic elements: elaboration and clarification, support with examples, building on or challenging a partner's idea, paraphrasing, and synthesizing. Teachers can also provide conversation supports for students by using graphic organizers. Zwiers and Crawford (2011) suggest teachers use a unique graphic organizer for each element of academic conversations. These organizers should identify preselected prompts and response prompts that help students with the language necessary to participate in the conversation (Zwiers and Crawford, 2011).

There are also several ways to turn the opportunities for ELs within math CCSS into reality. Since the math CCSS build on what students have already learned, teachers of ELs can concentrate on scaffolding their daily instruction using the previously taught information as a starting point for new instruction. But how do teachers scaffold appropriately for differing language levels? Fairbairn and Jones-Vo (2010) state, "In order to facilitate successful student learning and demonstration of that learning, teachers must provide graduated, incremental scaffolding for students at each of the five language proficiency levels" (44).

At level one, beginning English language learners have very little or no English language experience, so they create unique challenges for teachers. Scaffolding for level-one ELs must provide comprehensible input at the student's current language and content level while exposing the student to the next language and content level (Fairbairn and Jones-Vo, 2010). This is especially important for math instruction, since math concepts build on previously attained skills and understanding. Thankfully, the CCSS have already created the large chunks of grade-level scaffolding.

Allowing level-one ELs to demonstrate knowledge, instead of explaining orally or in writing, is vital. Level-one ELs can understand much more language than they can speak or write. A level-one student who is not allowed to demonstrate their knowledge physically has no medium to convey their higher-order thinking. Allowing students to demonstrate their knowledge versus requiring them to speak or write is the difference between success and failure. A teacher who wants to assess a level-one student's learning might allow students: to place sequenced pictures of math concepts in order, to categorize images, to point to correct answers, and to draw or copy (Fairbairn and Jones-Vo, 2010).

Additional strategies for level-one ELs include prompting for nonverbal responses, prompting for short oral responses, allowing first language responses, providing extensive visual support, and using graphic organizers (Fairbairn and Jones-Vo, 2010). Examples of nonverbal responses include shaking or nodding of the head, thumbs-up or thumbs-down, pointing, acting-out, and drawing. Examples of short-answer responses include yes or no questions or answers that have two or three one-word options. Sometimes a response in the first language is valuable to check for understanding and to help students feel like they can participate in a meaningful way. Each teacher must decide when first language answers might be appropriate in the classroom. Visual support during a lesson and graphic organizers provide additional clues about the context while allowing ELs more time to process language and content since they are not guessing about the information being presented.

As with level-one students, level-two students need exposure to comprehensible input at their language and content level and exposure to language and content at the next level (Fairbairn and Jones-Vo, 2010). Level-two students communicate much more than level-one students, but their communication is usually limited to simple and repeated language (Fairbairn and Jones-Vo, 2010). Some important strategies for level-two math students might be appropriately weighting assessment components since listening and speaking skills are typically stronger at this stage, prompting for memorized or simple responses orally and in writing, allowing students to support their writing with drawings and visuals, using simplified, but correct English language for instruction, allowing appropriate time for responses, and providing sentence starters and sentence frames when needed (Fairbairn and Jones-Vo, 2010).

Level-three, level-four, and level-five ELs are proficient in social language, but are still developing academic language. Errors are common, but decreasing, and reading and writing skills are becoming increasing more complex (Fairbairn and Jones-Vo, 2010). Advanced ELs pose a particular problem in the classroom because they appear to speak English well, but in reality, "English learners appear to speak English well, in hall-ways, on playing fields, and in small talk before a lesson begins, but struggle to use English well in the classroom lessons or on tests" (Echevarria et al., 2010, 12). Math teachers need to be particularly adept at recognizing the difference between social language and academic language in order to help students develop the necessary academic language required by the math content.

Even though intermediate and advanced ELs are in the later stages of English language development, they still need extensive, scaffolded support in math content instruction. Teachers can help these students by providing extensive opportunities for collaborative work with proficient speakers, providing graphic organizers and outlines, creating language level appropriate study guides, explicitly teaching academic vocabulary, and by assuring that daily objectives include content and language goals (Echevarria et al., 2010). Even though the CCSS facilitate language and content learning by assigning specific math tasks to each grade level, teachers of ELs must extend that leveling and scaffolding in their daily language and content instruction.

Even if teachers are willing to implement these strategies for ELs, their efforts cannot be maximized unless administrators, schools, parents, and communities are willing to be part of the process. Garcia and Kleifgen (2010) argue, "we should recognize that the education of emergent bilinguals is a partnership with parents and community" (101). TESOL International Association (2013) advocates "For all students in the United States to succeed, all educators must now share the responsibility for teaching ELLs" (10). Furthermore, Garcia and Kleifgen (2010) state, "Research has shown that parents' involvement in their sons' and daughters' education leads to better attendance, higher achievement, improved attitudes about learning, and higher graduation rates" (93). No one person or organization can attempt to improve education for ELs and utilize the CCSS without the help of the other stakeholders.

Asking administrators, schools, teachers of all content areas, parents, and communities to work together to help ELs is a daunting task, but it can be done. Teachers can advocate for students by actively participating in community organizations, attending school and district leadership meetings, and sharing classroom activities with the community through public media sources (Herrera and Murry, 2011). Teachers also promote positive changes within their schools as they participate in their professional learning communities.

Implementing changes within schools is not enough. Teachers and schools must also increase family and community involvement. Garcia and Kleifgen (2010) suggest finding ways to take advantage of the unique knowledge families and communities possess, celebrating native languages, and providing the information necessary for parents and communities to understand how schools work and how to get involved. Even though the CCSS provide wonderful opportunities for ELs, these opportunities cannot be realized without the help of school leaders, the collaborative efforts of all teachers, and inclusion of parents and communities in the education process.

Unfortunately, ELs have not always had access to the same educational opportunities as other students. State standards attempted to help them, but left out important features such as language acquisition theory for content classrooms, the belief that language is a tool with a purpose, direction on academic vocabulary, and the need for building on prior knowledge. Fortunately, under the CCSS, there are many opportunities to close the achievement gap for ELs. Teachers now have more pieces to the puzzle and more clues for the riddle of teaching CLD students. The opportunities within the CCSS can only become a reality when administrators, schools, teachers, parents, and communities collaborate in order to finish the puzzle and solve the riddle.

REFERENCES AND RESOURCES

Bunch, George C., Amanda Kibler, and Susan Pimentel. (2012). "Realizing Opportunities for English Learners in the Common Core English Language Arts and Disciplinary Literacy Standards." Paper presented at Stanford University Understanding Language Conference, Stanford, California, January 2012.

Corestandards. (2015). "Common Core State Standards Initiative." http://www.corestandards.org.

Echevarria, Jana, MaryEllen Vogt, and Deborah J. Short. (2010). *Making Content Comprehensible for Elementary English Learners: The SIOP Model.* Boston: Allyn and Bacon.

Fairbairn, Shelley, and Stephaney Jones-Vo. (2010). *Differentiating Instruction and Assessment for English Language Learners: A Guide for K/12 Teachers.* Philadelphia: Caslon Inc.

Freeman, Yvonne S., and David E. Freeman. (2009). *Academic Language for English Language Learners and Struggling Readers: How to Help Students Succeed Across Content Areas.* Portsmouth, NH: Heinemann.

Garcia, Ofelia, and Jo Anne Kleifgen. (2010). *Educating Emergent Bilinguals: Policies, Programs, and Practices for English Language Learners.* New York: Teachers College Press.

Herrera, Socorro G., and Kevin G. Murry. (2011). *Mastering ESL and Bilingual Methods: Differentiated Instruction for Culturally and Linguistically Diverse (CLD) Students.* Boston: Allyn and Bacon.

Krashen, S. (1982). *Principles and Practice in Second Language Acquisition.* Oxford: Pergamon Press.

Levine, Linda New, and Mary Lou McCloskey. (2009). *Teaching Learners of English in Mainstream Classrooms (K–8): One Class, Many Paths.* Boston: Pearson Education.

TESOL International Association. (2013, March). *Overview of the Common Core State Standards Initiatives for ELLs.* Alexandria, VA: Author.

U.S. Department of Justice and U.S. Department of Education. (2015). *Ensuring English Learner Students Can Participate Meaningfully and Equally in Educational Programs.* Joint Guidance issued in January, 2015. Washington, D.C.: U.S. Government.

Vygotsky, L. S. (1978). *Mind in Society: The Development of Higher Psychological Processes.* Cambridge, MA: MIT Press.

Zwiers, Jeff, and Marie Crawford. (2011). *Academic Conversations: Classroom Talk That Fosters Critical Thinking and Content Understandings.* Portland, ME: Stenhouse.

TEN

With New Standards in Mind

Selecting and Integrating Educational Technologies for Student Success

Seema Imam

In schools across the country, Common Core State Standards (CCSS) are now part of the landscape, with teachers and students embarking on the journey toward successful outcomes, very often through the selection and integration of educational technologies in the classroom. Gura (2014) explains, "The Common Core State Standards, an initiative that is about to redefine a good deal of what goes on in the intellectual lives of our students, is more than just another, better, standards document" (5). The classrooms of today, and teachers in particular, are swimming in a sea of educational and technological possibility, with so much to choose from and so much pressure to use technology. It is up to schools to provide the types of technology and access that will create classrooms of the twenty-first century. Teachers have the task of becoming proficient in a variety of ways, and this chapter will discuss four areas: model the use of technology, design technologically rich lessons, select appropriate technologies that involve learners in using technology, and engage creatively in teaching with strategies to best meet the needs of the lesson and the learners. It is important for teachers to become proficient in envisioning the lesson outcome and the nature of what students need and securing the best possibilities for learning in the digital age.

SETTING THE STAGE: A REALITY CHECK

Long before I heard the term CCSS, as an elementary education faculty member, I was an early adopter of teaching with technology and realized how rapidly the classroom would and has changed across the country. We never seem to go backward once we get a technology or a tool that enhances or changes the way we work or live. One would be challenged to revert to the days without our cell phones or the days of the desktop computer though neither are very far back in our past. Classrooms require the potential to be equally progressive in terms of what is now available. The wall map or pull-down world maps are less and less common and even less used once we realize that every possible type of map is a click away and can be displayed and marked on using the highlighting tools on the interactive whiteboard or computer screen and can easily be seen from the back of the room. Yes, better yet, it is possible for every student in the classroom with iPads, Chromebooks, tablets, or laptops to be on that same map doing their own personal learning with instantaneous feedback at varying levels. One example that kids love is the app Stack the States. It is one of many tools that gives immediate feedback as students drag and drop states to where they belong on the map. Students can repeat as much as they like. It is fun—you watch a timer and compete with yourself—but most importantly, learning happens. There is no grading, and no hassle. True, there is no going back; the American classroom is no longer the way it was when I went to school. In fact, classrooms where I spent sixteen years as a licensed educator are nothing like the classrooms I now prepare teachers for.

There are so many important ways to think about going forward, but for the purposes of this chapter, there is little reason to debate the CCSS and far more reason to put our hearts, heads, and minds together to be successful in the use of technology and the CCSS. The professional learning that has and is transforming our classrooms is essential and should be the priority. Professional learning can be focused toward systematic teaching and include the important voices of administration, teacher colleagues, students, and parents. In this chapter, however, these voices will not all be addressed, as I focus on teaching and teacher preparation.

With many initiatives, districts and schools have been somewhat overwhelmed by change, and I can personally identify with that, as we in teacher education are similarly immersed in twenty-first-century change and developments. So, being less and less willing to be frantic or allow the new trend or mandates to delay my approach to teaching, I prefer to go forward with focus and seek out the ways to embrace that future. It means that as a teacher of teachers I must focus my classroom on preparing teachers to teach CCSS through the use of educational technologies, prepare them for watching their own practice in a video format for their edTPA, and prepare them for teaching with skills necessary to reach children growing up in the twenty-first century. New teachers need to be prepared for a constantly and rapidly changing world just as much as veteran teachers will need to embrace new methodologies and teaching strategies in their transforming classrooms.

Additionally, this chapter is not going to focus on the preparations that schools must make aside from the teacher approach to planning and teaching with technologies, but it is certainly clear that school readiness is a factor of great concern. I suspect that by publication there will be new issues, and some of today's concerns will be solved because the world of technology is so rapidly evolving. Concerns I have as of now include access, students with special needs, and bandwidth. Students will have to have gained access to technology in order to have the necessary skill to use the computer to take the Common Core State Standards tests they are given. It is a necessity for technology to be made available for all students or risk a wider achievement gap where underserved populations will lack the technological skills required to compete in today's world. Teachers in classrooms without the availability of technology could benefit their students immensely if they were able to use what is available in the library, computer labs, or on computer carts but this is unlikely to be a viable solution. Second, though I do not hear a lot about students with special needs, having a special education background and teaching special education introductory courses reminds me that this is another extremely important area to consider. Third, the challenge of bandwidth in schools may not go away easily and may test us beyond the CCSS testing. Schools often struggle not having the bandwidth needed to serve hundreds of students. This alone presents some pretty hefty challenges. If we are to bring about the intended equity of CCSS, these three things are extremely important and we will have to find ways to ensure that all student needs are met, that technology is available, and that connectivity is consistent and adequate.

The fact that we are living at a time when information moves quickly means we must prepare young people to navigate the world and learn and interact in new formats, ones that look and feel like the world they are engaged with. Students need to attain digital literacy and become digital citizens with an understanding of what that citizen does and does not do in the electronic world. The Common Core State Standard tests require students to use a computer and take different actions to complete tests from the actions most often taken in the past. For example, today's tests will incorporate the need for students to generate the answer electronically while in the past answers were available in multiple-choice items and students chose one. Furthermore, students will investigate first and generate solutions through the use of Internet resources, so they will need to understand what is authentic and then write about it.

Teaching in the world where information is moving at such a rapid pace will mean that teaching has to look and feel different. To meet the needs of students who will be taking the Common Core State Standards test, it will be increasingly important what strategy is used, how the lesson is designed, which educational technology could best be employed, and how creativity and engagement is managed for the best possible results in student learning. In fact, I would like to think that all of these teaching foci are the new mode that will change education in ways that make learning meaningful and alive. I remember being in the classroom when Atari and Nintendo first came out and I began to notice a change in the students that I was teaching. This pales as I recall the changes in children as I raised my own children and now grandchildren, as well as what I have learned from being a former teacher, principal, and now teacher educator. I realize there are many significant changes in the way children learn and how learning in general has evolved rapidly, causing everyone to take note and focus immediate attention on education, on teachers and those who prepare educators worldwide. We must prepare the digital citizens and guide them to digital literacy.

Once we have accepted the need to change and to build the right infrastructures, then there are four key areas to discuss in this chapter with Common Core State Standards in mind. These relate to how teachers will need to meet the various challenges of becoming proficient, specifically: first, how to model the use of technology; second, how to design technologically rich lessons; third, how to select appropriate technologies that involve learners in using technology; and finally, how to engage creatively in teaching with strategies that best meet the needs of the lesson and the learners. These require teachers to become proficient in envisioning the lesson outcome first, preparing students to meet the standards while securing the best possibilities for learning. It follows then that teacher educators need to be preparing the next generation of teachers to enter these twenty-first-century classrooms with the necessary digital literacy teaching skills.

MODEL THE USE OF TECHNOLOGY

In what ways will teachers model the use of educational technology while integrating technology standards in their twenty-first-century classroom and teaching the CCSS? I believe there are important ways to model the use of technology in the classroom. First, it should be modeled in lessons; teachers can model the use of technology as an organizational tool, as well as a tool for professional development and personal productivity. The amount of skill required to model the use of technology will depend on each teacher or teacher candidate's own current skill set. Attaining these skills is a process and will not happen overnight. I think we should let go of the phrase "your students will know" when we refer to using technology. Over the years, many people have relied on the younger generation to access skills for the use of technology. It is my opinion that the time has come for teachers to move to the head of the class as they go beyond this and become facilitators and classroom guides in the appropriate and deliberate use of technology.

Next, teachers must model the use of technology in the lessons while teaching. Here we are not talking about the lesson but the skill to set up the lesson, which is often glossed over. This, of course, includes making connections to the Internet, using LCD projectors, and displaying the components of the lesson onscreen. In some of today's classrooms even connecting wirelessly is easy with the right tools. Students and teachers can share the screen from their iPads, for example. This means, perhaps, that the teacher uses multiple tools such as the laptop, iPad, Chromebook, tablets, or other devices with the class. It includes managing the lesson delivery using those technologies seamlessly, which is the goal and in some cases the current-day challenge here. Many lessons will require smoothly transitioning from displaying the slide of today's lesson outcomes to viewing a video, accessing a Web site, displaying a sample of the task the students will complete, and much more. Teachers will need to demonstrate capturing students' images as they work on video, or still photos, or scanning a lesson from one student to the screen to allow for classroom discussions. Teachers need to be knowledgeable about apps and software that can be used for skill building, for creating learning agendas, and for students to use to demonstrate what they have learned. All of this depends on teacher readiness.

Another area of setting up the lesson is deciding what students will do to demonstrate a newly developed skill. Gone are the days of writing assignments being the mode for demonstrating what was learned in the lesson. Teachers will need to be proficient and create work samples if their students will now demonstrate learning through a PowToons creation, a personal VoiceThread, a Vimeo, or simple iMovie that they have narrated, or created through still shots or live video recording. After teaching and after the students submit their work, assessment will also be enhanced by technology and will require its own focus as skills and understanding for assessment is another major component not taken on here. Throughout their teaching, teachers may also elect to send their video demonstrations of upcoming lessons via an e-mail or posting on a Web site to be watched before class and ask students to demonstrate their learning in class. This flipped model of learning, which is a newer tool or skill set for setting up the lesson, is more supportive for the learner as he or she has the teacher's support during the learning process in class when it is needed the most.

Using technology and modeling how teachers use technology as our own organizational tool will also be a strong way to model the use of technology for the students of the twenty-first century. When a student needs a copy of an assignment for a class missed it seems to me that the student will receive it electronically. Attendance will be taken electronically; communication with students, parents, administration, and other teachers will be electronic. It will provide a more immediate interaction. Social media sharing and texting are becoming common and frequent. Lesson planning will be done electronically, and teachers will share links that guide differentiation of lessons and post favorites on Instagram and Pinterest, thus allowing for more lesson organization within the use of technology. As teachers become guides and model how digital learning can best happen, this extra element of being electronically organized becomes paramount. Wireless backup drives, the Cloud, and various other Web sites help teachers and others to have the same material accessible on various devices. Teachers will be able to provide a static set of materials through the use of Web site pages, Pinterest, or social media as well as textbook Web sites and ultimately set the students up to become organized and to adopt organization skills that will later be used to enhance how they receive materials, curate materials, and interact during the lessons.

When classrooms do not engage in this way, in terms of being organized, it is easy to miss out on necessary components of learning. For example, gone are the days of the file cabinet and the many places we used to store the student material used for our lessons; the workbook certainly is not used the way it once was. While copies are still being made throughout the educational world, there are apps for signing, storing, organizing, and advancing one's own learning agenda, and a decrease in copies while electronic documents are on the rise. There are many apps such as Notepad, Studypad and Timelines that are replacing the student worksheet. In Google Docs alone, one can find document, quiz, form, and presentation tools that would easily replace the standard worksheet. When I consider the one app that was most valuable in my transition to teaching and learning in my university classroom with the iPad, for example, I think of the GoodReader app. It offers a highly organized platform that allows me to immediately open documents. It allows me to use file folders to organize work students submitted, but with online learning management systems, this is no longer needed for organizing student work. I still use GoodReader on the iPad to organize materials for one class or subject filed in one place. The idea of being organized in the twenty-first century while teaching the CCSS is an essential new way of looking at things. It will require us to take steps toward doing things differently and, for right now at least, embrace rapid and frequent change.

Professional development can be modeled as well. Students and parents are able to benefit when they see that teachers are lifelong learners. Today's technology-rich classrooms are great places to engage in professional development. It allows teachers and others to watch a webinar and use their time well. It's like children seeing that their teachers value reading. When children see their teachers use a video or webinar to learn something about use of the iPad or ways to work with art mediums in order for the teacher to then be able to use the information in classroom teaching, students will benefit in multiple ways. Professional development should be shared. I recently showed a video called "Austin's Butterfly" by Ron Berger, author of "An Ethic of Excellence," to pre-service teachers.

While we watched I realized that it could be shown to primary-aged students. It is an example of using a different kind of media to develop our own practice. Students in the video were learning about critique and revision. In another example, how often do we Google a question, read briefly to verify the answer's authenticity, and then use that new information instantaneously? There is so much available to learn online and getting information has become very different from the days of our youth. A good example is "Austin's Butterfly" because both teachers and students learn about critique, doing our best, and revising our work. While we once went to the encyclopedia, we now go to the Internet for learning. It is almost laughable at times when you see young children endeavor to turn a magazine page by swiping across it; modeling professional development could mean endless learning opportunities and a whole new world opened up to the students we teach.

Personal productivity is another area to model for students. When teachers are able to be productive quickly, for example, in getting student grading done electronically, students will take note of how quick it is. They will come to expect more rapid turnaround, but it feels productive. Being productive in using student photographs and creating a Web page or online book for parents to enjoy learning scenes from the classroom will mean a lot to families. While learning all these techniques does take time, once teachers have more and more technology skills and Web pages change daily and reflect an awesome classroom environment it creates a synergy and motivation that can go a long way. Whether it is about teacher productivity, professional development, organization or use of technology, all of the ways that teachers model the use of technology will enhance the classroom and student use of technology.

DESIGN TECHNOLOGICALLY RICH LESSONS

Teachers will design technologically rich lessons that provide strong student experiences and help them reach the desired learning outcomes, which is the most exciting part of teaching and learning with technology; the focus is on what teachers do. Teachers create and use technology-rich presentations for content material so that their teaching is engaging. Drapeau (2014) says, "The CCSS provide rigorous targets for what we want students to know and understand. . . . What this means is that teachers need to use their own elaboration skills to incorporate creativity . . . tweak their lesson plans so that they address critical thinking standards through the creative processing of information" (42–43). One element of incorporating creativity can be the use of the Internet. It offers extensive amounts of information and tools. As the use of digital technology increases all around us, teachers and students are both becoming creators and curators as well. They need to be able to create content and do so creatively, to locate their tools, to access what they create, and to easily and quickly locate specific activities to demonstrate all types of learning outcomes established as the expected outcomes of the CCSS. Teachers will use many digital tools and engage frequently with technology in designing technologically rich lessons. This discussion is about the use of a variety of digital devices, Web 2.0 tools, Google Docs, and other tools that build rich lessons. It will focus on three things: (1) What will I teach; (2) How will I teach; and (3) How will I know students have learned what I set out to teach? To answer these questions, we should explore real classroom experiences.

Taking time to deeply consider the classroom and what one will teach for each and every lesson is crucial in every teacher's experience. Anyone familiar with lesson creation and lesson planning will want to understand the desired outcomes for each lesson. Planning a lesson with technology then means we have to know what we are using the technology for. So, first off, the teacher will engage with the Common Core Standards that are to be met. The teacher might start class with a Glogster (electronic poster) that he or she created showing a community challenge such as diseased trees in the community and the plans for taking care of this problem. At the close of the Glogster presentation, the teacher could model the use of Skype by Skyping in the mayor for a "meet the class" discussion. This way they meet, and both the students and the mayor are thinking about this problem. This class would be delivered through technology-rich methods of teaching. To build on this opening, for example, to meet literacy standard suchs as ELA-Literacy CCSS.R1.4 and CCSS.R1.5 where students read information texts, students would be researching and learning through collaboration with others. Students will also need to know who can inform them. In this case, this would be a great place to use Skype in the classroom for collaboration and to hear, via computer, from the source we want to gather information from. Tree experts, park districts, or forest preserve attendants would be possibilities. Students would use Skype to conduct the interview process and through Skype and the interaction with experts, verify and collaborate on what they were learning from the informational texts. Students would set up the Skype meeting themselves and plan the discussion or any interview questions to be asked specifically. Since locally there could be issues where students could speak to park district specialists about diseased trees in the community, for example, students would be investigating relevant knowledge.

Students would need a research and resource or note-taking tool, which could be Google Docs or Evernote, depending on which functions they wanted to use most. Google presents itself so that students can share a document and write in the data or material simultaneously while sharing the document. Evernote does many things including setting up a shared notebook. In both cases, students also share the document with the teacher so that the teacher is on board with the progress throughout. Evernote is also a great tool for capturing the resources; in fact, one would expect students to collect and maintain the research materials and organize their resources in order to go back to them. Mobile phones and other personal devices that students typically bring to class are other ways of accessing Evernote in addition to the class computers or iPads, which is very helpful. Throughout the assignment, students would record their thoughts and keep this notebook or Google Doc to share their thinking with their teammates. As they move into the second phase, which would be an English Language Arts (ELA) writing standard such as ELA literacy CCSS.W.8.6, different tasks would be assigned. As the writing work is developed and students use their notes to then write the assigned papers they could also use an application called Easybib integrated with their Google Doc to create a bibliography. One way to differentiate in this project could be having students who need to achieve some different skill sets while working in groups create a poster in Glogster and demonstrating their learning in place of narrative paper assignments. The actual performance task would be different, but could be set up for the purpose of having students reach different goals and outcomes while still meeting the goal of collaboration that initiated the original lesson.

Teachers would want to demonstrate Skype meetings, perhaps on different topics, to practice the use of Skype, create a notebook in Evernote, a Glogster poster, a Google Doc, and an Easybib where students are involved. Students would see one example before they are asked to create their own. This is fairly easy and draws the students into the use of these tools. However, all of these tools would be ideal to use repeatedly throughout the year to meet a variety of reading, language, informational, and foundational skills in the CCSS. If teachers continue to say that students know more about technology than the teacher, this knowledge gap is a disaster. We must model the variety of tools at our disposal, in particular for special needs students but also because of the need for differentiation. According to Ray and Zanetis (2009), "For interactive lessons to be successful, certain ground rules must be established for classroom instruction" (4).

Thus, to have a technologically rich lesson, it will matter how the teacher teaches. Initially the teacher who is planning these lessons will be deliberate about the methodology and will immediately want to answer the questions, "what tools can be used to present content?" or "who makes or creates that digital tool?" Dougherty (2012) asks in her book, *Assignments Matter*, "What if students learned in environments where they could move easily between human-generated interactions and technology? The good news is that there are such schools, where students are learning with the help of technology and are learning to use technology to communicate their ideas to peers and those outside of school" (79). It seems to me that this validates the learning. To present content, the tools to use are many, and one would want to consider making demonstration videos, or instead of using video, the teacher may enhance the lesson by using apps with characters. (By characters, I am referring to programs that use cartoonish characters or those with simple avatars, which could also be used to represent an expert.) There are many ways of teaching that give the lesson more meaning and relevance. Creative media may grab student attention more readily. So, the teacher might create a Sock Puppet episode or a PowToons episode where several sock puppet characters or those found in PowToons interact and discuss the points that the teacher is teaching. This is modeling a methodology for students to engage with later. It is important for the teacher to model certain things in order to advance the classroom's thinking and to advance critical thinking about who is leading the classroom in the use of technology. By creating demonstrations such as PowToons, sock puppets, and Glogster, which was mentioned earlier, teachers are engaging in leadership in their teaching. Instead of teachers following the explorations and the lead of their students, this sends a stronger message and brings the teacher away from the old message that students, "know more about technology." In fact, using technology in this way and inviting students to be involved in real activities to validate their intelligence as students becomes even more engaging and teachers move to the head of the class.

Today's teachers record material for advance viewing in classes using the flipped classroom methodologies. It is an effective use of time, as Gagnon, Monroe, and Smith point out (2015) in their article, "Tales from the Flipped Classroom": "Since I've flipped my classroom, what I've noticed more than anything is that I have more time. I have more time with my students, and the feedback that I've gotten from my students is that I actually care more" (34). That is important and supports this approach. An app called Screen Chomp records either before or after lessons, but either way frees up time to work with the students. It is a tool that allows for simulating a whiteboard on the iPad screen. This app can also accommodate voice recording. An example of an instructional application is when a math teacher demonstrates how to work a problem. This recording could be e-mailed to a student, parent, or to the class for watching the evening before the lesson on long division is taught, as a flipped classroom example. Or it could be recorded in the classroom for a struggling student to watch again at home. When the student gets home in the second scenario, the student would then make their own Screen Chomp episode to show the teacher what they are thinking as they complete a different long division problem. These episodes can be posted on Web sites or e-mailed. For a deeper look at the flipped classroom, look into the flipped classroom professional learning network at flippedclassroom.org. Similarly, check out the popular Khan Academy for ready-to-use and easy-to-access videos for parents, math teachers, and students at www.khanacademy.org.

Similarly, there is Vimeo and VoiceThread, both of which are tools to record content in advance to be played either in the classroom as a group or on an individual basis. It could be a detailed vocabulary lesson, a math lesson, or a segment that shares knowledge about a tool that students would later use on their own. Vimeo is basically a video, VoiceThread uses still shots, and the teacher records over the still shots to demonstrate a skill such as the tool's use. These utilities answer the question, "what tools can be used to present material?" They are teacher-made in this case. Using Vimeo for creating a video is easy. Then teachers will need to decide where to upload their videos. Curating materials is very important. Most commonly, teachers use their own Web site or YouTube. These two demonstrations could be ready to access if uploaded with private settings to YouTube. The students benefit when a teacher can create something for differentiation. Some students don't need to hear a longer explanation. These students can engage quickly, but others need further explanation, and an already prepared and curated tool can help a variety of learners in the class.

A point that is far too important to leave out is that most of this type of teaching is more engaging. Students will not be listening to lectures or teacher talk in the way we are used to, but rather they will be actively engaged. Khan (2012) of Khan Academy says in his book, *The One World School House*, "My criticism is not of the institution but of the tired old habit of passive lecture. Replace that with active learning, and I believe that most and very possibly all of us are capable of taking in much more than is currently expected of us. . . . We can reach more ambitious goals if we are given the latitude to set goals for ourselves" (189). Teaching the CCSS with technology and at the same time deliberately taking time to consider the question "how will I teach?" is critical. We will not always teach with technology. When we differentiate, we are more likely to engage students in ways that they are capable of learning. This means we pace differently for different learners.

Finally, the third important point in understanding the technologically rich lesson is to understand how teachers will know the students learned what the lesson set out to teach. We discover our lesson success when we see how engaged the learners are. Lessons need to be productive, and it is important to consider what tool works best and how student assignments can be integrated into the learning in each of the lessons. Students learn when lesson connections are real. The performance task, assignment, or tool that students engage with to demonstrate learning will need to fit the lesson. The practice work that students are asked to complete requires purpose. According to Gura (2014), "while the technology itself may be of interest to the students, more often it is the authentic nature of the types of activities that it makes possible that offers the greatest value" (5). This is where we need to focus: on making authentic assignments and ensuring a wise use of time so that the result is engaged learning. Here we become responsible for what has been learned, not how much technology was used or how glamorous the product might be. Students will be asked to do specific tasks in the CCSS testing, so taking the time to carefully see what students have learned lesson by lesson will be the key that measures one's success.

Student learning will show in the digital assignment students have produced to demonstrate that learning. Yes, later they will be tested, but at the end of the lesson it is the blog, the Web site they created, the Vimeo, the video, the sock puppets episode, the storyboard, the script, the quick write, the animated cartoon, a PowToons episode, the persuasive writing, or the recorded session with the mayor that will show the teacher how much learning has transpired. Students in the twenty-first century will rely less and less on textbooks as we know them and we will be teaching more and more about the use of Internet. When using the Internet, according to Ray and Zanetis (2009), "Students need to be taught how to search on the Internet so that the time they spend online is productive and beneficial to their research" (4).

The activities that result from technology-rich classrooms allow students to produce new, original digital media. It is important to do this because of the world we now live in. Engaging students meaningfully in school, in a creative environment where students love learning and sincerely want to be involved in the classroom, is awesome. It is important to guide students so that they themselves can understand what they have learned, and all can excel in different ways while meeting the same standards. This is why I encourage teachers to post the outcomes for the day for students to see. It is important for students to have goals for themselves, to desire to read, to want to create a digital book, a video or a digital episode to tell a story, and to value doing these activities well. I think it helps students to discover the importance of learning and to remain eager to be engaged day after day in order to achieve what is needed for the success in life and testing in the CCSS. Every student's multiple experiences and constant interaction with learning through the use of digital tools will enhance their success and readiness for a college experience, which should be a natural progression of the same type of valued and meaningful learning.

SELECT APPROPRIATE TECHNOLOGIES

Selecting appropriate technologies will be important to both the teachers and students. As teachers develop a skill set that enables their effective use of technology, it is important to not waste time, money, or energy on trying first one thing and then switching to another unnecessarily. The International Society of Technology Education (ISTE) has long discussed the necessary readiness for institutions. On their Web site (www.iste.org), they publish a list of Essential Conditions (www.iste.org/standards/essential-conditions) for implementing the ISTE. Since we are all aware that there is an increasing variety of technologies being used in schools, and the realm of possibility is huge, gaining the right skills is important in order for teachers to build their teaching and learning skill set in a logical way and to be productive with their students in CCSS learning. Introducing too many things too quickly or things that ultimately are not used is not fruitful. It is not unusual to meet teachers who currently do not use much technology, so I know firsthand that a lot of attention is needed in selecting appropriate technologies. Here technologies include devices, software, apps, and 2.0 options. As teachers teach in schools where electronic devices have been selected and the teachers are all more or less on the same page, perhaps, then it becomes easier to move ahead with certain types of professional development that guides everyone involved toward success with CCSS. The first part of the decision is not likely up to the teacher alone. Will the school do a one-to-one distribution of iPads, tablets, mobile devices, or laptops or will the teacher have his or her own device to teach with while students use only occasional devices from shared sets or labs? Once this major decision is made many more decisions will follow about how to select the supportive technologies, which include projection devices, printers, apps, software, and Web sites to be used in the classroom.

Given that students will need technology skill for the PARCC tests and assessments, appropriate technologies are a must. The learners will be forever developing their skills in using technology. This will be a priority throughout the school year. Throughout the year, students should receive their instruction in less and less traditional ways and be involved with technology as a tool to access the content material. This challenge will vary in degree according to the school's decision to provide the technology and then also will depend on the preparation of teachers. Lessons will become those that integrate the use of technology so that the test items will be familiar and students will know how to go about taking the tests.

Classrooms will not only need those devices, but in addition will need a selection of software, apps, or Web 2.0 opportunities in order to prepare students for the tests taken electronically. Will students be well-versed and comfortable? The answer is "yes," if the classroom instruction is smooth, integrated, and done by knowledgeable teachers. Miller (2014) addressed this:

> For example, teachers can use Edmodo or Socrative for formative assessments that look just like the end of course assessment in any course. Or a teacher might use Poll Everywhere to ask multiple choice questions or short-response questions to check for understanding at the end of a lesson. By embedding "test prep" into the curriculum, not only are teachers preparing students for the PARCC or Smarter Balanced assessments, they are also using it as a meaningful component of instruction and assessment. (42)

Selecting and embracing technology is part of the shift toward a purposeful integration that will focus on student learning and support for the school curriculum and teacher readiness as well. According to Miller (2014), "Common core assessment readiness isn't just about being prepared in terms of the infrastructure, it's about exposing students to meaningful technology integration and using technological assessments in a meaning and intentional way" (42).

Schools can potentially select technology that provides for reading e-books on mobile devices. In this scenario, as students develop digital literacy, they would be able to use their device to read, use a dictionary electronically, search the text, note and highlight in the e-book, and more as they access learning seamlessly. According to Larson (2015), "Perhaps the greatest advantage of e-books is the ability to differentiate literacy instruction for all learners" (42).

The technology choice is drastically changing from whether or not to teach and learn with technology to which technology to use. In *Educational Leadership*'s May edition, the theme was Teaching with Mobile Devices. Warschauer and Tate (2015) explain, "Digital technology in education is here to stay. It's no longer a question of whether to allow digital devices, but rather which devices—and more important, how to implement them" (65). Each school and district will need to gauge where their teachers are and assess the necessary professional development needed as they select which devices to adopt in order to best deliver the curriculum and achieve the CCSS goals.

ENGAGE CREATIVELY WITH TEACHING STRATEGIES

When teachers engage creatively with teaching strategies, it is critically important that they seek out the ways to best meet the needs of the lesson and the learners. The teacher will explore all the necessary outcomes of the lesson in order to determine how best to teach the lessons in the context of other lessons that day or lessons throughout the week or unit. There are so many possibilities, and the teacher is the one who knows the context of their classroom and thus becomes the expert in selecting the teaching strategies to best meet the needs of all of the students. Teachers will take into account the variety of possible teaching strategies that will most accurately address the learning modalities, special needs, time frame, digital tools, classroom space, and more in deciding which strategies will be most likely to engage the learners creatively.

Planning for instruction includes a lot of thinking, and the teacher actually develops the mindset for strategizing. Some of the important questions I ask pre-service teachers to consider are:

1. What digital tool might I use to make the lesson interactive?
2. In what ways will I achieve the necessary differentiation for all students?
3. Will part of the lesson require students to be self-directed or independent, and what technologies or digital tools will students use?
4. In the actual lesson, will listening be an appropriate amount of time in comparison to the time students will engage interactively or independently?
5. Will I use video, PowerPoint, Prezi, Vimeo, or VoiceThread or other digital tools in teaching? What part of the lesson will use other types of medium or manipulatives?
6. Which style best suits the lesson, using video in advance and engaging with the flipped concept of learning or video as the introduction or in a closing?
7. How do I believe this lesson aligns with the CCSS being addressed?
8. Does the lesson invite student voice, parent voice, or other stakeholders like special education assistants who might work in the classroom?
9. Have I planned for auditory, visual, and tactile learners?
10. Does the lesson make real-world connections, and how will I connect the lesson to previous lessons and future lessons?

In order to think about how these questions are answered by teachers, I will introduce some of the choices teachers may ponder in determining how they plan. The first example is of a social studies lesson where the teacher is using the literacy skills of reading, writing, and listening and speaking. Students would listen to several famous speeches on YouTube, reading a trade book or novel about the person, for example, Abraham Lincoln, President Obama, or Malcolm X. Then students would write a short speech of their own and record it on Vimeo or VoiceThread, using their own still shot or creating a short video while delivering their own short speech. The teacher would make a variety of differentiation decisions about some students with special needs but would keep in mind that even students with speech difficulties, for example, often prefer to engage in the activity fully. It is up to the teacher to create the kind of learning environment where all children feel welcome and validated and where peers treat one another with respect throughout the day. Here we must imagine an eager and studious youngster with a speech challenge. They may prefer recording the speech at the computer than facing the class while speaking.

To be practical, a teacher will most readily engage with tools that work with ease. Take the example of a reading teacher planning for strong literacy skills. It is important to get students to read as much as possible. Gura (2014) explains the need to reach all students, "Many of these students have had limited success with reading, so I promote interesting, fast-paced books that deal with compelling teen-life situations" (17). Gura's literacy discussion goes on to suggest, in this case, using Goodreads (www.goodreads.com), which may be quite beneficial because it offers its virtual bookshelves across numerous genres and age levels as well as skill levels. Students and teachers can organize their own bookshelves, read, answer questions, read blogs, or participate in blogging on the Web site. If the goal is for students to enjoy reading and find something of interest, the Goodreads option does both. It also delivers an interactive school community for students to validate their own thoughts as they read. I have used Goodreads and have found that the selections, though the books are electronic, have a great amount of appeal. Since one of the goals for CCSS is to attain digital literacy, the exercise of reading electronically is an appealing and practical activity for most students. Students will practice skills here that they will apply later as they demonstrate literacy skills of reading and synthesizing reading materials. The teacher who decides to help students make this shift for some pleasurable reading will be doing them a great service. This strategy is both engaging and creative. Students will have tools for highlighting, and can hover over a word for its meaning. It's easy to imagine that more children may engage in looking into word meaning, since it is instantaneous.

In another scenario, as an ELA teacher began planning language arts lessons, it would be important to consider what CCSS is to be covered. Gura (2014) discussed in "Teaching Literacy in the Digital Age" how the CCSS can be seen in a variety of ways but hopes, "the Common Core standards will be seen instead as a rationale for doing wonderful projects and activities that foster student expression and creativity and that are highly engaging" (6). Take, for example, a teacher who is teaching the standard that covers reading information texts. The teacher might decide that the best strategy includes having students write a persuasive essay. The teacher then decides this lesson is project-friendly. It can include reading the informational texts (RI) and writing (W), but still further, it is possible through using the same investigation into the informational text that students would also cover speaking and listening (SL) and record their voice for a short video or TV special on the topic they have selected. After students access the material for reading on their topic, they would then synthesize this and persuade their reading audience to agree with their own perspective. They would then add digital images, links to expert sources, and record their own voice in stating the most convincing details. Students could enjoy this type of integration, which is creatively engaging. The writing assignment could be specifically writing and editing a script in draft and then final versions. A script and peer-editing tool can be found at: www.teachwithvideo.com/download_archives/Sports_ Skill_Peer_Resp.pdf.

The purpose here would be writing and editing. Students have some opportunity to engage in topics of their own reading interest. The levels and degrees to which each student does all of the components is where the teacher makes some determination around differentiation. The teacher may reduce the length of the writing or reading or may allow students to opt out of some of the project's components altogether. It is part of the teacher's understanding of the ways to best meet the needs of the lesson and the learners.

Finally, a teacher in middle school is using the CCSS in language arts, language, writing, listening and speaking, and reading informational texts, but is engaging the student creatively by asking them to analyze and evaluate and to think critically about solving some real-world problems. These lessons will prepare students of the twenty-first century for business, government, and more by asking students to engage creatively and critically to better understand today's water supply worldwide. The end result that the teacher has assigned is a documentary video. Each week, a section of the assignment is submitted for a progress check. Students will integrate core understandings they have of time, regions, science, current efforts to sustain water supplies, and more. They will prepare to become experts and the outcomes will demonstrate not only their knowledge but also their digital skills. There are many digital skills and it cannot be emphasized enough that care be taken in selecting what will help students meet the standards, not just engage with digital technologies. A digital tool resource for the movie-making skills can be found at www.teachingwithvideo.com/movie-rubrics.html.

CONCLUSION

After discussing modeling the use of technology, designing technology-rich lessons, selecting appropriate technologies, and engaging creatively, it is obvious that teachers and pre-service teachers are the most important players on the field. Each teacher's own focus on the digital journey is key to the future of our classrooms. Each one must be cognizant of their own opportunity and be willing to build their own personal skills to help them swim in the sea of possibility. Teachers are great visionaries. And positive energy can result in major successes. Teachers possess tremendous power and I am confident that, given more tools, they will do a great job embracing the challenges discussed in this chapter. With careful planning it is possible to create new learning spaces that embrace twenty-first-century learners. Teachers are not alone in the need for embracing technology; it has swept the country and the world into a new sort of information age. As we engage in the process of teaching the CCSS while selecting and integrating educational technology, what resonates the most with me is that if we are doing CCSS because we have to, at least we can enjoy the fact that the standards generate opportunities for students to engage digitally with awesome projects and stay deeply involved with their learning. Maybe the new synergy and way of life in the digital world doesn't appeal to everyone, but to me, at least, I feel that never before has education had the potential to be so personalized and so personally rewarding. The production of digital media alone is not just satisfying; it is far-reaching and has great potential.

REFERENCES

Dougherty, E. (2012). *Assignments Matter: Making the Connections That Help Students Meet Standards*. Alexandria, VA: ASCD.

Drapeau, P. (2014). *Sparking Student Creativity*. Alexandria, VA: ASCD.

Gagnon, D., Monroe, M., and Smith, R. (2015 May). "Tales from the flipped classroom." *Tech and Learning 34*(10): 34.

Gura, M. (2014). *Teaching Literacy in the Digital Age*. Eugene, OR: International Society of Technology in Education.

Khan, S. (2012). *The One World Schoolhouse: Education Reimagined*. New York: Hachette Book Group.

Larson, L. (2015). "The learning Potential of e-books." *Educational Leadership 72*(8): 42–46.

Miller, A. (2014). "It's bigger than the backbone: 4 steps to prepare teachers for CCSS assessments." *Tech and Learning 34*(10): 40.

Ray, K., and Zanetis, J. (2009). *Interactive Videoconferencing*. Eugene, OR: International Society for Technology in Education.

Warschauer, M., and Tate, T. (2015, May). "Going one-to-one, 2.0." *Educational Leadership 72*(8): 60–65.

WEB RESOURCES

"Achieve the Core" has articles, tools and resources: www.achievethecore.org.

Berger, R. "Austin's Butterfly." www.youtube.com/watch?v=hqh1MRWZjms.

Teaching Channel Videos for success in the CCSS: teachingchannel.org/videos?categories+topics_common-core.

ELEVEN

Formative Assessment Strategies

An Essential Element for Effective Classrooms

Katherine S. McKnight

The term "formative assessment" has been tossed around for years, at least since 1967 when Michael Scriven explained how information gathered from evaluation can contribute to changes in a program and its teaching method (Greenstein, 2010).

The Council of Chief State School Officers (CCSSO) defines formative assessment as "a process used by teachers and students during instruction that provides feedback to adjust ongoing teaching and learning to improve students' achievement of intended instructional outcomes" (McManus, 2008).

It's clear from this definition, formative assessment isn't one particular classroom strategy or technique. Frequent quizzes can be an element of formative assessment, but they don't begin to represent the full scope of it.

In a 2013 interview with Catherine Gewertz of *Education Week*, Margaret Heritage, a well-respected authority on formative assessment and its role in the classroom, discussed this misconception:

> Margaret Heritage, the assistant director for professional development at CRESST, a center for assessment research based at UCLA, dismissed the common view that formative assessment is about "giving more frequent mini-tests."
>
> She said it is a set of practices that are designed not only to figure out how well students are learning as they go along, but to provide feedback to them in concrete, actionable ways that enable them to make progress. Part of the work, too, Heritage argued, is to teach students to

self-assess, self-monitor and self-regulate, so they are more empowered learners. Too often, she argued, the education field discusses teaching and learning in a way that frames students as passive recipients.

"People still talk about delivering instruction to children, as if they're mailboxes into which learning will be delivered," she said. (Gewertz, 2013)

Instead of referring to one type of testing or one kind of teaching technique, formative assessment refers to an ongoing process of gathering information about students' understanding and using that information to adjust teaching or learning. Formative assessment is a process that creates a feedback loop between teacher and student that fosters student growth and achievement. It requires flexibility on the part of both student and teacher. Just as a teacher can adjust based on data gathered during formative assessment, so can a student. Because every circumstance is different, effective formative assessment shows up in many guises.

So much of what happens in a well-functioning classroom requires formative assessment. Every time a teacher designs a review activity using a different instructional strategy to help a struggling student grasp a concept, that's formative assessment in action. When the teacher gives a "pop quiz" at the end of class, discovers there is some confusion about one aspect of the material and so reviews that material the next day, that is formative assessment. When students are encouraged to share what they already know about a particular topic before it's presented so the teacher can gauge how to introduce the material, that's formative assessment. Likewise, when a student self-reflects on a classroom activity, acknowledges when and if "a light bulb went on," that is formative assessment.

To the untrained eye, they may not look like they have anything in common. But formative assessment, especially as it is applied to the new standards-aligned classroom, has five distinct attributes:

1. *Learning Progressions*: Learning progressions should clearly articulate the sub-goals of the ultimate learning goal.
2. *Learning Goals and Criteria for Success*: Learning goals and criteria for success should be clearly identified and communicated to students.
3. *Descriptive Feedback*: Students should be provided with evidence-based feedback that is linked to the intended instructional outcomes and criteria for success.
4. *Self- and Peer-Assessment*: Both self- and peer-assessment are important for providing students an opportunity to think meta-cognitively about their learning.
5. *Collaboration*: A classroom culture in which teachers and students are partners in learning should be established. (McManus, 2008)

We'll examine these attributes one by one.

LEARNING PROGRESSIONS

As a student learns, his or her skills grow and they're able to grasp concepts of increasing complexity. In the new standards, examining an anchor standard's relationship to its grade articulations can best exemplify this progression.

The anchor standard represents the "big picture"—the goals that all students will strive toward in order to be considered college and career ready when they leave school after twelfth grade. The grade articulations are the steps along the way. Grade articulations offer the teacher and learner clearly expressed short-term goals. These short-term goals help in both lesson planning and assessment.

The following example is from the Common Core State Standards (CCSS), but similar examples can be found in almost all the newly adapted standards.

Before we look at an example, it will be helpful to review a few things about the CCSS. First, college and career readiness is the overall objective. It's what every student is aiming for—even kindergarteners. Second, it's important to recognize that all CCSS standards, whether anchor standards or grade-level articulations, are student centered. That is, they are written from the students' perspective and they enunciate the students' goals. In other words, the teacher's job is to help each student achieve the goal. The standards are not goals for the teacher to achieve.

As we explore the first writing standard we can see how it is broken down into its grade articulations. The learning progressions are clearly visible:

Anchor Standard *(College and career ready students are expected to)*:

> Write arguments to support claims in an analysis of substantive topics or texts, using valid reasoning and relevant and sufficient evidence.

Kindergarteners *(are expected to)*:

> Use a combination of drawing, dictating, and writing to compose opinion pieces in which they tell a reader the topic or the name of the book they are writing about and state an opinion or preference about the topic or book (e.g., My favorite book is . . .).

Grade 1 students *(are expected to)*:

> Write opinion pieces in which they introduce the topic or name the book they are writing about, state an opinion, supply a reason for the opinion, and provide some sense of closure.

Grade 2 students *(are expected to)*:

Write opinion pieces in which they introduce the topic or book they are writing about, state an opinion, supply reasons that support the opinion, use linking words (e.g., because, and, also) to connect opinion and reasons, and provide a concluding statement or section. a teacher's philosophy, and a mindset.

Grade 3 students *(are expected to)*:

Write opinion pieces on topics or texts, supporting a point of view with reasons.

    a. Introduce the topic or text they are writing about, state an opinion, and create an organizational structure that lists reasons.

    b. Provide reasons that support the opinion.

    c. Use linking words and phrases (e.g., because, therefore, since, for example) to connect opinion and reasons.

    d. Provide a concluding statement or section.

Grade 4 students *(are expected to)*:

Write opinion pieces on topics or texts, supporting a point of view with reasons and information.

    a. Introduce a topic or text clearly, state an opinion, and create an organizational structure in which related ideas are grouped to support the writer's purpose.

    b. Provide reasons that are supported by facts and details.

    c. Link opinion and reasons using words and phrases (e.g., for instance, in order to, in addition).

    d. Provide a concluding statement or section related to the opinion presented.

Grade 5 students *(are expected to)*:

Write opinion pieces on topics or texts, supporting a point of view with reasons and information.

    a. Introduce a topic or text clearly, state an opinion, and create an organizational structure in which ideas are logically grouped to support the writer's purpose.

    b. Provide logically ordered reasons that are supported by facts and details.

    c. Link opinion and reasons using words, phrases, and clauses (e.g., consequently, specifically).

    d. Provide a concluding statement or section related to the opinion presented.

Grade 6 students *(are expected to)*:

Write arguments to support claims with clear reasons and relevant evidence.

    a. Introduce claim(s) and organize the reasons and evidence clearly.

    b. Support claim(s) with clear reasons and relevant evidence, using credible sources and demonstrating an understanding of the topic or text.

    c. Use words, phrases, and clauses to clarify the relationships among claim(s) and reasons.

    d. Establish and maintain a formal style.

    e. Provide a concluding statement or section that follows from the argument presented.

Grade 7 students *(are expected to)*:

Write arguments to support claims with clear reasons and relevant evidence.

    a. Introduce claim(s), acknowledge alternate or opposing claims, and organize the reasons and evidence logically.

    b. Support claim(s) with logical reasoning and relevant evidence, using accurate, credible sources and demonstrating an understanding of the topic or text.

    c. Use words, phrases, and clauses to create cohesion and clarify the relationships among claim(s), reasons, and evidence.

    d. Establish and maintain a formal style.

    e. Provide a concluding statement or section that follows from and supports the argument presented.

Grade 8 students *(are expected to)*:

Write arguments to support claims with clear reasons and relevant evidence.

    a. Introduce claim(s), acknowledge and distinguish the claim(s) from alternate or opposing claims, and organize the reasons and evidence logically.

    b. Support claim(s) with logical reasoning and relevant evidence, using accurate, credible sources and demonstrating an understanding of the topic or text.

    c. Use words, phrases, and clauses to create cohesion and clarify the relationships among claim(s), counterclaims, reasons, and evidence.

    d. Establish and maintain a formal style.

    e. Provide a concluding statement or section that follows from and supports the argument presented.

Grade 9–10 students *(are expected to)*:

Write arguments to support claims in an analysis of substantive topics or texts, using valid reasoning and relevant and sufficient evidence.

    a. Introduce precise claim(s), distinguish the claim(s) from alternate or opposing claims, and create an organization that establishes clear relationships among claim(s), counterclaims, reasons, and evidence.

    b. Develop claim(s) and counterclaims fairly, supplying evidence for each while pointing out the strengths and limitations of both in a manner that anticipates the audience's knowledge level and concerns.

    c. Use words, phrases, and clauses to link the major sections of the text, create cohesion, and clarify the relationships between claim(s) and reasons, between reasons and evidence, and between claim(s) and counterclaims.

    d. Establish and maintain a formal style and objective tone while attending to the norms and conventions of the discipline in which they are writing.

    e. Provide a concluding statement or section that follows from and supports the argument presented.

Grade 11–12 students *(are expected to)*:

Write arguments to support claims in an analysis of substantive topics or texts, using valid reasoning and relevant and sufficient evidence.

    a. Introduce precise, knowledgeable claim(s), establish the significance of the claim(s), distinguish the claim(s) from alternate or opposing claims, and create an organization that logically sequences claim(s), counterclaims, reasons, and evidence.

    b. Develop claim(s) and counterclaims fairly and thoroughly, supplying the most relevant evidence for each while pointing out the strengths and limitations of both in a manner that anticipates the audience's knowledge level, concerns, values, and possible biases.

    c. Use words, phrases, and clauses as well as varied syntax to link the major sections of the text, create cohesion, and clarify the relationships between claim(s) and reasons, between reasons and evidence, and between claim(s) and counterclaims.

    d. Establish and maintain a formal style and objective tone while attending to the norms and conventions of the discipline in which they are writing.

    e. Provide a concluding statement or section that follows from and supports the argument presented. (NGA and CCSSO, 2010).

When we examine the above grade articulations, for example, we are likely to imagine that fourth-grade student writing assignments are likely to focus on grouping related ideas to support a purpose. That's one of the differences between the third-grade articulation and the fourth-grade articulation. But do the students understand what that means? Do they understand the value of that skill? Can they recognize the grouping of related ideas when other writers do it? Do they believe that they have the tools to make that leap in their own writing? If not, what tools are they missing? These are the questions that are asked and answered during formative assessment.

Formative assessment then, refers to the methods teachers and students use to determine what their skills *are*, what they are *expected to be*, and what the difference is between the two. This leads us to the next attribute of formative assessment.

LEARNING GOALS AND CRITERIA FOR SUCCESS

It stands to reason that students are unlikely to achieve goals that aren't clearly articulated. Everyone wants students to be "better writers," for example. But what does that mean? What exactly is good writing? How will a student know when they're doing it? How will the teacher know?

A sports analogy might be helpful here. Consider the difference between a coach and a cheerleader. A cheerleader shows up on game day, stands on the sidelines, and yells, "Win, team, win!" But a coach makes certain that each and every player understands the game, knows how to score, and has practiced the necessary skills. Then and only then can the coach stand on the sidelines and yell, "Win, team, win!" An effective teacher is a coach, not just a cheerleader.

It's imperative that a teacher be able to enunciate clear goals, give students the necessary tools to achieve the goals, and allow time and opportunity for practice. Clearly articulated standards, like those in the above CCSS example, help make this possible. Effective formative assessment requires the teacher to confirm that each student understands exactly what is expected of him or her. The criteria must be communicated clearly, in language the students understand. And the students, in turn, need to confirm their understanding of the goal. This will determine the nature of the instruction and practice.

DESCRIPTIVE FEEDBACK

Formative assessment demands that teachers provide timely, specific feedback to each student. Rather than comparing his or her work with the work of other students or measuring it against a predetermined "average," however, descriptive feedback is most effective when it compares individual's work to the learning goal. Remember, the point of formative assessment is not to rank or compare students; it is to compare each student's skills to the skills articulated in the goal.

Some teachers encourage students to ask three questions during this phase of formative assessment:

- Where am I going?
- Where am I now?
- How can I close the gap?

Descriptive feedback can happen at any time. In fact, it often happens repeatedly and spontaneously. Feedback that happens while the student is working is often the most effective. And, as with learning goals, feedback must be communicated clearly, in language the students understand.

Regardless of which formative assessment strategy is used, it's important that the feedback be focused on the learning goal rather than reflecting personal judgment. This is important for all students, but especially for students who have a history of achieving below grade level. Education is about more than learning facts; it's about learning to question and reflect. In order for these to become lifelong habits, students need to take ownership of the process. That's unlikely to happen if students adopt a defensive posture. And defensiveness is only one of the common reactions to negative or judgmental feedback. Another response, especially prevalent during peer-assessment but often seen in reaction to teacher-assessment as well, involves doubting the motives of the person giving feedback. Or students may develop what's often called "selective hearing" or "selective reception." Simply put, that means that people who fear judgment often hear only what they want to hear.

Feedback that focuses specifically on the three elements addressed in the above questions, however, empowers students. Experience shows that empowered students are engaged students. Working toward a clearly defined goal builds confidence and confidence leads to success.

SELF- AND PEER-ASSESSMENT

Descriptive feedback doesn't have to come from the teacher. In peer-assessment, students provide feedback to each other. In self-assessment, students assess themselves.

The greatest challenge most teachers find with peer-assessment is creating an opportunity for students to give each other meaningful feedback while also maintaining a safe classroom environment. Giving students guidelines and rubrics to encourage them to focus on the learning goals is useful for this purpose. But the single most valuable thing a teacher can do is to model appropriate feedback. When a class observes the teacher giving constructive, specific feedback that encourages student improvement, they're more likely to be able to do it, too. And, of course, one of the greatest benefits of peer-assessment is that students really do learn from their classmates' successes and mistakes.

Self-assessment encourages students to think self-reflectively by examining their own work based on the feedback they've given to others. When students think meta-cognitively about their learning in this way, they begin to accept responsibility for lifelong learning. They learn to plan for their own education and monitor their own progress. This is the ultimate goal of formative assessment and education in general. It has been argued that assessment methods that leave out this valuable component are insufficient because they lose their effectiveness whenever the teacher (or other evaluator) is removed. As educational theorist D. Royce Sadler famously pointed out:

> A key premise is that for students to be able to improve, they must develop the capacity to monitor the quality of their own work during actual production. This in turn requires that students possess an appreciation for what high quality work is, that they have the evaluative skill necessary for them to compare with some objectivity the quality of what they are producing in relation to the higher standard, and that they develop a store of tactics or moves which can be drawn upon to modify their own work. It is argued that these skills can be developed by providing direct authentic evaluative experience for students. Instructional systems which do not make explicit provision for the acquisition of evaluative expertise are deficient, because they set up artificial but potentially removable performance ceilings for students. (Sadler, 1989)

COLLABORATION

Students who see themselves as partners in the learning process are going to be involved in their own learning. This means a culture of trust and open communication must exist. The classroom needs to be a place of mutual respect and appreciation. A collaborative classroom is characterized by a sense of trust among all participants. Once again, a teacher who models this in his or her interactions with students is much more likely to see it in his or her students' interactions with each other.

W. James Popham, one of the gurus of assessment and its various roles in the American classroom said in his 2006 paper, "Defining and Enhancing Formative Assessment":

> Teachers need to tell their students that "There's a new testing game in our class, and its only function is to help you learn better the things you need to learn!" I suspect you can see that if non-graded formative assessments are made a constant component of what takes place in a classroom, and the thrust of all such formative assessment is to help kids learn, a decisively different atmosphere ought to prevail in that classroom. Students can, sans embarrassment, reveal they don't know something. That's because there is a clear commitment on the part of the teacher to help all students learn what they need to, and the heart of this learn-better game is formative assessment. (Popham, 2006)

In an ideal situation the collaborative nature of education would extend beyond the classroom walls. Entire schools and school districts would support each student's individual learning process, encouraging self-assessment, peer-assessment, and open communication between teachers and learners.

These five attributes of formative assessment make it clear that formative assessment is not one particular kind of measurement or tool. Rather, it is a process that is integral and fundamental to the effective practice of teaching and learning.

GENERAL CLASSROOM STRATEGIES

General classroom strategies emphasize communication—between teacher and student and among the students themselves. There are many ways to explain the connections between what students already know and what they're expected to discover in a particular lesson. The most obvious strategy is, of course, to ask them. Ask them what they understand and ask them what confuses them. This can be done through individual or small group conferencing or as part of a whole class discussion.

Stop Wait Go–Self Assessment

Consider the Stop Wait Go, or traffic light communication, in which students use sticky notes to communicate with the teacher at the end of every class period. The classroom door displays a construction paper "traffic light" with green, yellow, and red circles. Students are instructed to write at least one sentence describing:

- What they learned in class today—post it on the green light;
- What they want to know more about—post it on the yellow light;
- What confused them or stopped their learning—post it on the red light.

Another way to use the traffic light communication is by giving each student a red, yellow, and green popsicle stick. Each student begins the class with a green stick in front of them. If they want the teacher to slow down or repeat a concept, they switch the stick to yellow. If they have a question, they switch the stick to red. This is especially effective for shy students or younger students who might be reluctant to express confusion in front of their peers.

A variation of this communication technique is the simple thumbs up, thumbs down, thumbs sideways. Students give the teacher a "thumbs up" signal anytime during the lesson to indicate that they understand the material. Thumbs down indicates that they're confused or they've lost connection to the material. Thumbs sideways means that they understand the material, but would like additional examples or further explanation.

All three of these strategies encourage students to self-assess. They require them to think meta-cognitively about their learning and determine the difference between grasping a concept, needing reinforcement, and really being "lost." Students who claim to be totally confused can learn to identify exactly where they became puzzled and oftentimes learn to recognize patterns in their own learning. For example, a student who realizes that, "I usually understand the math concepts until we get to the second or third example," might be well on his way to realizing that he's more comfortable manipulating whole numbers rather than fractions. With a little reinforcement, he's likely to be able to recognize that fractions behave like other numbers and don't affect the procedure.

Small group and whole class discussions provide additional learning opportunities while aiding in formative assessment. Consider dividing a class into groups of four or five students and providing each group with samples of student work with the teacher's feedback written on slips of paper. As the students match the feedback to the work sample, they discuss the reasons behind their decisions.

Think Pair Share–Peer Assessment

Similarly, the Think Pair Share activity, which was developed by Frank Lyman in 1981 and has been adopted and adapted by many writers in the field of cooperative classroom development, promotes communication and encourages class participation (Lyman, 1981). It is a great way for teachers to explore students' previous knowledge before a lesson, check students' understanding of material during a lesson, or encourage students to reflect on recently acquired information after a lesson. It's a simple, three-step activity:

1. The teacher poses an open-ended question to which there are a variety of possible answers. The students are given "Think Time"

to independently contemplate the question. This step is vital. Research indicates that students retain more information if they are given time to mull it over.

2. After independent thinking, students turn to face their partners. The pairs work together to share ideas, possibly challenge each other, and clarify their individual answers. Students find themselves having to make sense of their partner's ideas as they relate to their own prior knowledge. Misunderstandings are often revealed and resolved during the sharing phase. The teacher should walk around the classroom during this phase, listening to the discussions but resisting the impulse to interfere with the conversations.

3. The pairs share their ideas with another pair or with the whole class. It's important that each student be given an opportunity to share their *partner's* answer instead of their own. The ability to listen closely and paraphrase their partner's answer is one of the most important skills developed in the Think Pair Share activity. The teacher can adjust the lessons to address misunderstandings or adapt to previous knowledge, as it is expressed during the sharing step.

Regardless of what general strategies a teacher uses on any given day, formative assessment takes time. It requires two-way communication. Group communication is faster than daily individual conferences with each student, but still, teachers have to allow room in their schedule for the assessment itself as well as any changes that might result from what they learn. Formative assessment often requires teachers to rephrase lessons and rethink activities. And students often find themselves requesting more detailed explanations, which teachers have to provide. But the results are worth it. Positive interdependence, individual accountability, class participation, and the ability to adjust learning and teaching to meet individual needs are invaluable steps toward achieving the goals of the new standards.

It's important to note that while these skills are important for all students, students who fall within the achievement gap are especially vulnerable. Oftentimes, students who are at risk and within the achievement gap have had difficult experiences in school. They are particularly vulnerable to punitive, threatening assessment systems. In addition to mastering the material, they need to know how to build skills. In other words, they need to learn how to learn. This kind of formative assessment approach is generative, not punitive. It encourages curiosity and thereby creates the opportunity for learning.

SPECIFIC FORMATIVE ASSESSMENT STRATEGIES

Formative assessment is more than one strategy or collection of strategies: *it's a mindset*. A collaborative classroom, in which students and teachers are equal partners in learning, needs to employ a variety of communication tools. Students need to be aware of their objectives for each lesson, each unit, and each school year. Teachers need to determine students' prior knowledge before starting a lesson; they need to frequently check in with the students to determine if the lesson is working; and they need to adapt the presentation of material accordingly. In addition to the general classroom strategies discussed above, there are myriad specific strategies that can be adapted for a range of circumstances.

Say Something/Ask Something

This strategy is a great way to focus large- and small-group discussions. Essentially, it involves instructing students to make a statement about what they learned during their discussion ("Say Something") and then ask a question precipitated by their discussion ("Ask Something"). Say Something, Ask Something is an effective metacognitive strategy, prompting students to analyze and synthesize what they've learned from a discussion. It encourages students to develop speaking and listening skills as required in most new standards. And, as an element of formative assessment, this activity gives teachers the opportunity to check for student understanding and modify the lesson if necessary.

In a high school-level American history class, it might look something like this:

Teacher—Initiates the activity by asking something: "Who do you think was the smartest founding father?"

Student A—Says something: "I think Thomas Jefferson was the smartest of the founding fathers because he was able to take everyone's ideas about independence and include them in one document: The Declaration of Independence." Then asks something: "What would Thomas Jefferson have written in the Declaration of Independence if he didn't have to include other people's ideas?"

Student B—Says something: "We can't know what he would have done, but I think Thomas Jefferson would have chosen to free all the African slaves if he could have written whatever he wanted to. He was very concerned with freedom and we know he wrote the preamble about how all men are created equal, all by himself." Asks something: "Why didn't Thomas Jefferson just write whatever he wanted?"

Student C—Says something: "I think the Continental Congress was set up kind of like our Congress today. Thomas Jefferson just represented the colony of Virginia. The Declaration of Independence had to be approved by representatives of all thirteen colonies or it wouldn't count." Asks something: "How did they get the idea to set up the Continental Congress the way they did?"

Student D—Says something: "I have no idea how they decided to set up the Continental Congress the way they did! But if I had to guess, I'd guess that England was doing something like that. The founding fathers were all English citizens, so they'd be familiar with English stuff." Asks something: "How did they get the idea to set up the Continental Army the way they did? Was that the way they did it in England, too?"

Student E—Says something: "I bet the army was set up the way the English did it because I'm pretty sure George Washington was an officer with the English army during the French and Indian War, so that's what he would have been familiar with." Then asks something: "Did a lot of the founding fathers participate in the French and Indian War?"

The activity continues like this until every student has had a chance to participate. Notice that the conversation is allowed to flow naturally, as long as it stays more or less on topic. For example, the discussion is allowed to veer into the French and Indian War, but the teacher would intervene and bring the students back to task if they started to discuss the upcoming basketball game. Notice, too, that students are encouraged to guess if they don't have an answer to a question.

Because the activity is serving as a formative assessment, at the end of the activity this history teacher would probably correct some misunderstandings and clarify confusion. For example, these students appear to have forgotten that Thomas Jefferson was a slave-owner. They don't seem to realize that the French and Indian War ended only eleven years before the first meeting of the Continental Congress, so most of the congressional delegates would have been adult men during that conflict. The teacher can use this opportunity to review or maybe use this as a springboard into the next unit of study.

Stop and Write

Like so many of the formative assessment strategies, the Stop and Write activity serves more than one purpose. It allows students to self-reflect on their learning, it gives teachers the opportunity to determine how students are progressing, and it gives students the opportunity to work toward their reading and writing standard goals.

A Stop and Write requires students read a text and reflect on it by filling out a two-column grid: "What I Know" and "What I Think." This flexible strategy is highly adaptable. The text can be book-length or as short as a paragraph. The student-writing can be as short as a sentence or as long as a paragraph. Under most circumstances, when students are reading a text that is two to three pages in length, it's sufficient to ask students to stop and record what they know and what they're thinking about the reading approximately four to five times.

In the first column, under the heading "What I Know," the student should record simple information about the text. Being able to repeat back information indicates the most basic level of comprehension. In the second column, under the heading "What I Think," the student should make predictions about the text. When students are able to anticipate an author's upcoming points, they are reading on a more inferential level. This indicates a higher level of comprehension. But it's not all about reading comprehension skills. Students are also developing writing skills. They are using writing to record details and to document their thinking about a text and what they are learning. Writing informative/explanatory texts to examine and convey complex ideas and information clearly and accurately through the effective selection, organization, and analysis of content is the goal of the CCSS writing standard 2.

It is important that the students choose when to stop, rather than reflecting at predetermined stopping points chosen by the teacher. Experienced teachers know that when students have some kind of choice about their work, they become more engaged and motivated. In addition, leaving this decision up to the student is also a type of formative assessment in and of itself. Where a student pauses reveals how he or she is thinking about the content. Most of us tend to stop and reflect when we are confused or when we grasp a new point. An effective teacher will look for patterns in his or her students' choice of stopping points. *Where* students choose to stop and write is often as informative as *what* they stop and write.

Four Corners

Four Corners is known as a way to improve critical thinking and develop students' decision-making skills. Here is how this commonly employed strategy is explained by the West Virginia Department of Education:

> Four Corners is a quick strategy that can be used effectively in the formative assessment process for gauging student understanding. It can engage students in conversations about controversial topics. The four corners of the classroom can be labeled as Strongly Agree, Agree,

Disagree, and Strongly Disagree. Present students with a statement, like "All students should wear uniforms to school," and have them move to the corner that expresses their opinion. Students could then discuss why they feel the way they do. The teacher can listen to student discussions and determine who has information to support their opinion and who does not. Another way to use Four Corners is associated with multiple-choice quizzes. Label the corners of the classroom as A, B, C, and D. Students respond to a teacher-created question by choosing the answer they feel is correct. They must be able to give a reason for their answer. ("Four Corners," n.d.)

This strategy is popular because it's easily adapted to any grade level, from kindergarten through university-level classes. Depending on the prompt, it can be used in almost any class. It requires little teacher preparation, but it yields a lot of formative assessment information. And the active component encourages full participation from kinesthetic learners.

Learning and Response Logs

Learning logs are a great way for teachers and students to have private conversations. They are particularly well-suited for adolescents who might be reluctant to express themselves in front of their peers. Students maintain a log (like a diary or "captain's log") with a record of their learning. Entries can include achievements, personal goals, reflections, and questions about specific lessons. The teacher has access to the log and reads it to monitor progress toward mastery of the learning targets. In addition, the teacher occasionally writes feedback to the student's entries. Teacher response can include encouragement, clarification, or other descriptive feedback. This focus on metacognition, students thinking about their learning, is coupled with valuable and constructive teacher input.

Whereas learning logs are similar to those kept by scientists, response logs originated in the field of literature study. They offer students a place to respond personally to a text, to anticipate what will happen next, to reflect, and to compose their thoughts about text. They are generally kept private and, as such, are valuable self-assessment tools. They can easily be adapted to other fields of study.

Learning logs and response logs are a simple way to incorporate formative assessment into the classroom. Because entries can be written and read at any time, their use doesn't interfere with otherwise tight classroom scheduling.

This strategy can also be adapted for peer-assessment. Traditional logs can be shared among classmates, of course, but they can also be shared digitally. Some teachers have adapted logs as an online tool in which students enter their reflections on personal blogs. These blogs can be shared with others in the class. Older students in particular benefit from reading each other's insights. Recognizing that others experience the same struggles during a particular course of study has proven to be a powerful motivator.

Entrance Slips

Entrance Slips are particularly useful as a means of assessing students' prior knowledge. As with most formative assessment strategies, it's widely adaptable to a variety of uses. Consider the following examples of how an Entrance Slip could be used.

At the start of a new unit on the solar system, a third-grade science teacher may give each student an index card with request, "Please draw a sample of what you think the solar system looks like." Each student is expected to sketch on the card and turn it in as an "admission ticket" before class the next day. This will provide the teacher with a pre-assessment so that she can begin the unit instruction at an appropriate level. If, for instance, most entrance slips indicate that there are multiple planets circling the sun, the introductory element of the lesson can be covered very quickly. If a significant number of students appear to be confused by the request, the teacher knows to start with basic information. If, however, many of the entrance slips include drawings of galaxies, rocket ships, and astronauts, the teacher will prepare to harness the students' enthusiasm for science fiction and support it with scientific fact.

Before beginning a lesson on the U.S. legislative branch, a ninth-grade civics teacher might ask students to fill out a questionnaire as an entrance slip. Questions on the slip might include:

- What do you think the phrase "parliamentary procedure" means?
- Have you ever watched congressional proceedings on C-Span, YouTube, or other video providers? If so, what do you remember most about it?
- Have you ever watched a movie or TV show about the U.S. Congress? If so, which one?
- Do you know the name of at least one of your U.S. Senators or Representatives? If so, please list it here. If you don't know one, why do you think that is?
- What do you want to learn about the legislative branch of the federal government?

The teacher can then use this information to plan lessons and tailor them to the needs and experiences of the students. The nature of the questions also encourages students to begin contemplating the material even before class starts.

A high school literature teacher is planning to have his class read a few scenes from Shakespeare's *Romeo and Juliet*. Their Entrance Slip to class includes the following instructions:

Now that we've discussed Shakespeare's *Romeo and Juliet*, we're ready to read a few scenes aloud in class. Please rank the following characters from 1 to 7. (1 means you would MOST like to read that role, 7 means you would LEAST like to read that role). This is "gender blind" casting, so boys and girls can request to read any role. Note that you may not get your top request but all students will have an opportunity to read aloud! TIP FROM THE TEACHER: you may want to look over the scenes (Act I sc. 3, Act II sc. 1, and Act II sc. 2) before you make your choices!

_____ Benvolio
_____ Juliet
_____ Lady Capulet
_____ Mercutio
_____ Nurse
_____ Romeo
_____ Tybalt

The teacher has noticed that giving students some voice in what role they'll be assigned significantly increases their enthusiasm. It also encourages them to review the scenes that they've been discussing in class and prompts them to consider them from various viewpoints. By examining the roles that they request, the teacher also gains insight into which characters the students most identify with.

Exit Slips

Exit Slips work much the same way as Entrance Slips. Instead of assessing students' prior knowledge, however, they are more valuable in assessing students' understanding of academic content or indicating students' comfort level or attitude about the material. As with Entrance Slips, they are easily adapted to different classes and different grade levels. Consider the following ways an Exit Slip could be used.

A second-grade teacher hands out exit slips before the end of the day. Each slip includes these instructions, which the teacher reads aloud:

Write about or draw the favorite or most exciting thing that you learned in school today. We might learn more about it tomorrow!

The students have ten minutes to reflect and complete the exit slips before dismissal. They put their exit slips in the basket by the door as they leave for the day. The teacher examines all the exit slips and is pleased to find out that a large number of students enjoyed using rulers to measure various objects around the classroom. Most students were able to measure to the nearest half-inch with little difficulty and they enjoyed comparing the sizes of the books on the library cart. Since they enjoyed measuring so much, the teacher decides to leave the jar of rulers on the bookcase so students can use them during tomorrow's free study time. The teacher also makes note of which students chose to draw an answer as opposed to writing about it. She notices that a few students are attempting to print out complete sentences, including capitalization and punctuation. Because her school focuses on integrated curriculum, she's able to use information from the exit slip to make a formative assessment regarding both the English language arts (ELA) and math standards.

Throughout a forty-minute social studies period, a class of seventh-grade students discusses daily life in Olmec civilization. They discuss the benefits and limitations of pile dwelling, palisades, and mound building as methods of construction; consider the importance of maize as a major food crop; and examine the difficulties of river transportation. Five minutes before class is over the teacher gives each student an exit slip with a single question. The students are expected to hand the exit slip to the teacher on their way out the door. Correct answers get a "high five" hand slap. Incorrect answers get an immediate correction or prompt the teacher to ask, "What would be your second guess?" The completed exit slips look something like this:

- Question: You're a twelve-year-old Olmec youth. What will you probably be eating for dinner tonight? Answer: Maize.
- Question: You live in an Olmec settlement. How will you probably get home from school today? Answer: Canoe or raft.
- Question: You're a fourteen-year-old Olmec youth. What is your favorite sport? Answer: Mesoamerican ballgame.

The next day the teacher randomly distributes the exit slips and the students take turns reading them aloud during what the teacher calls "classroom round table." This serves as a quick refresher of the material and prepares the students to move on to that day's discussion of Olmec religion, artwork, ethnicity, and language. If students have any questions about the previous day's material, they are encouraged to ask each other during this "round table" conversation. The teacher has discovered that the exit slip strategy takes up just about as much time as the "pop quiz" strategy she used to use, but the students find it much more engaging. The playful, egalitarian aspect of it also seems to encourage students to reflect on their own understanding and ask questions if necessary. The round table discussion also helps students work toward the speaking and listening goals as enumerated in the new standards.

An integrated eleventh- and twelfth-grade physics teacher requires her students to turn in exit slips after every class. These slips of paper include a simple checklist:

My name: _____
Today we learned about _____.
_____ I totally understand this and I'm ready to move on.
_____ I'm starting to understand this.

_____ I'm confused. Help!

Comment (optional): _____.

These slips provide both the teacher and the student with a lot of information. Summarizing the day's topic into a few words requires the student to reflect on what exactly was covered in class and how that material fits into the curriculum. If, for example, the point of the class was to examine the difference between mechanical waves and electromagnetic waves, a student who says they learned about and totally understand "light waves" might not understand the material as well as they think they do. The three checklist items encourage the students to evaluate their understanding and also provide the teacher with valuable information as she prepares for differentiated instruction. She's likely to follow up with a group activity that combines students that are beginning to understand and students that already understand the material. Meanwhile she can remediate the students who admit to being confused. The optional comment section is an ideal place for students to ask for clarification on specific aspects of the material. Because older adolescents are often overwhelmed by real and imagined competition, the comment section also provides a safe place for students to admit frustration. An exit slip like this is an ideal tool to prepare each student for his or her impending role in college and the workplace.

In addition to the strategies that have been explained here, many other classroom activities can be adapted for use as formative assessment tools. Consider how graphic organizers, in-class discussions, group projects, individual projects, pop quizzes, and even doodle art could be used to gather information about a student's understanding. Then imagine how that information could inspire adjustments to teaching and learning.

Appropriate and effective use of formative assessment requires both students and teachers to be flexible, creative, and cooperative. And because every situation is different, formative assessment can be expected to look different in every classroom.

REFERENCES AND RESOURCES

"Four Corners." (n.d.). Four Corners. West Virginia Department of Education. Retrieved from wvde.state.wv.us/teach21/FourCorners.html.

Gewertz, Catherine. (2013, 8 April). "Busting Up Misconceptions About Formative 'Assessment'" *Education Week*. Retrieved from blogs.edweek.org/edweek/curriculum/2013/04/httpwwwwestedorgonline_pubsres.html.

Greenstein, Laura. (2010). "Chapter 1 The Fundamentals of Formative Assessment." In *What Teachers Really Need to Know about Formative Assessment*. Alexandria, VA: ASCD.

Lyman, F. (1981). "The responsive classroom discussion: The inclusion of all students." In A. Anderson (ed.), *Mainstreaming Digest*. College Park: University of Maryland Press.

McManus, S. (comp.) (2008). "Attributes of Effective Formative Assessment." Formative Assessment for Students and Teachers (FAST) and Council of Chief State School Officers (CCSSO). Retrieved from www.ccsso.org/Documents/2008/Attributes_of_Effective_2008.pdf.

National Governors Association (NGA) Center for Best Practices and Council of Chief State School Officers (CCSSO). (2010). *Common Core State Standards (ELA)*. National Governors Association Center for Best Practices and Council of Chief State School Officers. Washington, DC: Authors.

Popham, W. James. (2006, 15 September). "Defining and Enhancing Formative Assessment." Consortium for Policy Research in Education (CPRE). Retrieved from www.cpre.org/ccii/images/stories/ccii_pdfs/defining%20formative%20assessment_popham.pdf.

Sadler, D. R. (1989). "Formative assessment and the design of instructional systems." *Instructional Science 18*(2): 119–44.

TWELVE

College and Career Readiness in the Classroom

Elizabeth Knost and Elizabeth Perry

Teaching in today's world poses many challenges. Teaching in a building where 72 percent of your students are on free/reduced lunch and in a classroom where most read anywhere between one and eight years below grade level is daunting. With the changes in state standards in all subject areas shifting to a college and career readiness approach, closing the achievement gap in these "low" students becomes even more critical. The majority of high school English Language Arts (ELA) teachers are not reading teachers and are required to deliver a complex level of text to their students at the grade level in which they are currently enrolled. Many of these students cannot effectively read or comprehend at grade level. This chapter will focus on closing the achievement gap in the classroom while emphasizing the role of complex texts in the era of new college and career readiness standards.

WHO WE ARE

We, Elizabeth Knost and Elizabeth Perry, teach ninth-grade English Language Arts at a public high school, with a population of roughly two thousand students. Nearly five hundred of these students are freshmen who are divided among seven ninth-grade English Language Arts teachers: four teachers have three sections of ninety-minute blocks, two teachers have nine sections of forty-five-minute blocks between them, and we have one teacher who has self-contained classes which are also in ninety-minute blocks. Approximately 50 percent of freshmen are in ninety-minutes blocks; they have either failed the state standardized test in English Language Arts the previous years or have been identified as those that need special education services either in self-contained classes or in Regular Education Initiative (REI) classes that contain a co-teacher. Some of these freshmen are also selected to receive their education in one of two alternative settings: Success Academy, which is housed within the high school, or COMPASS, which is the alternative school off campus where students are in smaller classes and receive counseling services as well as instruction in English Language Arts, mathematics, and physical education.

I (Perry) teach in an alternate setting within the high school. Success Academy, a school within a school, consists of freshmen and, up to the 2015 to 2016 school years, also housed a small group of sophomores. The Success Academy offers small-class size (typically no more than eighteen students), opportunities for one-on-one instruction, a team of six teachers, and an intense focus on closing the achievement gap while meeting the needs of the students psychologically and emotionally. Oftentimes these students are not able to function in the "regular" school setting and are anywhere from one to eight years behind their grade level in reading. Success Academy has its own dean and instructional coach in order to meet the needs of these students. Math and English Language Arts classes are blocked in ninety-minute sections rather than the traditional forty-five-minute sections to provide a more intense focus on curriculum. Students have been placed in the Success Academy based on previous academic performance, behavior performance, Lexile levels, state standardized test scores, and recommendation of previous teachers and administrators. We also have the ability to absorb some students who have Individualized Education Plans (IEP); however, this number on average totals no more than a handful of students in the Academy's population. Seventy-six percent of our students are on free/reduced lunch and primarily come from the lower-income demographic of the town. Many of my students have been in the Success Academy since junior high school and continue to stay in it at the high school level until they phase out at the end of the semester or end of year into "regular" school. In order for this to happen, students need to have good behavior, good grades, good effort, and be reading on or above grade level. We also use formative and summative assessments to determine whether or not a student should be moved out of the Academy as well as teacher recommendation.

I (Knost) am a ninth-grade English Language Arts teacher. I teach in an REI co-taught classroom. This means that my students are a combination of neuro-typical and special education students, and there is a special education teacher in the classroom to help differentiate instruction. We have roughly a one-to-one ratio of neuro-typical to special education students. Beginning in the 2015 to 2016 school year, my classes are housed in a "Freshman Center," an area of our school building designated for only ninth graders. Mine is the only ninth-grade REI class in the building. Because my students are well below grade level (in some cases barely decoding with little or no confidence or ability to comprehend and analyze literature), my classes are all double-blocked: students are in my room for ninety minutes a day rather than the typical forty-five minutes. Selection for REI classes is based on standardized test scores, Lexile levels, grades, teacher recommendation, and IEP mandate. While 88 percent of my students are on free/reduced lunch, I have the added "challenge" of meeting the requirements of IEPs and Behavioral Intervention Plans for many of my students. In order to meet these specific student needs and help close the seemingly insurmountable achievement gap in larger (twenty-five- to thirty-student) classes; it is evident that student-directed instruction that includes differentiation of text materials and frequent formative assessment is essential.

INTEGRATED LITERACY MODEL

Historically, the secondary English classroom has been a very traditional setting: desks in rows, novels, worksheets, textbooks, lectures, and so forth have been the norm. While this model seemed to be a very effective and efficient one, research by educators such as Sheryl Feinstein (2009) have shown that we need to "place less emphasis on textbooks and more on projects. Take away sedentary seat time and actively involve them in learning." Students today, and particularly those in special education and alternative settings, are finding it increasingly difficult to thrive in such a teacher-centered setting.

Rather than utilizing the more traditional classroom atmosphere, we have moved to an Integrated Literacy Model in our classrooms. The Integrated Literacy Model uses varied instruction and alternative seating arrangements in order to best support even our most struggling students, especially in the areas of reading and comprehension. An Integrated Literacy Model is one in which a teacher combines all aspects of writing, reading, speaking, listening, and college and career readiness, into the curriculum every day. This is done so that students see a connection between topics and ideas, and so that standards are taught as companions to one another, rather than each standard being its own isolated unit. The Integrated Literacy Model places a significant emphasis on teacher modeling and gradual release of responsibility (GRR) as a means to support and elicit positive work habits, which are foundations of skill development and academic independence, as articulated in Indiana standards 9-10.RL.1 and 9-10.RN.1, which speak specifically about literature and nonfiction texts, but which both state that "by the end of grade 9, students interact with texts proficiently and independently at the low end of the range and with scaffolding as needed for texts at the high end of the range. By the end of grade 10, students interact with texts proficiently and independently." And, 9-10.RV.1 states that students will be able to "demonstrate independence in gathering vocabulary knowledge when considering a word or phrase important to comprehension or expression." We practice the gradual release of responsibility in a series of somewhat methodical steps. Typically in our classes, we begin with a mini-lesson, which may be somewhat or entirely teacher led, after which students work in small groups or pairs to practice utilizing the tools we are teaching. It is sometimes after these small group or partner pairings that we move into centers, where students do work individually. Because of its structure, the gradual release of responsibility model is also sometimes called the "I do, we do, you do" model. Due to it being essential that students move from the hand-holding of the teacher-centered model and become independent thinkers and learners, we use a variety of methods with increased responsibility, including the following:

- Literature circles
- Close reading strategies
- Sticky notes
- Audiobooks
- Journaling
- Sustained silent reading with choice of novels
- Text structure

We also incorporate a lot of direct instruction elements into our mini-lessons and small group instruction. These techniques not only serve as a guide while we are discussing content, but also as a reference for our students once they are released to work independently. Some of the direct instruction supports we typically use are:

- Anchor charts
- Choice
- Graphic organizers
- Essential questions
- Content-related bell ringers

Because standardized testing will be conducted using grade-level readings, and because we know that the best way to improve reading skill is to read more, we are expecting our students to read eight to ten complete works throughout the year. Our hope is that even our most reluctant readers will move closer to grade-level by the end of the school year. In a traditional classroom setting, our particular students would drown in their own confusion. In an Integrated Literacy Model classroom, they are not only thriving under this level of academic rigor, but they are closing in on grade-level reading skills at an incredible rate.

One of the techniques that we use frequently in our classrooms is a center approach. Centers are used regularly in elementary school classrooms, but are unfortunately often dropped from curricular norms at the middle school level in favor of a more rigid teacher-centered structure. In a secondary classroom where students are expected to master grade-level appropriate skills, but in which many students are reading well below grade level, centers are a marvelous differentiation technique. Not only are students able to choose literature that is interesting to them in a center model, they also allow students to work at their individual reading levels, while working on the same skills as other students without the frustrations of text confusion in the face of lower comprehension.

In Knost's classroom, centers are used on a nearly weekly basis. We begin utilizing centers within the first two weeks of school, in an attempt to establish them as a routine part of the classroom. In my classroom, it is very essential that everything we do be routine from as close to day one as possible. Because of the emotional and academic exceptionalities of many of my students, anything out of the ordinary quickly becomes a road block and I do not want centers to be something that causes them to shut down. Being that my students have such varied reading levels, it is imperative that they also read texts at varied levels. This poses a problem not only for instruction but for assessment as well. One way I have gotten around this potential roadblock is by creating objective-based centers, in which students complete tasks specific to their individual reading while also showing objective mastery. On a typical center day, I will have three to five centers, or stations, set up around the room.

Each center is labeled with very specific step-by-step instructions, so that even after they are released to work, students always have the directions and the goals available. Often my centers are some combination of a vocabulary center, a characterization center, a plot center, a mood or tone center, and a speaking or listening center, during which students complete several assignments to show mastery. In the picture below, students are participating in characterization and vocabulary centers.

In my class, the rotation of students throughout the room always follows the same predictable pattern, so that students quickly become accustomed to the routine of centers. Students move in groups around the room, often based on the texts they are reading. Moving them with students who are reading similar, or the same, texts allows them to discuss as they work and move. This collaboration during centers aids significantly in text comprehension as well as improving students' ability to speak and think critically about a text.

When first setting up a center-modeled classroom, I was very anxious about participation, engagement, and noise level. I expected that these three aspects of the center model would be performed much differently from what was normal in everyday more teacher-centered classrooms. What I did not expect was for my students to surpass their typical classroom behaviors in all of those areas. I immediately discovered that when set up carefully and explained thoroughly, the center model is actually

Figure 12.1.   Students Participating in Characterization and Vocabulary Centers.

very engaging and mostly quiet, with extremely high levels of participation! Because students tend to stay more on-task while using this model, class time actually flows very smoothly and with few interruptions. There is a lot of necessary set up for sure, and centers do not always work perfectly, especially the first time, but with practice and careful execution they support students much more effectively than does a teacher-centered approach. Because most students are used to more of a lecture-style classroom, gradual release of responsibility will need to be very well-modeled and carefully implemented in order for centers to work well.

Unlike Knost, I do not begin the school year immediately with using centers on a weekly basis. Much like GRR, I have to ease my students into the center model of instruction. Because I have several students with Behavior Plans and psychological impediments such as Oppositional Defiant Disorder and Attention Deficit Disorder, my approach to centers has to be thoroughly planned and thought out. Gradually throughout the year, we move to a more centered approach to learning and by the end of the year, my students are able to get up and transition smoothly to the center model. Due to the constantly evolving attendance of my students, sometimes centers are a complete and epic failure and then sometimes there is great success. Once implemented, the center model becomes quite effective in the classroom and the students love those days. In the beginning, I set up no more than two centers and we spent a lot of time modeling how to move back and forth between the centers, how to look for the directions, how to get started on the task at hand, and then how to choose the best representation of their work to turn in for assessment.

The centers I usually begin with are vocabulary and some kind of literary device work that relates to the text such as characterization. Because I begin the first week of school with vocabulary strategies, by the time we begin center work (about six weeks into the school year), I can work directly with the center on literary devices. As time goes on, I add another center usually working with context, and then another one regarding comprehension of the text, then finally, a catch-up center. Because my classes are smaller in size, the most I have working in a group at a center is four students, and I typically do not set up more than five centers. My students become increasingly overwhelmed and try to race the clock if they cannot complete all the tasks at hand. This model, for my students, has increased engagement in the classroom and raised reading and comprehension. It has also instilled confidence in learning with my students.

They continuously learn how to work together and students are grouped based on the book they have chosen for literature circles or ability level. There have been times when I let the students create and run the center themselves (after conferencing with me and showing me that it relates to the content we are reviewing in the classroom). This gives them more of a buy-in to their education. Centers are a lot of hard work. You are constantly moving in the beginning and modeling, for the students, behaviors, how to work together well, how to disagree politely, how to accomplish the task in the given amount of time, how to transition, and how to choose the best representation of their work. The rewards are significant. Students are more engaged in the classroom, you are working smarter and not harder by having less to grade, students are more reflective (eventually) about their work, and you begin to see the achievement gap narrow at an increasingly rapid pace.

When conducting assessments using the center model, teachers (and students) initially feel that collecting and grading every piece of paper is imperative. This would, however, greatly increase the teacher workload and simultaneously create the potential for inflated or deflated scores based more on completion than mastery. In an effective center model, a teacher will often ask a student to hand in just his best work, or his best and most challenging work, or some other combination of assignments. If properly structured, the center model will allow students to conference with teachers during class, so formative assessments can be immediate and provide positive one-on-one interaction between students and their teachers. This actually allows the teacher to cut the paper load, and also gives the student not only choice, but the opportunity to be a voice in his own education. The center approach specifically, and the Integrated Literacy Model in general, are very useful in aiding our students in becoming college and career ready.

DATA

Closing the achievement gap at the secondary level seems almost impossible. Regarding reading and comprehension, it seems insurmountable as (previously mentioned) English teachers are not reading teachers. Our school uses Scholastic Reading Inventory (SRI) three times a year to progress monitor our students' reading levels. SRIs are given in August, January, and May. Many of our students begin the year reading one to eight years below grade level. One of the hardest things to do is close the achievement gap and get secondary-level students to attain massive growth in reading and comprehension. Typically, most students at this level (high school) tend to grow only a few points a year. Lack of interest in reading and non-advantageous use of technology has aided the decline in student growth. Information is received fast and in rapid succession in today's world; thus the idea of taking the time to sit down, read, and comprehend a book is becoming a novelty. By using the SRI data that we collect at the beginning of the year, curriculum is then tailored to best meet the needs of our students.

In the past, we have also used Acuity testing to determine whether or not our students are mastering the standards as put forth by the state. Combined with SRIs, Acuity also gave us an idea of where our students were performing on standards and whether they had achieved the status of mastery, proficient, developing, or basic. One advantage Acuity testing gave us was the ability to pinpoint where each student struggled regarding a specific standard. We were able to utilize the overall classroom report to see across the board where the students performed regarding standards and then break down each student's performance. This was a resourceful tool that aided in tailoring and differentiating instruction in the classroom. Acuity has posed its own problems regarding our academically low students as the district does not feel it is tailored to meet a more "true" read of our students' intellect. Beginning in 2015 to 2016, students will take the Northwest Evaluation Association (NWEA) assessment which questions at the individual student level and thus provides a more accurate assessment of where our students are academically.

Another source of data we use in the classroom is department-wide mini-assessments. These assessments are typically done every three weeks and are conducted over a specific number of standards. Teachers then receive their individual classroom data and can tailor their instruction to go back over skills not at a proficient or mastery level.

Techniques also used in the classroom include putting students in charge of their own data. Not only is this one way to integrate basic math skills into the curriculum, but the students always know where they are data wise and we work on setting their individual goals. Students are given a sheet on which they keep track of their quarterly grades, semester grades, NWEA scores, Lexile levels, and overall goals for the quarter. Included is a section where the students reflect on their performance and determine if they need to tailor their goals. It is discussed in class what the overall Lexile-level goal is for their particular grade level and then a conference is held between the teacher and student to set Lexile-level goals individually. Overall averages are discussed with the students and strategies are brainstormed between the teacher and the student regarding what can be done to help them close their achievement gap. It also gives responsibility to students to take charge and have a say in their education.

Between SRIs, Acuity (now replaced by NWEA), and mini-assessments, teachers are able to progress-monitor their students more effectively. The results of these assessments give a more in-depth look at the student and their proficiency level regarding college and career readiness. It also gives the classroom teacher information needed to differentiate instruction in order to help that student close the achievement gap. We also have to take into account classroom performance. For many of our low students, if they are having a bad day or they are frequently absent, their assessment reflects this. The following example shows the results of one class's Acuity diagnostic assessments. This test was created by the state, covered various standards, and was comprised of two sessions: session one was reading comprehension and session two was grammar. As you can see, students moved up more toward the middle of the year, then toward the end of the school year, they became tired and, while some improved, some went down in scores. This is why it is important to track many different components of data for students.

CASE STUDIES

Success Academy

Adam

Adam came to my class as a freshman with quite the attitude regarding education. He did not want to do anything: did not want to read, did not want to write, and did not want to be anywhere in a classroom if he could not sleep. After testing, it was discovered that Adam was reading and comprehending at a beginning, or BR, reading level. He also qualified for special education services and had an Individualized Education

Name	Acuity A	Session 1 (18)	Session 2 (12)	Acuity B	Session 1 (18)	Session 2 (12)	Acuity C	Session 1 (18)	Session 2 (12)
*Student A		NA	NA		44%	42%		56%	58%
Student B		39%	75%		50%	67%		67%	50%
Student C		33%	22%		56%	50%		56%	25%
Student D		52%	58%		44%	50%		39%	58%
Student E		4%	58%		28%	58%		39%	42%
Student F		17%	42%		61%	50%		50%	33%
Student G		39%	58%		56%	58%		44%	17%
Student H		35%	42%		56%	50%		33%	17%
*Student I		22%	42%		28%	50%		28%	17%

Figure 12.2.   Students Who Came to Success Academy at Semester. Tier 1 (0–25 percent) is beginning level; Tier 2 (26–50 percent) is developmental level; Tier 3 (51–75 percent) is proficiency; Tier 4 (76–100 percent) is mastery level.

Plan (IEP) that teachers were to follow. Adam was placed in Success Academy for a more inclusive classroom situation. The special education classes were already at their maximum amount of students allowed per teacher and Adam needed the smaller class size and different support the Success Academy team was able to offer. It was not easy getting Adam to believe in himself and that he could, indeed, do the work. When conferencing with Adam, I was able to find out that he was embarrassed that he struggled in reading and comprehension and was tired of always being directed toward what he referred to as "the baby books." In doing a student interest inventory with him, a love of sports, music, and even poetry was discovered. I searched through my shelves and came up with several books that catered to Adam's interests. He looked at me with a big grin on his face and said, "Mrs. Perry, these ain't no baby books at all!"

Throughout the semester, Adam worked very hard and began to participate in class and small group discussions. Using the sticky note strategy when talking to the text helped Adam a lot, as did working in centers.

Centers created a nonthreatening environment where *all* of the students helped each other learn the task at hand and where Adam could get help without it being noticeable. Adam thrived in this environment and by January was reading and comprehending at a second-grade reading level, even though curriculum was at a ninth-grade level. Continuing to utilize sticky notes, close reading, centers, and really working on an integrated literacy model with reading, speaking, listening, and writing, and by offering choice, Adam was growing in confidence and in academics. Modeling and utilizing the gradual release of responsibility model helped Adam and many other students as well. It helped immensely if I would model the lesson first then we would all do the lesson and I would then walk around during the independent part of the lesson aiding and assisting as needed. By using the gradual release of responsibility strategy, Adam gained confidence in asking questions and the achievement gap continued to narrow. By May, Adam was at a fourth-grade reading and comprehension level. He had gained nearly four and a half years in just one year. It was the use of the integrated literacy model, centers, gradual release of responsibility, sticky notes, and choice that contributed to his success academically, emotionally, and intellectually.

David

David began his year in Success Academy frustrated that he was not in "regular" school and could not understand why he was up with these other students. During his eighth-grade year, David had experienced some behavior problems and was put in Success Academy to hopefully resolve those issues so he could go to "regular" school. With disgust and a sour countenance, David walked into my room on the first day and said, "I don't care what you do, I hate reading. I *hate* reading. Nothin' is going to make me want to read and I'm not gonna read. Period." My response was "okay, but I've heard this before and I promise you I will at least get you to appreciate reading by the time school's over." David disagreed with me wholeheartedly. I began that day to see what David enjoyed and wanted to do in life. He, like so many of my students, came from a broken home and was living with grandparents.

However, David really enjoyed playing sports, football especially. He knew he had to keep his grades up in order to be eligible to play football—but he still did not like to read. David's Lexile level was that of a beginning eighth grader—on the lower end of the spectrum. After the first assessment, David became very frustrated and wanted to know why his score was what it was. I always explain Lexile levels to my students and help them to understand the purpose behind teachers assessing their reading consistently. David was given his data sheet at the beginning of the semester and at our conference, I sat down and showed him where he was and where we would like him to be regarding his reading. He very

politely folded his hands and said, "Miz Perry, you just don't understand. I hate reading. I don't enjoy it, you just need to quit trying with
me." David actually had one of the higher reading levels in my class
compared to many of the other students.

He was grouped with a pretty active class of students that responded
to more of a hands-on approach to learning. With David, I began to bring
in articles regarding the sports he loved and we would read them together during Silent Sustained Reading and then me, being the non-sports
person that I am, would ask David what this meant and could he "act" it
out with some of the Minions and Pokémon toys I had in the room. I
learned more about defense and football positions that year and more
importantly, David was reading, comprehending the text, *and* enjoying it!
In my class, he enjoyed expressing his opinion and helping other students that were struggling. He became a natural leader in the classroom
and one not afraid to raise his hand and ask for clarification.

My not so outspoken students began to want to work with David as
they could see he was having the same confusions as they were. As with
Adam in the previous case study, David also enjoyed the center model
more as it gave him opportunity to move around and to do more hands-
on activities. Centers also gave him an opportunity to be a leader and to
help his fellow classmates and they became a team in the classroom.
Assessments took the form of projects as I began to give this particular
group alternate choices for assessing. David was also assessed in January
and in May regarding his Lexile level. Although he did not make massive
growth (seventy-three points), the fact that he grew and used strategies
such as sticky notes, talk to the text, alternate assessments, and that I
tapped into what he enjoyed learning and reading, made all the difference. By the end of the year, David was reading closer to a ninth-grade
reading level and admitted, "Aw, Miz Perry, reading isn't all that bad. I
still don't like it very much, but I can appreciate it more now."

Regular Education Initiative Class

Dawn

Dawn is a mild-mannered girl who has never enjoyed English class
because it has always been very difficult for her. She came to my class as
a freshman, and was very quiet and extremely hesitant. When we first
tested reading levels, Dawn tested at a fifth-grade level. She had not read
more than one or two books ever and those only because she had to for
school. Her standardized test scores were in the 20-percentile range early
in the school year. Dawn felt like she was really behind in reading, but
admitted that writing was a little bit fun, at least when she was allowed
to write what she wanted. I quickly discovered that she was a great
writer and a fantastic thinker, and her difficulty with reading seemed to

be as much a confidence issue as it was difficulty with comprehension. Dawn had tons of questions, and when she was reading the "voices in her head" were loud. In class, we took advantage of her strengths.

We utilize a literature circle method quite frequently, and I gave her a "Discussion Director" job, where she could not only show off her leadership skills, but she could invite other students into the discussions she was already having with books. In my classroom, literature circles are sometimes discussion groups and sometimes center groups. As I circulated among groups, particularly on discussion days, I was always careful to mention to Dawn how great her questions were, and to encourage the other students to try to think of more questions like hers. No matter who was in her group, Dawn pushed the other students to think deeper than the words on the page, and encouraged them to come up with questions of their own during discussion. Dawn loved the leadership role, and really thrived on hearing that the thoughts she was having as she read were not only helpful but also insightful. As the year progressed, Dawn's confidence as a reader, a leader, and a student grew tremendously. By May, Dawn's reading level had jumped three grade levels, to an eighth-grade level. While still not quite up to grade level, she felt confident in her own ability, and was choosing to read increasingly complex books independently. For Dawn, small group instruction, literature circles, centers, and choice all made a very strong impact on her educational and social journey.

Mark

Mark walked into my classroom in August with a 602 Lexile level, no desire to participate in class and a real apathy toward academics. As a basketball player with a lot of athletic potential, he was confident he would skate through high school and into a college ball career whether he could read effectively or not. His experience with school had been one in which he was passed on and passed on because of his basketball ability and his "rough life" with no real motivation to push himself academically, and it showed. Mark not only read at a third-grade equivalency, he also struggled to participate in group activities, did very little class work, and often slept through classes.

Despite being a bright student, Mark was not motivated to push himself academically, and definitely did not take kindly to others trying to direct his learning either. Mark was the kind of student that often gets pushed aside. He did not seem to want to learn, and he was often a disruption in class. By the end of first quarter, not only was Mark still reading at a third-grade level, he was also failing ninth-grade English. It was just after the start of second quarter that Mark began to get comfortable in class. He started to participate in group discussions on occasion, read his literature circle novels sometimes, and he even sometimes stayed awake for whole class periods. Mark voluntarily moved his seat away from students that were distracting him, and decided he was going to try to make a name for himself in the classroom, not just on the basketball court. It would be easy if the story ended there and Mark immediately became a model student, but he was a transient student, one whose family often lived in basements or shared houses or even cars. His family did not have electricity for the majority of the third quarter, and had running water for only a few weeks of the fourth quarter. Because of the challenges Mark faced outside of the classroom, his academic work began to again suffer. Mark struggled to stay awake in class most days again, and I knew that if there was a day he dozed frequently, there was probably something going on in his home life.

On several occasions, I took Mark to the hallway and gave him pep talks. Although he was a strong, tough basketball player who stood about a foot taller than me, Mark would often crumple to the floor in tears as he told me about what challenges he was currently experiencing. I would remind him that while basketball might be his "out," he wouldn't get there if he didn't do well academically. He would promise to do his best, and we would have weeks of classroom compliance. Mark spent most of his second semester in this yo-yo, striving to gain control of both his life and his academics. While Mark's reading level didn't increase as drastically as many of my other students (he ended the year with a Lexile level of 825, up 223 points), he was able to pass ninth-grade English with a B for second semester.

Despite starting ninth grade six years below grade level in reading, Mark pushed himself to overcome, and overcome he did. He read six complete books on his own throughout the school year, learned to have positive collaborations with fellow students in a classroom environment, learned to trust his classmates and teacher in the English setting, and became a much more confident reader and student. Although the achievement gap is still quite large for Mark, he now has many of the college and career ready skills he will need to thrive in the rest of his educational career and beyond, as well as the confidence to push himself academically and socially.

CONCLUSION

With students entering their high school years already academically behind in their reading levels, self-motivation and self-monitoring are skills they severely lack. These skills do not magically appear overnight. We get these students at the beginning of the year, most of them hating English Language Arts, complaining of how hard it is, and astonished at the amount of reading of complex texts we expect in the curriculum. One thing you have to understand is that while we discuss Gradual Release of

Responsibility, the Center Model, and working in an Integrated Literacy Model, it takes a lot of time to get the students to the point where everything works seamlessly.

The first quarter of the school year is spent modeling a lot with these students the strategies and skills they will need to be successful in closing the achievement gap. It is not easy. We have students who will be moved to other classes, other teachers, and especially with Success Academy and REI students, it is not unusual to pull a student partway through the quarter and put them in class where they can get more one-on-one instruction and the smaller class size. It is also difficult when students leave the REI classes or Success Academy to go into a more "regular" school-type setting. We are given a new influx of students to take the place of the ones that left and we begin again.

Motivation and high expectations of the students add to their success. Many of our students do not have a champion or solid support system outside of the school environment, so we do a lot of self-esteem building and helping them achieve an "I can" attitude versus an "I can't" one. Our students also do not have solid schema when entering the classroom, so along with building confidence, we also work on helping the students learn to make those connections with the texts they are reading and to think about their own thinking. Because so many of them do not have the confidence to do this, there is modeling done weekly and sometimes daily with close reading strategies.

Being consistent and establishing trust are other factors that help our students. Students that perform at a lower academic rate than others tend to need a more structured learning environment. Trust is an issue in which many of our students struggle. They come into the classroom not believing that we truly want them to succeed and become better readers. This is a consistent characteristic we see in our students due to the inconsistencies in many of their home lives. They have been raised to believe they will only go so far in life and no matter how hard they try, no one truly cares. School is viewed as something they have to do in life, not as a tool that will give them success in the real world. With so many reading below grade level, trust in teacher and trust in self has to be built carefully. This is done through consistency on behalf of the teacher and established routines and norms. Once that trust and consistency is established, the students become more comfortable and the classroom begins to run itself as the teacher becomes more of a facilitator in the roles of guide and motivator.

Choice of reading materials and a variety of complex texts is another element that contributes to the success in closing the achievement gap. In our classrooms, we have a selection of high-interest low-level novels, grade-level novels, and other text sets that might include periodicals and poetry. Students need to feel in charge of their reading choices. By allowing them to have choices, it promotes a higher interest in reading and then the amount of complex texts becomes easier for students to break down, especially when utilizing strategies such as close reading, sticky notes, centers, and such. The achievement gap begins to narrow as these strategies are utilized more and more in the classroom.

We have experienced success in closing the achievement gap by implementing these strategies in our classrooms and including choice. With the new era of standards, we, as teachers, are being called upon to achieve what seems the impossible with students who are performing well below grade level. Our district requires us to follow the curriculum, yet we are given some leeway in tailoring it to our students' needs and to do whatever it takes to get them there. We have found through implementing the integrated literacy model, incorporating centers, and not teaching standards as isolated units, we are reaching above and beyond students' perceived potential and achieving great gains in closing the achievement gap.

REFERENCES AND RESOURCES

Feinstein, Sheryl. (2009). *Secrets of the Teenage Brain: Research-Based Strategies for Reaching and Teaching Today's Adolescents*. Thousand Oaks, CA: Corwin Press.

THIRTEEN

Fast Forward

College and Career Readiness for All

Katherine S. McKnight

Closing the student achievement gap is a challenge that consistently vexes educators. Searching for solutions, educators in many schools tirelessly work toward lessening the gap. In this text, expert educators from their respective fields offer insight in what the college and career readiness movement means. Like many educational movements, there are opinions as to how to best accomplish academic and career success for all students.

As I consider the contributions of the authors, and how their expertise and experiences inform us of pathways for closing the achievement gap in the era of college and career readiness-focused standards, the discourse is largely centered in two areas: affective and cognition. The affective domain largely deals with our attitudes and feelings. The cognitive domain focuses on learning how to think and develop skills for critical thinking. In the twenty-first century, students need to develop greater confidence to create solutions with independence, which is where the cognitive and affective domains intersect.

THE AFFECTIVE IMPORTANCE

Students need to feel confident and competent in order to learn. This is largely addressed in several chapters. Richard Cash asserts in his chapter, "Self-Regulation for Learning," that "educators, curriculum developers and policy makers need to understand the holistic impact self-regulation has on student learning and achievement." Students *must* develop the mindset for learning and school. Without self-regulated learning and a growth mindset, no initiative, textbook, or new program can raise achievement. Creating the kind of environment where students can develop self-regulated learning can be achieved by emphasizing the process and outcome of student work, and providing choices for students. This creates a more motivating environment where children can develop feelings of success and a "can-do" attitude.

LeAnn Nickelsen also addresses the impact of the affective domain and mindset on students who live in poverty in her chapter, "Empower Poverty-Stricken Students for Common Core State Standards Mastery." Nickleson explains that chronic exposure to poverty causes changes in the brain that affect learning. Neuroscience research indicates that environments affect the brain. Enriching school environments can promote student achievement. Schools where there is positive emotional support, nutritious diet, and best practices in curriculum design and instruction can promote a growth mindset in students that fosters achievement.

A growth mindset is manifested in the messages we send to students. Using generative and positive messages about effort are critical to student success. I have often encountered students who are enrolled in remedial classes who don't believe that they can be successful. They often express that they are "doomed" for constant failure. Yet, we see classrooms like Elizabeth Perry's and Elizabeth Knost's, where students are growing a mindset that is resulting in greater academic success. As anyone who works in education knows, students who enter high school reading below grade level and lacking self-motivation or self-monitoring skills present special challenges.

This is particularly true of students whose families have fallen between the loosely woven threads of our nation's social "safely net." In chapter 12, "College and Career Readiness in the Classroom," Knost and Perry describe how four students—Adam, David, Dawn, and Mark—benefited from the integrated literacy classroom model. Practices like small group instruction, kinesthetic learning models, gradual release of responsibility, manipulative use, scaffolding strategies, and the non-threatening peer-supportive environment of classroom literacy centers benefitted those students who were struggling with family transience, homelessness, poverty, and the sleep deprivation that comes with it.

The teachers employed more detailed summative assessment tools and more frequent formative mini-assessments to monitor student progress. This enabled them to differentiate instruction to accommodate the needs of each student. And, in an especially inspired move, the teachers permitted students to help manage their own data. This allowed teachers not only to integrate basic math skills into the curriculum but it gave students a sense of control over their own progress toward their personal goals. It was a double win: teachers integrated basic math skills into the curriculum, and the students were empowered to monitor their own achievement.

Knost and Perry discovered that their early trepidation about the use of varied instruction and alternative seating was unfounded. Rather than losing control, they found that students embraced the less traditional, student-centered learning environment. In fact, the teachers found that students surpassed their previous levels of classroom participation and engagement, and noise levels dropped, when they were allowed to work in learning centers. As is so often the case, struggling individuals respond to being offered more choice, rather than having their options restricted. Their success is largely due to the pairing of outstanding instruction, rooted in the principles of differentiated instruction with a growth mindset that promotes self-regulated learning and academic achievement.

Knost and Perry's classrooms are exemplars for Cash's assertion that *success breeds confidence which breeds success*. Their classrooms also embody how generative environments can break the often causal relationship between poverty and student achievement as discussed in Nickleson's chapter.

THE COGNITIVE IMPORTANCE

The new standards have addressed the reality that American students are failing to meet grade-level proficiencies in reading and mathematics. In response, the new standards are designed to promote more academic rigor to develop the mathematical and literacy skills that students need for the twenty-first century. This is in response to a significant body of research, indicating the level of texts assigned to students in the K–12 classroom has decreased in the last forty years. Consequently, more than 11 percent of students entering college must enroll in remedial reading classes. Even Advanced Placement courses generally require reading that is not rigorous enough for college, and, at one point, paralleled the rigor of newspapers (Hayes and Ward, 1992). In one study, reading achievement in the United States is dire among K–12 students and those who live in poverty face an even greater challenge as described in the Common Core State Standards:

> It should be noted also that the problems with reading achievement are not "equal opportunity" in their effects: students arriving at school from less-educated families are disproportionately represented in many of these statistics (Bettinger and Long, 2009). The consequences of insufficiently high text demands and a lack of accountability for independent reading of complex texts in K–12 schooling are severe for everyone, but they are disproportionately so for those who are already most isolated from text before arriving at the schoolhouse door. (CCSS, 2010, ELA Appendix A, 4)

The Common Core State Standards as well as many state standards indicate that students must engage in more complex texts in order to be better prepared for college and career. The lack of student achievement in mathematics is just as dire as literacy.

Historically, mathematics curricula in the United States tend to be unfocused and lack coherence. Consequently, students are often disengaged with mathematics since it becomes an exercise in mechanical computations rather than a means to solve complex problems. In response, the Common Core State Standards, with input for the National Council of Teachers of Mathematics, created a list of Eight Standards for Mathematical Practice that is also often referred to by other state standards. These are:

1. Make sense of problems and persevere in solving them.
2. Reason abstractly and quantitatively.
3. Construct viable arguments and critique the reasoning of others.
4. Model with mathematics.
5. Use appropriate tools strategically.
6. Attend to precision.
7. Look for and make use of structure.
8. Look for and express regularity in repeated reasoning. (CCSS, 2010, Mathematics, 6)

Michael Troop's chapter, "High-Leverage Practices in Math Education that Bolster Academic Achievement," outlines how the new mathematics standards, rooted in the mathematical practices, impact student achievement. Gone are the days where students completed dozens of computation-based problems. Instead, the emphasis is on how to use mathematical concepts to solve more complex and inquiry-based problems. The standards encourage rigor and conceptual understanding in mathematics as each grade builds on the other for deep comprehension and application of mathematical practices. For mathematics teachers, there is a greater emphasis on application and contextualization of mathematical practice to solve complex problems.

Eileen Murphy, a Chicago educator and founder of ThinkCERCA, also explains the deep cognitive aspects of the new standards and how this is connected to college and career readiness. Like the new mathematics standards and practices, critical thinking and evidence-based argumentation promote a student's ability to apply skills and discipline-specific knowledge to solve complex problems in a wide variety of contexts. Through the innovative Web-based ThinkCERCA platform, which encourages collaborative thinking and debate.

Promoting the critical literacy skills required to develop an effective written argument is one of the most important skills in our personal, academic, and professional lives. Students need to be able to read critically, evaluate and synthesize information from different media, and express what they know and understand through many mediums. When students possess strong skills in critical analysis and evidence-based written argument, success in college and career becomes more attainable. As Murphy argues, this is a key factor in closing the student achievement gap.

For students to be able to think critically in all disciplines, our students must have strong reading skills. The state of reading achievement in the United States is alarming. The majority of our students are not reading at grade level.

Regardless of which standards (whether it's Common Core State Standards or individually developed state standards) our students are aiming for, we teachers have the same goal: develop student literacy skills in order to open doors to all content knowledge. Whether college- or career-bound, all students are going to spend a lifetime bombarded with text. They'll need sophisticated reading skills to sort it all out. And the surest way to achieve it is practice. The "number of pages read" continues to be the most valuable indicator of student literacy achievement. But because not all students read at grade level, educators have to expend time and effort to help them select "just right" texts—that is, texts that are comprehensible and yet appropriately challenging.

The Common Core text complexity model is valuable for teachers in any state. By giving equal weight to qualitative measures and reader and task considerations, in addition to quantitative measures like Lexile scores, the CCSS authors give teachers the authority to tailor text selection to individual students. Scaffolding techniques that incorporate gradual release of responsibility (GGR) support students as complex reading skills are broken down into manageable chunks. Centers-based learning and Fix It Up strategies are two of the most effective ways to incorporate this into the classroom. As Nickleson and Cash assert, when students develop independence and feel good about what they are learning and why they are developing certain skills, students have higher rates of achievement. But whatever instructional methods are used, a strong sequence of skill development combined with plenty of practice time (that also fosters greater student independence), leads to comprehension and mastery for *all* students.

KEY PEDAGOGICAL PRACTICES FOR GREATER STUDENT ACHIEVEMENT

As we move toward these more rigorous standards and ensuring that all of our students become college and career ready, there are other pedagogical practices that are integral to closing the achievement gap: intelligent and strong technology integration to foster rigorous learning experiences, differentiated instruction in order to meet the needs of all of our students and formative assessment which nurtures what Cash calls a "growth mindset" for students.

As Seema Imam writes in her chapter, "With New Standards in Mind: Selecting and Integrating Educational Technologies for Student Success," that twenty-first-century students who have access to seemingly limitless amounts of information require a different education than their parents did. Fact-finding is less of a struggle than sorting through a barrage of data. Consequently, the demand for digital literacy is taking its place beside the demand for traditional literacy. Innovations like flipped classroom learning open up previously unimagined possibilities. Imam explains that teaching, by necessity, now looks and feels different than it did a generation ago. Teachers not only have to align lessons with new standards, they have to determine which classroom technologies students will use, and figure out ways to differentiate delivery to accommodate their students' range of learning styles and abilities.

There is no one simple way to meet all the demands of contemporary teaching. Veteran educators and new teachers alike are required to explore new methodologies and strategies in order to stay apace of rapidly changing technology. Ever more powerful educational resources are bound to replace today's Instagram, Pinterest, social media, and textbook Web sites. Flexibility, innovation, and creativity are key. Teachers have an obligation to be familiar with whatever digital tools are developed because each and every student deserves lessons that make real-world connections. Technology, as Imam asserts, never replaces great pedagogy that promotes rigor and critical inquiry.

Flexibility, innovation, and creativity are common themes that echo through the contributing authors' discussions of college and career readiness in the era of new standards and our most vulnerable students. Our classrooms are more diverse than ever and teachers know that reality firsthand. Our students are not cookie-cutter children who all perform on the same academic level. One of the great joys about teaching and education is that our classrooms are beautifully diverse. Yet, how do we avoid "teaching to the middle" and meet the needs of all of students in the midst of increasing demands and fewer resources?

Melissa Dickson, a veteran public school educator, discusses how differentiated instruction can close the achievement gap and promote greater rigor and success for our students. Differentiated instruction increases the likelihood of student success in standards-based classrooms and enables teachers to reach and teach more learners. Differentiation is doing what is fair for students, sometimes different things for different students.

When research-based differentiated instructional practices replace ineffective instruction techniques, teachers know their students and have established a learning environment that values growth, acceptance, and respect. In these classrooms, teachers, pre-assess to determine what, how, and who to teach, use student-centered best-practice methods, use formative assessments to aid teaching choices, and analyze data to determine student mastery and effectiveness of instruction. Teachers do this with standards and data about each student to plan instruction. When teachers combine the science of teaching with art of teaching, students achieve.

ALL OF OUR STUDENTS CAN ACHIEVE

As an educator for over thirty years, I have always believed that *all* students can achieve and learn. Oftentimes national educational initiatives focus primarily on regular education students. Populations such as English language learners and students with special needs are conspicuously absent from these initiatives. Three educators from Farmington, New Mexico, offer us insight and voice for these students.

As Diane Arrington explains in chapter 9, the rigor of the new standards and college and career readiness offers the opportunity to achieve academic success. Arrington explains how the rigorous academic demands of the new standards, with their focus on skills and higher-order thinking, provide all students, including English language learners (ELLs), an opportunity to excel academically. Historically, ELLs were denied access to high-level content until they were deemed "ready." By isolating one population of learners based on one single factor, ELL students were prohibited from accessing grade-level texts and mathematical concepts until they could prove proficiency. But by accepting *language as a tool for understanding*, rather than a prerequisite goal, the new standards challenge the long-held idea that ELLs lack the ability to process content.

Indeed, the CCSS acknowledge that, "Teachers should recognize that it is possible to achieve the standards for reading and literature, writing and research, language development and speaking and listening without manifesting native-like control of conventions and vocabulary" (CCSS, 2015, Addendum for English Language Learners). Collaboration, an important strategy for all students, is critical to ELLs' development. Traditional conversational support leads to academic conversation and written communication. Technical developments in the classroom also contribute to creating a hospitable environment for language learners. And adoption of the textual complexity model, particularly the aspects of qualitative measures and reader/task consideration, acknowledge teachers' ongoing commitment to helping these students develop the necessary content background for understanding complex texts.

Similar to English language learners, there have been assumptions about students with special needs. As Nicole Lambson and Brenna Sherwood detail in chapter 8, the best practices of the special-needs classroom are essentially the same as every other classroom. Moreover, they are easily incorporated into the new standards-aligned classroom. Activities

like Concept Charades, Four Corners, Thirty-Second Expert, graphic organizer support, and centers-based learning encourage students of all
ability levels to explore content while working toward the same reading,
writing, language development, speaking, and listening goals. As independent learning and self-monitoring become routine, all students discover ways to monitor their own progress, visualize targeted goals, self-
adjust, and self-reflect.

In the new standards, there's no difference between the goals of the
special needs student and those of a "regular" student. The pathway may
bend and twist in different places, and the teacher may need to provide
additional scaffolding, but the target is the same. Just like all educators,
teachers in special-needs classrooms have to express clear expectations
and allow time for active processing and practice. By providing descriptive feedback the teacher models the necessary skills self-monitoring and
thereby sets the student on the path toward lifelong learning. But most of
all, the teacher in a special needs classroom has to provide plenty of
opportunity for success. No child enters school wanting to fail. Professional educators have the obligation to employ motivating, realistic, and
easy strategies that will assist all students on their pathway toward twenty-first-century citizenship.

FLEXIBILITY, INNOVATION, AND CREATIVITY

The student achievement gap has continuously vexed educators. As I
recently wrote in a blog post about the Common Core State Standards:

> There's no magic spell that can transform students into learners. Strong
> standards alone can't do it. Strong standards combined with inspired
> teaching, committed schools, a limitless supply of learning materials,
> and supportive communities can't do it either. Students *themselves* need
> to be ready to learn before learning can happen. This means they have
> to have the emotional and social skills to master basic academic tasks,
> and they have to find meaning in the tasks that teachers ask them to
> perform. Each student needs to independently develop his or her own
> reason to grow. (McKnight, 2015)

As I collaborated with the contributing authors for this volume, it
became increasingly evident how to develop high-achieving students
who are college and career ready is through our ability as educators to be
flexible, innovative, and creative.

When I followed my mother's professional path and became an educator thirty years ago, I was well aware that my career choice would be
packed with challenges. Like my mother, I have witnessed many educational fads and initiatives and as these waxed and waned I always
thought about students, particularly our most vulnerable ones who were
trapped in the achievement gap. When Common Core first emerged in

2010, I was suspicious. Still feeling the professional bruising from No Child Left Behind, which I felt caused more damage to our struggling educational system, I was leery about Common Core.

As I delved into this new framework for college and career readiness, I realized that it was grounded in research-based methodology. In fact, as I reflected on this new framework, I knew in my head and heart that it reflected good teaching and learning. As I have written about Common Core and college and readiness and met thousands of fellow educators and discussed it, we often acknowledge that much of this is not new. In fact, great teaching and learning is based in the balanced literacy model and the mathematical practices that Common Core and other state-based models promote.

Yet, as this book was developed and written, the college and career initiative has been under attack. I find many of the arguments are riddled with incorrect information and hearsay. As such, I feel it is more necessary to remind us all that great teaching and learning always originates with teachers who are able to be flexible, innovative, and creative. This foundation, along with research-based methodology, a nurturing learning environment, and rigorous expectations can and will close the achievement gap. All students can achieve and all students can be college and career ready.

REFERENCES AND RESOURCES

Bettinger, E., and Long, B. T. (2009). "Addressing the needs of underprepared students in higher education: Does college remediation work?" *Journal of Human Resources* 44: 736–71.

Hayes, D. P., and Ward, M. (1992, December). "Learning from texts: Effects of similar and dissimilar features of analogies in study guides." Paper presented at the 42nd Annual Meeting of the National Reading Conference, San Antonio, TX.

McKnight, K. (2015, 7 November). "Social-Emotional Learning and the Common Core." *Free Spirit Publishing Blog.* Free Spirit. Retrieved from freespiritpublishing-blog.com/2015/11/02/social-emotional-learning-and-the-common-core.

National Governors Association Center for Best Practices and Council of Chief State School Officers. (2010). *Common Core State Standards for English Language Arts.* Washington, DC: Authors.

National Governors Association Center for Best Practices and Council of Chief State School Officers. (2010). *Common Core State Standards for Mathematics.* Washington, DC: Authors.

Selected Sources for Further Study and Exploration

1. INTRODUCTION: HOW DOES THE COMMON CORE ADDRESS THE NEEDS OF ALL STUDENTS?

Bae, S., and Darling-Hammond, L. (2014). *Recognizing College and Career Readiness in the California School Accountability System.* Stanford, CA: Stanford Center for Opportunity Policy in Education.

Quoted Abstract:

"Changes in education funding and accountability policies in California provide new opportunities to end the false dichotomy of preparation for college *or* career and support students in graduating from school well-equipped with twenty-first-century skills. This research describes practical and measurable indicators of career as well as college readiness that the state and districts can look to as they develop accountability plans."

Calkins, L., Ehrenworth, M., and Lehman C. (2012). *Pathways to the Common Core: Accelerating Achievement.* Portsmouth, NH: Heinemann.

One of the first books to analyze the Common Core State Standards and its potential impact on students. The authors explain the English Language Arts standards and the potential to accelerate and raise academic achievement for students.

Darling-Hammond, L., Wilhoit, G., and Pittenger, L. (2014). "Accountability for College and Career Readiness: Developing a New Paradigm." *National Center for Innovation in Education Faculty Publications.* Retrieved from uknowledge.uky.edu/ncie_facpub/1

Quoted Abstract:

"As schools across the country prepare for new standards under the Common Core, states are moving toward creating more aligned systems of assessment and accountability. This paper recommends an accountability approach that focuses on meaningful learning, enabled by professionally skilled and committed educators, and supported by adequate and appropriate resources, so that all students regardless of background are prepared for both college and career when they graduate from high school. Drawing on practices already established in other states and on the views of policymakers and school experts, this paper proposes principles for effective accountability systems and imagines what a new accountability system could look like in an imagined '51st state' in the United States. While considerable discussion and debate will be needed before a new approach can take shape, this paper's objective is to get the conversation started so the nation can meet its aspirations for preparing college- and career-ready students."

Fields, R. (2014). *Towards the National Assessment of Educational Progress (NAEP) as an Indicator of Academic Preparedness for College and Job Training.* Washington, DC: National Assessment Governing Board.

Report from the National Assessment of Educational Progress documenting the level of academic preparedness of K–12 students in the United States.

Porter, A., McMaken, J., Hwang, J., and Yang, R. (2011). "Common core standards: The new US intended curriculum." *Educational Researcher,* 40(3), 103–16.

Quoted Abstract:

"The Common Core standards released in 2010 for English language arts and mathematics have already been adopted by dozens of states. Just how much change do these new standards represent, and what is the nature of that change? In this article, the Common Core standards are compared with current state standards and assessments and with standards in top-performing countries, as well as with reports from a sample of teachers from across the country describing their own practices."

Tomlinson, C. A., and Imbeau, M. B. (2014). *A Differentiated Approach to the Common Core: How Do I Help a Broad Range of Learners Succeed With a Challenging Curriculum?* Alexandria, VA: ASCD.

The authors examine how the Common Core State Standards promote "deeper learning" and offer suggestions, strategies and solutions for diverse learners to meet the more rigorous demands. Deeper learning creates the expectation that all students can think in creative and innovative ways. Since these rigorous expectations are expected of all learners, how can educators create curriculum and instruction for all students to develop this intellectual mastery?"

2. EMPOWER POVERTY-STRICKEN STUDENTS FOR COMMON CORE STATE STANDARDS MASTERY

Jensen, E. (2013). *Engaging Students with Poverty in Mind: Practical Strategies for Raising Achievement.* Alexandria, VA: ASCD.

Quoted Abstract:

"In this galvanizing follow-up to the best-selling *Teaching with Poverty in Mind,* renowned educator and learning expert Eric Jensen digs deeper into engagement as the key factor in the academic success of economically disadvantaged students."

Jensen, E. (2009). *Teaching with Poverty in Mind: What Being Poor Does to Kids' Brains and What Schools Can Do About It.* Alexandria, VA: ASCD.

Quoted Abstract:

"In *Teaching with Poverty in Mind: What Being Poor Does to Kids' Brains and What Schools Can Do About It,* veteran educator and brain expert Eric Jensen takes an unflinching look at how poverty hurts children, families, and communities across the United States and demonstrates how schools can improve the academic achievement and life readiness of economically disadvantaged students."

Jensen, E., and Nickelsen, L. (2008). *Deeper Learning: 7 Powerful Strategies for In-Depth and Longer-Lasting Learning.* Thousand Oaks, CA: Corwin Press.

Quoted Abstract:

"With the amount of content that teachers have to teach, how can we ensure that students gain a deep and lasting understanding of what they have learned? Based on the most current research on cognition and the brain, this exciting book provides teachers with a systematic, reflective approach to incorporating powerful learning and content processing techniques into everyday instruction."

3. SELF-REGULATION FOR LEARNING

Colvin, G. (2008). *Talent Is Overrated: What Really Separated World-Class Performers from Everybody Else.* London: Penguin.

Quoted Abstract:

"Asked to explain why a few people truly excel, most people offer one of two answers. The first is hard work. Yet we all know plenty of hard workers who have been doing the same job for years or decades without becoming great. . . . What really makes the difference is a highly specific kind of effort, 'deliberate practice.'"

Dweck, C. (2006). *Mindset: The New Psychology of Success.* New York: Random House.

Quoted Abstract:

"World-renowned Stanford University psychologist Carol Dweck, in decades of research on achievement and success, has discovered a truly groundbreaking idea—the power of our mindset. Dweck explains why it's not just our abilities and talent that bring us success."

Tough, P. (2012). *How Children Succeed: Grit, Curiosity, and the Hidden Power of Character.* New York: Mariner Books.

Quoted Abstract:

"Why do some children succeed while others fail? The story we usually tell about childhood and success is the one about intelligence: success comes to those who score highest on tests, from preschool admissions to SATs. But in *How Children Succeed,* Paul Tough argues that the qualities that matter more have to do with character: skills like perseverance, curiosity, optimism, and self-control."

Schunk, D. H., and Zimmerman, B. J., eds. (2012). *Motivation and Self-Regulated Learning: Theory, Research and Applications*. New York: Routledge.

Quoted Abstract:

"This volume focuses on the role of motivational processes—such as goals, attributions, self-efficacy, outcome expectations, self-concept, self-esteem, social comparisons, emotions, values, and self-evaluations–in self-regulated learning."

4. DIFFERENTIATED INSTRUCTION: A FRAMEWORK FOR LEARNING SUCCESS

Cash, R. M. (2010). *Advancing Differentiation: Thinking and Learning for the 21st Century*. Minneapolis, MN: Free Spirit Publishing.

Quoted Abstract:

"Create a thriving, student-centered classroom with this powerful resource. The book guides teachers to develop a rigorous, concept-based curriculum that is differentiated for all learners across content areas, and to build students' thinking skills."

Tomlinson, C. A. (2014). *Differentiated Classroom: Responding to the Needs of All Learners* (second edition). Alexandria, VA: ASCD.

Quoted Abstract:

"Although much has changed in schools in recent years, the power of differentiated instruction remains the same—and the need for it has only increased.

"Today's classroom is more diverse, more inclusive, and more plugged into technology than ever before. And it's led by teachers under enormous pressure to help decidedly unstandardized students meet an expanding set of rigorous, standardized learning targets."

Wormeli, R. (2007). *Differentiation: From Planning to Practice, Grades 6–12*. Portland, ME: Stenhouse Publishers.

Quoted Abstract:

"The author demonstrates how to weave common and novel differentiation strategies into all subjects and offers clear advice about what to do when things don't go as expected."

Wormeli, R. (2006). *Fair Isn't Always Equal: Assessing and Grading in the Differentiated Classroom*. Portland, ME: Stenhouse Publishers.

Quoted Abstract:

"Differentiated instruction is a nice idea, but what happens when it comes to assessing and grading students? What's both fair and leads to real student learning?"

5. READING, THE FOUNDATION FOR *ALL* LEARNING

Bitter, C., O'Day, J., Gubbins, P., and Socias, M. (2009). "What works to improve student literacy achievement? An examination of instructional practices in a balanced literacy approach." *Journal of Education for Students Placed at Risk 14*(1): 17–44.

Quoted Abstract:

"A core assumption of the San Diego City Schools (SDCS) reform effort was that improved instructional practices, aligned with a balanced literacy approach, would be effective in improving student outcomes. This article explores this hypothesis by presenting findings from an analysis of classroom instruction data collected in 101 classrooms in nine high-poverty elementary schools. The study found a prevalent focus on reading comprehension instruction and on students' active engagement in making meaning from text. Teachers' use of higher-level questions and discussion about text were substantially higher than that found by a prior study using the same instrument in similar classrooms elsewhere. Analyses of instruction and student outcome data indicate that teacher practices related to the higher-level meaning of text, writing instruction, and strategies for accountable talk were associated with growth in students' reading comprehension."

Jensen, E, and Nickelsen, L. (2013). *Bringing the Common Core to Life in K–8 Classrooms: 30 Strategies to Build Literacy Skills.* Bloomington, IN: Solution-Tree.

This book outlines research-based strategies to foster the development of skills as articulated in the new standards.

McKnight, K. S. (2014). *Common Core Literacy for ELA, History/Social Studies, and the Humanities: Strategies to Deepen Content Knowledge (Grades 6–12).* San Francisco: Jossey-Bass.

McKnight, K. S. (2014). *Common Core Literacy for Math, Science, and Technical Subjects: Strategies to Deepen Content Knowledge (grades 6–12).* San Francisco: Jossey-Bass.

Quoted Abstract:

"In this age of the Common Core State Standards, all content area teachers must integrate literacy standards into their curriculum. This book offers resources and strategies for developing literacy skills and content knowledge in English and social studies in one volume, and addresses mathematics and science in a separate volume."

Zygouris-Coe, V. (2012, January–March). "Disciplinary Literacy and the Common Core State Standards." *Topics in Language Disorders 32*(1): 35–50.

Quoted Abstract:

"The article highlights possibilities and challenges associated with national efforts to prepare students for success in college and the workforce. Information is presented on the basis of a selected literature review of disciplinary literacy, adolescent literacy, student achievement, and the common core standards. Instructional strategies also are presented for developing students' disciplinary literacy and meeting common core goals. This article calls for collaborative inquiry and shared accountability among stakeholders to ensure that all students' literacy and learning needs are met in a new era of educational reform."

6. THE CERCA FRAMEWORK FOR CAREER AND COLLEGE READINESS

Graff, G., and Birkenstein, C. (2007). *"They Say/I Say": The Moves that Matter in Persuasive Writing*. New York: W. W. Norton and Company.

Quoted Abstract:

"The book that demystifies academic writing, teaching students to frame their arguments in the larger context of what else has been said about their topic—and providing templates to help them make the key rhetorical moves."

Hillocks, G. (2011). *Teaching Argument Writing, Grades 6–12: Supporting Claims with Relevant Evidence and Clear Reasoning*. Portsmouth, NH: Heinemann.

Quoted Abstract:

"Argument writing can be difficult to teach, but it may be the most important set of skills we teach in English. According to the National Common Core Standards, by the end of high school, students should be able to write arguments to support claims with clear reason and relevant evidence—and they should be able to do so *well*.

Designed for middle and high school students, the activities in this book will enable students to *write* strong arguments and *evaluate* the arguments of others. When they are through, students will be able, as the Common Core Standards ask, to 'Delineate and evaluate [an] argument and specific claims...including the validity of the reasoning [and] the relevance and sufficiency of the evidence.' Developed by George Hillocks, Jr. and others in diverse inner city classrooms in Chicago, students are easily engaged in the lively problem-solving approach detailed in this book."

7. HIGH-LEVERAGE PRACTICES IN MATH EDUCATION THAT BOLSTER ACADEMIC ACHIEVEMENT

Gurl, T. J., Artzt, A. F., and Sultan, A. (2013). *Implementing the Common Core State Standards through Mathematical Problem Solving*. Reston, VA: National Council of Teachers of Mathematics.

Quoted Abstract:

"The 37 problems and tasks for students in this book are organized into the major areas of the Common Core for grades 6–8: ratios and proportional relationships; the number system; geometry; statistics and probability; and expressions, equations, and functions. For each task, teachers will find a rich, engaging problem or set of problems to use as a lesson starting point, with accompanying discussions that tie the tasks to specific Common Core domains and clusters."

Other grade levels books are included in this NCTM series.

Lee, J. (2012). "College for all: Gaps between desirable and actual P–12 math achievement trajectories for college readiness." *Educational Researcher 41*(2): 43–55.

Quoted Abstract:

"This study addresses missing links in 'college for all' debates by investigating gaps between actual and desirable math achievement trajectories for students' college readiness. Linking multiple national data sets across P–16 education levels, the study estimates college readiness benchmarks separately for two-year and four-year college entrance and completion."

National Council of Teachers of Mathematics. (2014). *Principles to Actions: Ensuring Mathematical Success for All*. Reston, VA: National Council of Teachers of Mathematics.

"NCTM has defined and described the principles and actions, including specific teaching practices, that are essential for a high-quality mathematics education for all students.

Principles to Actions: Ensuring Mathematical Success for All offers guidance to teachers, specialists, coaches, administrators, policymakers, and parents:

- Builds on the Principles articulated in Principles and Standards for School Mathematics to present six updated Guiding Principles for School Mathematics
- Supports the first Guiding Principle, Teaching and Learning, with eight essential, research-based Mathematics Teaching Practices
- Details the five remaining Principles—the Essential Elements that support Teaching and Learning as embodied in the Mathematics Teaching Practices

"Identifies obstacles and unproductive and productive beliefs that all stakeholders must recognize, as well as the teacher and student actions that characterize effective teaching and learning aligned with the Mathematics Teaching Practices."

8. WHAT DO THE NEW STANDARDS MEAN FOR STUDENTS WHO RECEIVE SPECIAL EDUCATION SERVICES?

Haager, D., and Vaughn, S. (2013). "Common core state standards and students with learning disabilities: Introduction to the special issue." *Learning Disabilities Research & Practice, 28*(1), 1–4.

Quoted Abstract:

"As is often the case with large-scale educational initiatives, how to include students with disabilities arises as an additional consideration.

Though the language of this document indicates that that the standards apply to *all* students, the burden is on teachers in classrooms to determine when and how to make the standards accessible."

9. HIGHER ORDER THINKING SKILLS FOR ENGLISH LANGUAGE LEARNERS

Bright, A., Hansen-Thomas, A., and de Oliveira, L. C. (2015). *The Common Core State Standards in Mathematics for English Language Learners: High School*. Reston, VA: National Council of Teachers of Mathematics.

Quoted Abstract:

"For ELLs to have a voice in secondary mathematics classrooms, they must be given opportunities to comprehend grade-level content and share their learning journeys. ELLs need this support to express their mathematical thinking, including their insights, conjectures, comparisons, and questions.

"This book focuses on ways to tailor instruction to capitalize on the strengths of each ELL while aligning teaching and learning with the Common Core State Standards for Mathematics. It explores some of the ways in which high school mathematics content can be made accessible to ELLs by building on the strengths that they bring to the classroom and scaffolding their opportunities to learn."

Bunch, G. C., Kibler, A., and Pimentel, S. (2012). "Realizing opportunities for English learners in the common core English language arts and disciplinary literacy standards." Stanford, CA: Understanding Language Initiative. Retrieved from ell.stanford.edu/sites/default/files/pdf/academic-papers/ 01_Bunch_Kibler_Pimentel_RealizingOpp%20in%20ELA_FINAL_0.pdf.

Quoted Abstract:

"This article, a joint effort between two researchers with expertise in the education of ELs and one of the writers of the Standards, represents an attempt to explicate some of the predominant challenges facing ELs in the Standards and to provide guidance and recommendations based on relevant research and theory."

10. WITH NEW STANDARDS IN MIND: SELECTING AND INTEGRATING EDUCATIONAL TECHNOLOGIES FOR STUDENT SUCCESS

Hamilton, B. (2015). *Integrating Technology in the Classroom: Tools to Meet the Needs of Every Student*. Arlington, VA: International Society for Technology Educators.

Quoted Abstract:

"Teachers possess unique skills, knowledge and experience. So why should their approaches to classroom technology look the same? In *Integrating Technology in the Classroom*, author Boni Hamilton helps you discover technology tools and projects that resonate with your teaching style, classroom context and technology skill level—all while helping students achieve academic growth. In this book, every teacher can find new and immediately applicable ways to integrate technology in the classroom."

Solomon, G., and Schrum, L. (2014). *Web 2.0: How-to for Educators*. Arlington, VA: International Society for Technology in Education.

Quoted Abstract:

"Finding tools and apps for the classroom is easy. Understanding how to use them effectively in a lesson—that's another story. This revised edition of *Web 2.0: How-To for Educators* not only introduces an expanded list of Web 2.0 tools, but it expertly leads you through classroom and professional applications that help improve student and teacher learning. From Google tools and virtual environments to apps such as SoundCloud, explore the very best Web 2.0 has to offer for educators."

11. FORMATIVE ASSESSMENT STRATEGIES: AN ESSENTIAL ELEMENT FOR EFFECTIVE CLASSROOMS

Frey, N., and Fisher, D. (2011). *The Formative Assessment Action Plan*. Alexandria, VA: ASCD.

Quoted Abstract:

"[The authors] outline a clear-cut, realistic, and rewarding approach to formative assessment. They explain how four discrete steps work in tandem to create a seamless, comprehensive formative assessment system, one that has no beginning and no end. This ongoing approach enhances an active give-and-take relationship between teachers and students to promote learning."

Marzano, R. J. (2009). *Formative Assessment and Standards-Based Grading*. Bloomington, IN: Solution Tree Press.

Quoted Abstract:

"Dr. Robert Marzano provides the specifics. He explains how to design and interpret three different types of formative assessments, how to track student progress, and how to assign meaningful grades, even if a school or district continues to use a traditional grading system. He brings each concept to life with detailed examples of teachers from different subject areas applying it in their classrooms."

12. COLLEGE AND CAREER READINESS IN THE CLASSROOM

Burns, C. C., and Garrity, D. (2012). *Opening the Common Core: How to Bring All Students to College and Career Readiness*. Newbury Park, CA: Corwin Press.

Quoted Abstract:

"The authors helped lead their district—Rockville Centre in Long Island, New York—in closing achievement gaps and increasing the number of students who completed four-year college programs. The results of their efforts show a remarkable increase in both excellence and equity in English language arts, math, and science."

13. FAST FORWARD: COLLEGE AND CAREER READINESS FOR *ALL*

Conley, D. T. (2010). *College and Career Ready: Helping All Students Succeed Beyond High School*. San Francisco: John Wiley and Sons.

Quoted Abstract:

"*College and Career Ready* offers educators a blueprint for improving high school so that more students are able to excel in freshman-level college courses or entry-level jobs—laying a solid foundation for lifelong growth and success. The book is filled with detailed, practical guidelines and case descriptions of what the best high schools are doing.

- Includes clear guidelines for high school faculty to adapt their programs of instruction in the direction of enhanced college/career readiness
- Provides practical strategies for improving students' content knowledge and academic behaviors
- Offers examples of best practices and research-based recommendations for change

The book considers the impact of behavioral issues—such as time management and study habits—as well as academic skills on college readiness."

Index

About the Editor

Dr. Katherine S. McKnight is a dynamic presenter, dedicated teacher, and award-winning author. In addition to speaking at professional development conferences, she is a regular consultant in schools and classrooms all over the country and in Europe. Administrators and teachers welcome her expertise, witty good humor, and hands-on approach to education.

McKnight currently serves as a Distinguished Professor of Research at National Louis University. A passionate student advocate, McKnight stays true to her roots in the Chicago Public Schools where she began her career. She is recognized for her in-depth knowledge of the Common Core State Standards, and is known to delight educators with her observation, "Good teaching is good teaching, no matter what standards we're aiming for!"

She has authored many books that support teaching strategies to engage all learners. Her titles include the best selling *The Teacher's Big Book of Graphic Organizers*, winner of the 2013 Teachers' Choice Award. She's also written *The Second City Guide to Improv in the Classroom*, *Teaching Writing in the Inclusive Classroom*, and the twin volumes: *Common Core Literacy for Math, Science, and Technical Subjects*, and *Common Core Literacy for ELA, History/Social Studies, and the Humanities: Strategies to Deepen Content Knowledge (Grades 6–12)*. In 2015, she received the Teachers' Choice Award for professional development.